WHY WE TALK FUNNY

ALSO BY VALERIE FRIDLAND

Like, Literally, Dude:
Arguing for the Good in Bad English

“WHY WE TALK FUNNY”

The Real Story Behind Our Accents

VALERIE FRIDLAND

VIKING

VIKING
An imprint of Penguin Random House LLC
1745 Broadway, New York, NY 10019
penguinrandomhouse.com

Designed by Nerylsa Dijol

LIBRARY OF CONGRESS CATALOGING-IN-PUBLICATION DATA
Names: Fridland, Valerie, author
Title: Why we talk funny: the real story behind our accents / Valerie Fridland.
Description: New York, NY: Viking, 2026. |
Includes bibliographical references and index. Identifiers:
LCCN 2025035615 (print) | LCCN 2025035616 (ebook) |
ISBN 9780593830482 hardcover | ISBN 9780593830499 ebook
Subjects: LCSH: Accents and accentuation—History
Classification: LCC P231 .F75 2026 (print) | LCC P231 (ebook)
LC record available at https://lccn.loc.gov/2025035615
LC ebook record available at https://lccn.loc.gov/2025035616

Printed in the United States of America
2nd Printing

The authorized representative in the EU for product safety and compliance is Penguin Random House Ireland, Morrison Chambers, 32 Nassau Street, Dublin D02 YH68, Ireland, https://eu-contact.penguin.ie.

To Craig

CONTENTS

WHY WE TALK FUNNY

INTRODUCTION

When I was a little girl, one thing was very obvious to me. Unfortunately, it wasn't that green pants and blue shirts don't go well together. That little nugget I simply learned through the school of hard knocks. Instead, what was obvious to me as the daughter of immigrants growing up in the South was that we couldn't go anywhere without my parents' accents getting noticed. Whether from the mouths of friends playing at my house or the woman at the bank, every new encounter brought the same question: "Where you from?" The subtext being "Not from around here."

Of course, they were right. My parents were foreign, and French was the first language for them both. They had moved to Memphis for work, and, in the 1970s, if you didn't speak with a Southern accent, you definitely attracted attention. While French might have made them seem exotic, it didn't make them immensely popular at parties because, as every Southerner who's been the butt of *Deliverance* jokes knows, accents lead people to form opinions about you, mostly without you having much say in the matter.

The most curious thing was not that my parents spoke with an accent, but that I didn't. Or at least not an accent that stood out, which is probably why my neighborhood BFFs were so blown over by the lilting French way my mother called out my name when it was time to come inside for dinner. I sounded pretty much just like all my peers—and, of course, none of us knew we also had accents until we encountered snarky non-Southerners. Having been too absorbed in important things like Barbie, bikes, and then my SAT scores, it never occurred to me I might sound funny until I left for college and was surrounded by people from the North. It was there that I first came to the striking realization that, for most people, the pronunciation of *lawyer* and *liar* didn't rhyme and saying "Ima" for *I'm going to* was not everyone's short-form stand-in. My first thought? What's wrong with you people! But then I realized I was the odd accent out.

Really what my younger self was discovering was a small insight into a much larger linguistic lesson: what provides a sense of belonging in every human society on the planet is the way we sound—and it's when our own variety diverges from that spoken by another community, nation, or people that we really notice its power to make us feel connected to those sounding like we do and isolated from those who don't. While our speech can differ in big ways, like when speaking completely separate languages, it's the small ways—the pronunciation differences that ride shotgun to social differences otherwise known as accents—that tend to impact our social lives more in the day-to-day.

Of course, there are also the fun accent-related mysteries like why "vahzes" sound so much pricier than regular vases and how "warshing" for *washing* ever became a thing. Never fear, we will definitely talk about those. But this book is really about a much bigger mystery: How is it that we unconsciously learn to speak using patterns of sounds that come to define us in extremely important ways—i.e., as smart or uneducated, as Black or White, as local or foreign? And what larger evolutionary and social purposes might these sound differences serve? As we will discover, from the day we are born, our accents are a huge part of how we come to understand where we fit, and who we fit with, in our neighborhoods, our schools, and our workplaces. Yet most people know surprisingly little about the science and history behind the way we talk, unless they've happened upon a sociolinguist like me at a dinner party or in a stray class at college.

Stick with me, and while you may not get cocktails or college credit, you will get a fascinating trip through the social and linguistic forces that drive the way we sound and how that, in turn, has shaped the way we listen.

THE SCIENCE OF SOUND

As a linguistic mutt myself, I am deeply intrigued by the question of what makes us sound the way we do and, even more, why, as the trade-off for being old enough to drink and cast a vote, our accents become so hard to adjust. In college, I decided to become a language and linguistics major, which, if I'm being totally honest, was mainly because I wanted to take the fewest math classes possible. But it turned out to be a fortuitous decision, even if a lazy one, as it was there that I was first turned on to phonetics and phonology, the linguistic fields dedicated to unlocking the secrets of sounds. By the end of graduate school, I had also discovered the surprisingly social side of sounds, something studied in a field we nerdy linguist types call *sociophonetics*.

For most people, phonetics sounds a lot like the once popular method of teaching kindergarteners to read. But phonetics is actually the scientific study of sounds as they are spoken. Phonics is the name of the program designed to teach little munchkins things like that the written letters "c" and "k" often both sound like "k" (as in *cut* and *kit*)—well, unless "c" is friends with an "h," and then it is a whole different ball game. In other words, phonics is about written letters and how to read them, not really about the sounds we speak. The reason kids need phonics in the first place is because of the weird mismatch between the letters we write and the sounds we say.

Letters are the graphemes we've adopted to write English down, but our ABCs often do not represent the sounds as we say them. For instance, "eye," "aye," and "I" all represent the same sound spelled differently, and the "y" in *you* and *happy* are different sounds but represented with the same letter. Since English has twenty-six letters but fortyish separate sounds (depending on dialect), you can see that sounds and letters cannot be the same thing.

A lot of these spelling/sound mismatches are a result of writing not keeping up with changes that occurred in spoken language, like the "ee" and "ea" spelling of what is now, but wasn't always, the same sound, e.g., *meet/meat*. English also got a bit creative with letters after shifting from a Runic to a Latin alphabet and trying to represent Germanic sounds—for instance, replacing Old English "þ" with that odd "th" double letter combo used for what is actually a single sound. In other cases, we introduced spelling/sound confusions when English borrowed words, their spellings, and some attempt at their original pronunciations from other languages, as with *ballet* and *sorbet* with no actual "t" pronounced from French. Uniquely American spelling conventions came about when Noah Webster decided to right some spelling wrongs by getting rid of that extra "u" in words like *colour* and *honour* and sensibly changing the "c" to "s" in *offence* and *defence* (now *offense* and *defense*), yet leaving us with *fences* not *fenses*. Geez. No wonder kindergarten is so hard.

This is why, when we want to discuss the range and mechanics of human speech, phonics won't do us much good. Phonetics, on the other hand, helps us understand and describe the speech sounds—rather than the written forms—that exist across all languages. We might want to know, for example, how the "l" at the beginning of a word is different from an "l" said at the end, as is noticeable when you say the word *lull*, a phonetic difference we linguists call a light versus a dark "l." Or why American "t" sounds in words like *metal* and *waiter* are strangely similar to the "d" sounds in *medal* and *wader*, a phonetic process we call *flapping*.

Why should those of us who are not linguists even care? Because, as part of the process of acquiring a language, our minds start to play tricks on us—mentally registering just one sound when in fact we say that sound in many different ways in phonetic terms. And this is where phonology enters the fray.

While phonetics is about studying the way sounds are made, phonology is about how they specifically pattern in different languages, i.e., what speakers "know" about which sounds are in their language. As a native English speaker, for example, I "know" that "r" and "l" are different sounds, but I have no idea that I also have a regular habit of making light "l" and dark "l" sounds. Since subtle variations like these, which can automatically arise depending on where sounds occur in words, have no impact on meaning in English, our brains filter them out and just register them both as one single "l" sound. But step out to learn another language, and these little phonetic differences can become extremely important because other languages divide up what counts as a separate sound in different ways.

This is why English speakers often notice that Japanese or Korean speakers struggle with "r" and "l" when learning English. In those languages, what our English-trained minds hear and categorize as a separate "r" sound is instead just heard as a variant of another sound, similar to the way that American English speakers produce both dark and light "l" sounds without realizing it. This then becomes quite the pain in the mouth when Japanese or Korean speakers learn English, which divvies up the sound spectrum differently and contributes to what Americans hear as their accent.

And even when we hear the "same" sounds, very small differences in how they are actually articulated in each language can still create crosslinguistic pronunciation problems. Going back to our "r" sounds, consider American English speakers' typically fruitless attempts at a Spanish trill ("perro"). While it once rolled off the tongues of our linguistic ancestors, it went the way of the linguistic dodo in English centuries ago and is no longer something most English speakers can easily get their tongue around. Likewise, that throaty slightly gargling "r" sound so popular among Parisians is not part of our typical American repertoire. So, when we modern speakers encounter a Spanish trill or a French uvular "r," we simply substitute our regular old "r" as our closest approximation. Voilà, we end up having an American accent while speaking Spanish or French.

You might be wondering why it would be that languages exhibit such variability in the way sounds are pronounced and understood. In large part it is the nature of the beast, meaning that our physiology—and the way speech sounds tend to affect one another when spoken together—naturally gives rise to alterations in how sounds are said. But just as crucial is the fact that such variation is incredibly useful from a social and evolutionary standpoint as it can be exploited to serve group signaling purposes. What we will learn as we march our way through the science behind our accents is that very little of what we hear around us as "different" is evidence of something wrong or even anything unusual in the long view of language.

Instead, for thousands of years, the very human drive to congregate based on what we have in common has coexisted with this regular variability in the sounds we use. It is this magic mix of variation driven by the way our mouths and minds work, along with our tendency to flock together and talk together, that forms the foundation for our accents and the social meanings they acquire.

THE SOUNDS OF EVERYDAY LIFE

Despite its centrality to explaining our accents, it might still be tempting to think that the scientific study of sounds is unimportant work in a world where "serious" science on climate change and Alzheimer's disease are headliners, but phonetics and phonology affect you every day no matter who you are or what language you speak in ways you probably never imagined. As I tell my bright-eyed students at the start of every semester, there is very little any of us do in life where the way we say things isn't super important.

For instance, think of how we change up our speech to caregiverese when we talk to tiny tots. Sure, it might be nauseating to everyone else around us, but we are doing the good work of modeling sounds and patterns for the next generation. Or what do you think speech therapists are working with as their building blocks when helping those who struggle to pronounce those tricky "r"s and "l"s? You have to understand the underlying phonetics to know how to assist with articulatory issues, the very reason why many of my students are speech pathology majors. Likewise, foreign language teachers must have an awareness of phonological information, so they know whether we need extra drills to practice trills. Less obviously, there are phonetics experts hard at work in the background in courtrooms and tech companies, helping you stay out of jail or trying to make sure you have a coherent conversation with Siri.

What's that? Speech sounds could land you in jail? Well, possibly, but more likely they could keep you out of it. One of the most famous cases where phonetics and phonology saved the day (at least for the defendant) was a case involving Pan Am Airways in the 1980s.

That case revolved around a series of bomb threats the airline had received over a period of several months, forcing it to repeatedly evacuate a plane on one of its most profitable routes. Suspecting an inside job, fingers got pointed at a disaffected Pan Am employee by the name of Paul Prinzivalli, who originally hailed from New York but worked as a cargo handler at LAX. On recordings made of the threats, the caller's voice sounded, to West Coast ears, like someone from the east, and coworkers suspected Mr. Prinzivalli. It probably didn't help that he had been cranky about his current work assignment and had made vague statements about "getting back" at his employer. With motive and an East Coast accent, Mr. Prinzivalli was arrested and put on trial under a prosecution theory that he was a disgruntled employee. His fate hinged, quite literally, on his voice.

Luckily for Mr. Prinzivalli, the defense team brought in Bill Labov, a renowned sociolinguist from the University of Pennsylvania who specialized in regional American dialects. After examining recordings of both the suspect and the threatening caller, Labov stunned the courtroom by pointing out several defining features on the bomb threat recordings that were clearly from a Bostonian, not a New Yorker, such as a distinctive merger between the traditionally different vowels used in words like *on* and *off.* This merger would make word pairs like *cot* and *caught* or *collar* and *caller* sound the same, but only for Bostonians, not New Yorkers. The conclusion was that it was impossible that they were recordings of the same speaker. Labov's testimony was pivotal to the case, and Mr. Prinzivalli was acquitted, in what, as the *LA Times* put it, was some sound judgment. This type of forensic linguistic analysis continues to be used in criminal cases for speaker identification to this day.

If the pursuit of liberty is not enough to convince you of the power and importance of understanding phonetics and phonology, let's turn instead to the fact that one needn't ever type again now that voice dictation has arrived. Linguists have been working tirelessly to find out how our tendency to vary the way we pronounce things messes with our phone's ability to understand us. On a recent Apple discussion board about texting troubles, one hapless user, upon grabbing an out-of-town neighbor's mail, found himself in hot water when voice-to-text misheard "I have two envelopes for you" as "I have two on the lips for you."

How could this have happened? Go on, try saying "envelopes" slowly, and now fast: "on-ve-lips." You've probably said it quickly just like that many times at the post office, but context made all the difference in how you were understood, unless you scored an unexpected date with the postman. Our recent shift from face-to-face to face-to-phone speech makes everything rest solely on the sounds our phone picks up, without the contextual nuances or body language hints that old-school conversations involved. And that's just considering our phone's issues with the little phonetic adjustments we tend to make when speaking quickly. For those with less familiar accents, foreign or otherwise, research shows our phones perform even worse. For example, linguists have found that voice recognition programs do not do nearly as well for those with Southern or African American accents. Speech-to-text technology has been a boon, but Siri's comprehension remains an issue because the sounds we say are far from as straightforward as we believe them to be. In fact, variation is all around us, and phonetically speaking, the sounds we say compared to what we (not just Siri!) think we hear are rarely an open-and-shut case.

UNDERSTANDING OUR SHIFTY NATURE

Despite the myth in the United States that, somewhere out on the great Midwestern plains, there exists a bastion of unaccented speech, it is simply not true.

We all vary in the way we say things depending on where we are from, and if you've ever heard someone from Cleveland pronounce the word *pop*, you already know better. And, of course, even the least noticeable American accent is strikingly different from any British English accent. This is why when traveling abroad, you are an easy mark for pickpockets and tourist scams, as your accent sets you up before you even have a chance to stash your cash in your hot-pink fanny pack. Even calling it a fanny pack is a dead giveaway, since "fanny" is a vulgar term for female parts in British (and Australian) English.

What else gives Americans away? In large part, the sounds we say: like the fact that we take "baths" rather than "bah-ths," we pronounce all our "r" sounds, listen to "toons" not "tyunes," and stick a "d"-like sound instead of a "t" in the middle of *water*. This type of variation that has evolved over time when we're separated geographically is something we are all familiar with.

Here's an example of how the same sorts of underlying articulatory processes also give rise to more subtle forms of variation that come to mark us in other socially salient ways: Have you ever noticed the tendency of some English speakers to say words like *string* or *street* more like "shtring" or "shtreet"? Now, notice here that "sh" is shortly followed by an "r," a sound that many speakers make by curling the tongue tip slightly back, something referred to as *retroflexion*. Say "sss" versus "rrrr" and feel the difference in where your tongue is. So what happens in some dialects is that speakers curl their tongue back a bit early, i.e., leading the "s" to sound more like "sh," a sound made with the tongue a bit farther back.

Who does this? Well, more and more speakers, it seems, since I get a surprising number of emails commenting on it. Also, recent research confirms that there are now more "shtreets" and "shtrings" in dialects like Cockney and, increasingly, in the speech of younger speakers from American cities such as Philadelphia, Pennsylvania, and Columbus, Ohio, and in some Southern dialects with a lot of Northern in-migration like Raleigh, North Carolina.

In these varieties, what started as a small underlying coarticulatory tendency becomes more prominent until it becomes the norm rather than the exception. Since novelty is rarely rewarded in speech, speakers whose accents include this feature are often heard as "mispronouncing" the "s" as opposed to the more traditional pronunciation. But the fact that the "sh" version is on the increase where it's been studied tells us that it has taken on some subconsciously attractive social meaning (at least for those using it) such as an urban, youthful, or chill quality. A desire to radiate such qualities leads to greater uptake, even among those who might originally not have been articulatorily predisposed to backing their tongues. In other words, it has become a socially driven variant rather than simply a phonetically driven one. For those who are not on the "sh" bandwagon, though, it can mark a speaker as non-standard or lower-class. This is why a most important application of phonetics and phonology is not just understanding how accents come to exist, but how they affect our perception of others' speech—and what we make of their backgrounds.

BEFORE WE GET MUCH DEEPER, though, let's clarify the difference between an accent and a dialect, since dialect is a much broader term than accent.

When we are talking about someone's accent, we are talking specifically about noticeable differences in how they sound; when we talk about someone's dialect, we mean that someone's language variety is different on many levels beyond just pronunciation, including vocabulary, like saying "soda" versus "pop," and sentence structure, like saying "they was" versus "they were." Though we are more than happy to judge people on those aspects too, research shows that we react to people's accents pretty much by the end of the first word they speak; we literally have them at "Hello." This is why it's pretty dang important to understand what we so often get wrong about what drives people to sound different than we do. For that reason, although we will be chatting about the dialects wherein these accents reside, pronunciation, rather than differences in words or grammar, will be our focus as we explore the many accents found in English.

Accents are certainly not the only thing about sounds that people are curious about. Sometimes people ask me things like why particular words trigger feelings of disgust (hello, *moist*!) or why certain languages sound especially attractive. So, in a quest to satisfy the range of sound-related queries you might have, we will periodically also cover some fun, slightly peripheral topics, in what I like to call a "sound bite." Even though most of our chapters will explore the accents that loom large in our experience, like those associated with region or class, these little sound bites will hit on some of the other interesting and unexpected ways sounds and accents shape the way we see the world.

Finally, there are also two very different types of accents we will be talking about: native accents and non-native accents. When we talk about accents within our own language, like Midwestern or Southern, we are talking about what are known as *first language* or *native* accents. These accents come about because of regionally or socially based variation in terms of how we pronounce the "same" sound in our language, as with the "street/shtreet" example we discussed earlier. Much of what we will explore in these pages will be how English emerged as such a tongue divided, and how social facts, like the place where we grew up, the race we belong to, or the social status we hold, became attached to the sounds we utter.

In addition to native speaker accents like these, we will also spend some time talking about the accents that brand us as outsiders when we leave our country of origin—like a noticeably American accent when trying to order phở in Vietnam.* Known as *foreign*, *second language*, or *non-native speaker* accents, these arise from differences in the distinctive sounds that each language uses, with "distinctive" referring to the sounds a speaker of that language would point out as part of their language (like hearing just a single "l" sound for both the light and dark "l" described earlier).

Out of the eight hundred or so possible speech sounds found across languages, we typically only use about twenty to forty in any one language. Of these, there are some sounds that we find in a lot of languages, like a "t" or "ee" sound, but many, like clicks (like a "tsk tsk" sound) or the "zh" sound in *rouge*, are less common. That means that a new language will pretty much always have some different sounds compared to the one you already know. In contrast to native speaker accents, this type of accent is less about the socio-stylistic identity moves we make with our mouths and more about the fact that, when a speaker learns an entirely different language, they encounter sounds that they've never used before, making sounding native-like as an adult a very difficult task.

* The closest Americans usually get to pronouncing this word "accurately" is something akin to "fuh," not "foe," though it still lacks the distinctive rising tone found on the vowel in Vietnamese.

LIVING BY OUR PRINCIPLES

Whether we're talking about native or non-native accents, linguists have discovered that there are two fundamental principles that seem to play a huge role in determining the ways that sounds end up changing over time and across accents: namely, *ease of articulation* and *ease of perception*.

Ease of articulation refers to the fact that the goal of speech is to communicate a message using a minimum of time and effort. In short, the point of yelling "Fire!" in a crowded room is not to show off your impressive articulatory skill set, but to get people running to the doors. Whether you say "fire" or something more like "far" as a Southerner would isn't important as long as people get the hell out. Though Southerners get a lot of grief for this tendency to shorten their vowel pronunciation, making *fire* and *bye* sound more like "far" and "bah," it is simply an example of the guiding principle of economy of effort that all speakers adopt from time to time.

Just think back to our hapless texter mentioned earlier who was misunderstood as saying "on the lips" because Siri was assuming "ve" stood for "the," a common substitution a lot of us make in fast everyday speech when we think no one's looking. One of the key findings of sociolinguistic research is that we don't just vary across groups but also within our own speech. We all drop a "g" sound here or there or sometimes say "doncha" for *don't you* because different linguistic styles—like being cool and formal or friendly and laid-back—are part of everyone's repertoire. What tends to garner notice most though is how often people follow this drive toward efficiency—with higher rates often associated with less highly regarded ways of speaking.

Now, you might believe yourself above such ease of articulation tendencies, but think again. How do you pronounce the words *immoral* and *immature*? Or how about *irregular*, *illiterate*, and, just to bring it up, *irregardless*? Notice a pattern? These are all cases where the original Latin-derived *in-* prefix, meaning "not," came into contact with a word starting with "m," "r," or "l" and lo and behold—sound smush happened! This type of sound blending is not limited to our past—it is found throughout our everyday talk. For instance, say "Bless you" or "Miss you" and, in normal speech, you are very likely to economically combine the "s" and the "y" sounds into a single "sh" sound, with "blesh-u" and "mish-u" the result.

This process, usually referred to by the more technical term *assimilation*, is one of the most frequent ways we make sounds easier to say—and it affects all languages, not just English. For example, the word for eight in Latin was *octo*, but, by the time Latin turned into Italian, the "k" had become a "t" sound to match the one right next door, giving modern Italians *otto* for eight instead. Human speech is constantly subject to such economy of effort and, as we will see as we look at sounds throughout history and in various accents, this is one of the main underlying reasons sounds shift the way they do over time.

And this is where our second principle, ease of perception, comes in. We only allow principle one to apply to our speech when doing so does not interfere with the perception of speech for those within our group. What that means is that we unconsciously allow for a certain amount of variability but with our listening audience in the back of our mind, limiting that variation to what can be fairly easily recovered by a listener.

Problem is, speakers in different social groups have developed differing senses about how much and what type of variation is "too much," and more standard accented speakers often suppress tendencies that are associated with socially disfavored groups, despite many instances of similar adjustments in their own speech. As a result, complaints about a lack of intelligibility are sometimes more about a lack of social status associated with a specific group of speakers than about true issues with comprehension.

The reality is that we are pretty good at using context to decode what speakers mean and also seem to have a keen ability to reconstruct sounds affected by articulatory efficiencies frequent in speech. So, for example, even though the "s" plural on words like *cats* and *dogs* are always said differently, i.e., as "cat**s**" and "dog**z**," a listener filters this variability out to perceive both of them as the same ending. But why do we get "hors**es**" and not "hor**ss**"? After all, that "e" is supposedly silent. One might politely surmise it is because we don't like its close proximity to another rather indelicate word, but one would be wrong. It's actually ease of perception. One longer "s" sound would be hard to discriminate, whereas if you stick a vowel in there, its plurality will not be questioned. And these patterns are not just about cats, dogs, and horses. Notice how you say *puffs*, *gloves*, and *buses* or *tacks*, *rags*, and *kisses*: they all have the same pattern of alternating "s," "z," and "ez" plural pronunciation—a perfect example of the delicate balance we are constantly striking between efficiency and clarity. Aren't we quite amazing?

Variation is built into the fundamental nature of the linguistic beast—and, without it, we would lack the ability to adapt to new situations and discern who's who by taking advantage of small unconscious linguistic adjustments that become socially recognizable and intelligible within our own group. Most such variation occurs as a result of the principles just discussed—not as an intentional act—and takes on no meaning. Then, when geographic or social distance enters the fray, little differences that start or are more widespread in one group as opposed to another can take on social notice. At first awareness might simply be that people A from the highlands sound a bit different from people B in the lowlands, i.e., simple cues to group membership. Over time, each group's perceived traits and habits come to be linked with the sound patterns in their speech, giving rise not to just accents, but also to the myriad meanings we've come to associate with them.

As we begin our journey together, we will be traveling the path of our accents as they first emerged from the babbles of babies and even follow the accent trail far back in time to see how our modern ones relate to the mutterings of ancient ancestors. Most fascinating, though, are the origin stories we will uncover of today's most recognizable accents, those spanning nation, region, class, and race. By the end of our trip, it will be clear how biology, psychology, and our fundamental social need to feel a part of something bigger came together to make the way we sound—and the way we sound different—matter. So, my friends, fasten your seat belts—we've got a lot of linguistic ground to cover.

ONE

BABY STEPS

As most parents will agree, there is nothing cuter than little toddler mispronunciations, like "wabbit" and "twee," even if potentially a bit embarrassing in public. I still cringe at the accidental swear word that enthusiastically came out for "truck" during a class birthday party before my son had mastered consonant clusters. Luckily, all tends to be forgiven coming from the mouth of those still in training pants because we understand that learning language is no small feat. Mispronounce "sheet" as "shit" as an adult though, and things don't usually go over quite as well.

For speakers of languages like Spanish that have fewer vowels than English, a.k.a. most languages, figuring out new vowel contrasts, like the ones in *sheet* versus *shit*, is not exactly a walk in the park either. That's because it is in our toddling years when our brains home in on the sounds that will end up being the ones we need to know. Tiny infants might babble all sorts of sounds, but by the ripe ol' age of one we have fine-tuned it down to only those found in our language by paying attention to the speech around us.

Remember those variations in speech we talked about, like the dark and light versions of "l"? As an adult, you might be completely unaware of those variations of the "same" sound, but that is only because a baby's first job on the way to adult language skills is figuring out what sounds are the important ones and which ones they can ignore. To do this, baby brains are wired to notice the way sounds pattern in the speech they hear, allowing them to work out which ones their language employs as distinct and which ones are just versions of the "same" sound, a process called *statistical learning*. And all this starts happening before they even understand what's being said! Is it any wonder they don't have time to bother with a toilet and utensils?

The crazy thing is, babies don't really seem to find this such an onerous task. In fact, they seem delighted by their newly emergent language skills (and our desperate need to record it for TikTok) and not at all bothered by the extraordinary amount of work it is to churn out all sorts of sounds, words, and fancy sentences. Even more impressive, they don't need much explicit help from those of us pointing the iPhones at them, other than hearing child-directed adult speech now and again. After all, do you recall ever getting pointers from Mom or Dad on how to make a "p" sound or which variant of "t" should be used in words like *train*? It's a "retroflex t," just in case you were wondering, something that's certainly an unlikely nugget of knowledge for a non-linguist mom or pop anyway. Babies seem to come primed for speech acquisition, figuring out how to produce the sounds and sentences of their language without much in the way of sophisticated instruction. Which is a relief to overburdened parents everywhere, because, take it from me, it would really stink to be responsible for not only keeping those little suckers alive but also for overseeing their proper "t" retroflexion.

Unfortunately, there is a downside to being infant language savants, which is that it doesn't last forever, and it makes language acquisition more difficult later on. Whatever the impetus that drives kids to be able to pick up all the intricate details of sounds and syntax by the time they enter kindergarten, it fades almost as fast as that dewy glow from spring break on the beach. In linguistic circles, there is still a lot of debate about exactly what this impetus is, ranging from Noam Chomsky's theory that we have innate linguistic skills to theories that suggest general learning mechanisms or greater cognitive plasticity help with language acquisition.

Regardless of the reason, after puberty, our ability to acquire language without much effort has dried up, leaving us as adults who have to painstakingly learn how to make the sounds of another language without the benefit of a brain attuned to implicitly picking up on the subtle patterns and variations. Babies have minds and mouths unhindered by past experience and primed to make any of the sounds possible in human language. In adulthood, years of practice with exclusively the patterns in our own language make it super hard to hear and say sounds that don't exist in our native tongue—like the "th" sound my parents still struggle with or, in turn, the rounded front vowels of French in words like *tu* or *peu* that I can't seem to respectably produce.

What this all means is that native-like fluency is about on par with doing a split for those of us past the golden age of adolescence. Still, despite reminding us of our lack of limberness, understanding the way babies learn language can offer us clues about which sounds will be the ones that give adults trouble and why.

NOTHING BUT ORGANIZED

In order to better understand how children learn to say things, we have to know a little something about the different classes or types of sounds we create. Let's start with some easily recognized groups, vowels and consonants. Not only do vowels get their own fun little ditty reminding us how they are written ("a, e, i, o, u, and sometimes y"), but, in speech, they also do the important work of forming syllables, something poor consonants can't generally do.

To see how this is an important difference, think of words you can say that are just a single vowel sound, like the "a" in *a book* or when saying "I." Now, tell me how many English consonants are able to live independent lives without a partner? Um. None. Those consonants are very needy little sounds, always demanding to have a vowel at their side. Why? Because all consonants are made with some blocking of air in the mouth (creating the pop of a "p" or the hisslike quality of "s") while vowels are made with relatively free-flowing air. This makes them louder and longer, and thus, they can stand on their own as syllables, which is what makes it possible for them to be their own words. As an added bonus, this also makes them easier for babies to say because they don't require as much motor control and coordination as consonants, which means they tend to be the earliest sounds babbled in infancy, especially the vowel sounds "ee," "ah," and "ew."

So what about consonants? Consonants are much more sophisticated, at least in articulatory terms, because they involve positioning the vocal folds, tongue, and lips simultaneously in unique ways to form each individual sound. Now get this: adults speak at a rate of about ten to fifteen consonants and vowels per second—with each consonant involving about a dozen concerted movements to create its unique acoustic signature. Some, like "p," "m," and "f" sounds, are somewhat more visible than others in terms of how this is done (i.e., we can see the lips move in making them). This of course is helpful to small children trying to figure out how the hell to make all these sounds their parents keep blabbing. Other sounds, like "sh" or "r," are less obvious, but involve moving parts of the tongue toward different areas in the front or back of the mouth.

Not surprisingly, some of these sounds are quite difficult for wee ones to figure out, but remarkably they keep babbling away. Eventually their mind and mouth work out the ones in their language and how to produce them. How babies do this is a bigger question and one hotly debated, but it likely involves something called *mirror neurons*, which prompt us to imitate or reproduce others' actions by essentially mapping them or embodying them in our own motor cortex system.

What all this means is that learning to speak is not an easy feat for anyone, babies included, and that some sounds require more cognitive maturity and motor control than others. Given the varying degree of mechanics and perceptual abilities involved, true speech sounds are generally not heard until a baby is about four to six months old, and we find an interesting similarity across languages in terms of the sounds that babies practice early on.

Vowels, as just mentioned, are some of the earliest speech sounds that infants make, and we also find babies tend to babble the same set of consonants, namely b, d, g, p, t, k, m, n, w, h, and j. In case you're wondering, the "j" sound mentioned here is the same one we often spell with "y" (as pronounced in *you*) but that is represented as /j/ in the International Phonetic Alphabet. All these consonants are typically babbled alongside vowels, creating sweet little basic baby syllables like "ba," "ta," or "ma." The choice of consonant doesn't depend on what language a child is learning to speak; in a study examining the order that emerged in infant/child speech across twenty-seven languages, these same consonants were always the earliest ones.

Why these in particular? These tend to be the most common consonants universally used in languages, which suggests there is something about them that makes them more easily produced and perceived. This is partially because of the simpler motor mechanics involved in making them. Most of these consonants come from a category linguists call *stops* or *plosives*, where the tongue makes contact with areas along the top of the mouth; this tongue contact briefly holds then releases the air, giving off an audible pop, which is what we hear as that sound (for example, say "p" or "k"). Sounds that involve more coordination among the muscles controlling the tongue to make different shapes, like "r," "l," or "th," take longer to figure out, so those sounds are often not accurately produced before kids are five, six, or even seven years old, driving cute toddler substitutions like "wabbit" and "wuv." These are also the sounds that tend to land kids in speech therapy, as they are harder to master even in the best of times.

A baby's native language may not end up including all the sounds they babble early on, and it isn't until about nine to twelve months of age that a baby narrows down which specific sounds their language uses and no longer makes sounds that their language doesn't have. In other words, early in life, babies are exercising their articulatory motor skills and are universal talkers in the sense of being similar to babies across languages, but, by their first birthday, they have become specific language speakers and are already starting to develop the accents of their native language.

OLD DOGS, NEW SOUNDS

Unfortunately, these amazing abilities that kids have to effortlessly acquire their native language end up becoming the accent albatrosses around our wrinkled and wattled necks.

When adults encounter a new sound, they have to figure out how to move their tongues and mouths in ways they haven't tried since maybe their first year of life. Sounds that are common across languages can be less problematic for adult learners because they are part of many speakers' first language, but sounds that are less frequent (like "th" or "sh") or those that are more complex and variable in how they are pronounced across languages (like "r" or "l") make our first language a hindrance rather than a help. This is a big reason why "l" and "r" contrasts are really hard to learn for speakers of Japanese—the "r"-like sound they produce involves a different tongue gesture than the English "r," so not only do they have to learn to *hear* "r" as a distinct sound from "l" in the first place, they also have to replicate a new tongue movement while trying to suppress their native language's articulatory instincts.

To top it off, languages also change up how a sound is pronounced in different situations—like American English speakers making a "t" a bit more "d"-like in words like *water* or *little*.* We don't have to think about the "rule" we use to do this when we speak, as it has become automatic because of our mad childhood linguistic skills. But put us in a language environment where this rule does not apply, say eating haggis in a pub with a bunch of locals in Glasgow, and it will out our American accent every time, because the downside of automaticity is that, well, duh, it is automatic.

Another example: when Germans say English words like *dog* or *had*, it typically sounds more like "dock" or "hat" because of an automatic rule that affects the way some consonants at the ends of words are pronounced in German. This transfer of a native language pattern becomes a recognizable characteristic of German-accented English. Such influence of our first language on our

* The unconsciously applied rule here is not related to any specific word but instead related to syllable stress, as "t" sounds become flapped when occurring right after a stressed syllable. For instance, compare how American English speakers pronounce *atom* (where "t" is after the stressed "aa" syllable) versus *atomic* (where it isn't).

second language is something known as *language transfer*, and it takes a lot of work and experience with a second language to decrease its effects.

GETTING PAST OUR PROGRAMMING

It might seem counterintuitive, but sometimes the more similar a native language's and second language's sounds are, the more difficult it can be to sound native-like compared to when languages have radically different sounds. For instance, coming from a language like Spanish, which only uses a light "l," the English dark "l" variant is very hard to replicate perfectly because it involves not just a different variant, but also suppressing the ingrained instinct from Spanish in those contexts.

On the other hand, while it would take a lot of practice, learning to make a "w" or "th" sound for a speaker of, say, Russian is a bit easier because there is no underlying competition from the native language, since Russian has neither sound. Even in this case, most Russian speakers will do things like substitute a "v" sound for "w" as part of their accent in English because it is the closest approximate sound that Russian does have. Adults often substitute the closest sounds in their language for non-native ones, especially early on. This doesn't signal ignorance or laziness, but simply the influence of a native language sound system that has been programmed since birth.

Babies likewise often substitute sounds they have already mastered for ones they are still learning (like saying "ting" for *thing*), but this stems from not knowing a sound yet rather than transferring from a system that is fully operational in another language. Yes, the substitutions might seem to be the same because of the principles that govern how sounds generally shift, as we touched on before, but the reasons are quite different. For kids, it's about maturational development of the mouth and mind. For adults, it's about interference from a native language, not to mention that adults simultaneously have to learn new vocabulary and remember where adjectives go and how verbs are conjugated over and above how to get their mouths around new speech sounds.

Another thing that contributes to our accents as adults is not just the sounds and patterns that our infant selves learned, but also what young kids come to know about which sounds can be pronounced together in their native language. So, for instance, in Spanish "sp" or "st" clusters never occur at the beginning of words—a constraint children pick up during their early language exposure. These are known as *phonotactic constraints* to linguists. These constraints are why, as adults, Spanish speakers say things like "es-tudent" or "es-panish" when speaking English, as they are influenced by what they unconsciously learned as children. Likewise, in English, we don't use combinations like "mb" or "mz" at the beginning of words, as can be found in Swahili in words like *mbwa* (dog) or *mzazi* (parent). English learners of Swahili usually stick an extra vowel in between, e.g., "muh-zazi," to make it conform to English rules, which makes them sound different from a native speaker.

Now you may not feel like you've ever been held back in life by your phonotactic constraints, but research tells us that they influence more than simply how you say things. When asked to listen to words with clusters like "st" or "mz" that never start words in their native language, listeners in such experiments actually report hearing vowels that are not there, like the "e" before "student" that pops up for Spanish speakers. Our early life language training is so strong that it affects not only our accent when speaking a foreign language but even makes us hear with an accent! In other words, childhood can screw with us in a number of ways when learning a second language as we get older, though it makes us pretty darn accomplished in our own.

Of course, one often hears anecdotes about somebody's neighbor's sister's roommate's friend who can sound like they were born speaking Mandarin after spending a year in Beijing, but this is an exception rather than the norm (which is why you heard about it in the first place). While focused training, motivation, and a Duolingo streak can absolutely increase fluency, it is much harder to achieve native-like pronunciation as an adult learning a language. That doesn't mean it is impossible, as research has shown that some adult learners are able to pass for native speakers, but they are by far the minority, not the majority.

For instance, one study examined whether twenty-four English speakers who learned German and were going to graduate school in Germany were able to pass for natives in pronunciation, finding that only one out of the twenty-four students did in fact fool the judges. What made him different from the rest? An intense fascination with the language and culture he was immersed in and the desire to sound German (and he was probably related to the neighbor's sister's roommate's friend). But motivation alone, while definitely shown to increase one's acquisitional abilities, is still often not enough to allow adults to sound native the way that children can. Certainly, these other twenty-three students were not slackers; after all, they were taking graduate classes in German, but they were simply not able to fully overcome the barriers imposed by their native language.

Given all of this evidence that accented speech is the norm not the exception and that it is related to the ways our mouths and minds soak up the language of our youth, the lesson we should be taking away is that sounding native-like is not a realistic or necessarily desirable goal when learning a second language. As these students in Germany surely knew, you can communicate quite well even with an accent! Our accents are what show the world we have successfully participated in the universal miracle of childhood language acquisition—and the only part of raising a baby that doesn't require a shit ton of work.

BABY, TALK TO ME

Accents don't just arrive on the heels of another language; they also arise as a by-product of becoming the socially attuned creatures that we are. Even within our first language, there is a lot of variation in how things are said. Some of this variation comes to be recognized as important, because either it points to a specific group (like a Southerner saying "far" for *fire*) or it points to a social meaning, like knowing that "got to" spoken with all its "t"s means business, while "gotta" comes off a lot more chill. But how is it that kids learn not just the sounds of their language, but which pronunciations are the ones they should use as well as when and where?

Well, moms and dads, you might have thought you were off the hook in this whole language learning thing, given the natural predisposition of infants we just discussed, but where would the fun in that be? You still have a linguistic role to play, at least until the teen years, and much of that involves teaching your kiddos the ins and outs of the social meanings associated with the sounds around them. I know, throw this on top of the need to feed them, clothe them, and monitor their social media and you're exhausted already, right? Never fear, you and your kid's natural language instincts are already hard at work, and I bet you barely even noticed.

When we look at how it is that kids learn not just a language, but the dialect of their environment and its socially relevant variation, we find that adults are the equivalent of linguistic Yodas, subtly providing life lessons through unconscious modeling in how we say what we say to kids. The secret sauce lies in what we fancy linguists call *child-directed speech* (CDS), or what people who actually have friends call baby talk or caregiver-ese. Yup, that elongated, repetitious, slowed down, singsongy drivel that we patty-cake to our babies seems to be part of the magic recipe for helping kids learn not just how to divide our speech into separate sounds and words, but also to understand the social patterning of those sounds and when they are important.

Now, I know there are often glossy parenting magazines or internet blogs that debate the value of baby talk, but, scientifically speaking, baby talk does seem to offer linguistic pointers to infants, helping them break down the stream of speech coming at them in various ways, and there is no evidence it holds babies back at all. Do we absolutely need to do it? Probably not, as babies in cultures that do not use baby talk are able to acquire language without issue. Instead, it merely speeds up a process that happens naturally and it makes us feel like we are connecting with our infants.

Not surprisingly, much of the research on baby talk focuses on mothers, possibly because male scientists are never home long enough to chat up their kids. Still, that research has pointed to some interesting patterns in the types of speech moms use with their babies despite pigeonholing them as baby raisers. For one, mothers tend to be hyperarticulate in terms of how they pronounce their vowels when talking to their baby, which is likely a way of helping the little bean learn to recognize the ones that are important in their language. They also have been found to emphasize contrasts between consonants like "t" and "d" or "k" and "g" more than when talking to adults. Again, this makes sense as an assist to babies in figuring out the basic categories of their language.

But the role of moms doesn't appear to stop with the highlighting of what sounds their language will have. Research suggests mom also models the latest in linguistic finery—early on using the most standard versions of sounds with her pumpkins, even if she rarely uses them when chatting with other adults. Linguist Julie Roberts looked at Southern pronunciations like those of "bah" for *bye* and "todd" for *tide* in the speech of moms in Memphis, Tennessee. She found that all the moms she studied used the more standard pronunciations when talking to their kids compared to when they were talking with the interviewer, a pattern echoed in other studies. For example, in a working-class town called Tyneside in Northern England, where residents are known as Geordies, researchers similarly found mothers using fewer local forms with their kids, especially in the earliest years, than they did when speaking to other adults.

Why would this be? It might be driven by mom's desire to teach her kiddo the speech forms that are most widely accepted, but since kids are often there when mom talks to adults using her more typical speech, it is also a way of introducing babies to the types of variability they will encounter and showing that "friend talk" involves the more local or casual variants—in other words, hinting at values that have become attached to forms. We also find studies that suggest that when moms repeat something, they often use a more reduced form than in their original saying of that word or phrase—"Is that your little toe? Where's ya' li' toe?"—which is a signal of intimacy and closeness. In contrast, when moms are in teaching or explanatory modes, they tend to use more full or standard forms. All of this modeling helps teach kids the basic sounds they need to command and provides clues as to how to interpret the different pronunciations they hear around them.

Interestingly, what moms highlight in terms of usage norms also seems to change over time. Research finds that moms decrease the use of hyperarticulate forms and standard pronunciations as babies get older. Going back to that study looking at mother/child interactions in Tyneside, moms started using more of the local

Geordie accent with their kids as they aged up from two to four years old. This suggests that the earlier pronunciations are focused on helping kids figure out the basic sounds their language has, and once that is accomplished, moms shift to using the specific accents that will prove socially valuable to their kids in their local environment.

Some evidence we have for this interpretation is the fact that moms often use more positively valued forms (like "talking" versus "talkin'") with girls than they do with boys, which tells us that they are trying to use the pronunciations that will prove most socially beneficial to their kids. In this way, moms are attending to the generalized cultural belief that girls need to be ladies, while boys can get a bump for being tougher or coming across as a bit more slangy. When we look at studies of adult speech, this pattern of women tending to use "better" pronunciations holds—women often use more standard forms of speech compared to men. Dads, on the other hand, don't seem to change up their speech when directed to children nearly as much—something that seems to reinforce the associations of more local or less standard speech as a boy thing.

All this brings us back to how we get regional, class, or ethnic accents within the same language. While moms and dads provide some of our initial training, their influence becomes less important once we discover something way more exciting: cool peers. What we find in sociolinguistic research on kids exposed to more than one dialect, say when moving to a new area, is that success in getting a new accent down depends greatly on two factors: the age when they move and their integration with speakers of the new dialect.

A number of studies have traced kids from the same families that have moved from one place to another where a different dialect is spoken and discovered that, as with acquiring a completely new language, the youngest kids are more successful at picking up native-like abilities in the new dialect compared to their older siblings. That success is in large part driven by their early exposure to a peer group in preschool or kindergarten, something that also explains why kids who are born into families with a different home language don't end up sounding like their parents.

One well-known study looked at kids who had moved to Philadelphia from elsewhere in the country at different ages and found that kids who moved before age four ended up sounding very similar to Philly natives. Those older than four picked up many accent features, i.e., they might drink "wooder," the iconic Philly pronunciation of *water*, but their accent was not completely native-like.

Interestingly, where one's parents were from made a difference even for locally born kids. Those with parents also from Philly were the only ones who were able to replicate all aspects of the local accent perfectly, while those with out-of-state parents were not. This doesn't mean that they couldn't pass for locals, but simply that, from a linguistic perspective, they were not completely conforming to the local dialect patterns. What this tells us is that our local accents start forming even before we are born, probably when listening to our mother's speech in utero, and are darn hard to get rid of even in the most perfect circumstances.

When we consider that most of us grow up and go to school with people from backgrounds, neighborhoods, and ethnicities similar to ours, the idea that it is somehow simple to just "pick up" a new or socially preferred accent is pretty ludicrous. Second dialect acquisition works similarly to second language acquisition—once your system is set, picking up another variety gets much more difficult because your mouth and mind have already zeroed in on specific sounds and patterns. Being surrounded by speakers of that new variety certainly helps, especially if you are strongly motivated because of your peer group, but that means most speakers will shift closer to the local accents of their friend group, not toward some other accent that teachers or principals use. And, since a lot of us don't move until we are adults, our ability to do the accent hokey-pokey is often close to nil. The gist is that much of the way we will sound—whether we are talking about a foreign accent or an English one—is related to our experience with language and its speakers in early childhood.

BABY, DON'T JUDGE ME

While they are busy learning the sounds and patterns that will become the accents of their future, kids are also forming social preferences via messaging they get from parents, peers, media, and institutions. We all know adults tend to be quite judgy when it comes down to the way others talk, but a good question is how much young kids notice, and have opinions about, the accents they hear around them. When do they start to see differences in pronunciation as providing some useful social information about speakers and situations, like that lil' Susie doesn't sound like she's from around here or that Jimmy is a bossy smarty-pants because he is always hyperarticulating his "t"s and "ing"s?

You might think kids don't yet know enough about the world to make any kind of social inferences. But research suggests that children are learning to categorize at the same time that they are learning to be linguistically savvy. What I mean by this is that, very early on, kids might notice and pick up linguistic variation without any real sense of its social relevance, but by the time they go to school, they start to notice that people are different in certain ways—there are girls versus boys or people who look similar and people who don't—and seeing these no longer simply as aspects related to individuals but as socially defined groups.

From there, it's not much of a leap to observe that these social differences ride shotgun to linguistic differences, and to judge speakers in terms of whether they are "like me" or "not like me," a first step on the road to developing language attitudes. By the time kids hit five years old, they are already pretty good at recognizing and associating accents with social facts like where someone is from. Of course, anyone who's fielded endless questions from kindergarteners about every inane detail of daily life may not be that surprised to learn of their keen sense of accent observation, but what might surprise you is that they don't just notice accents at a young age, they also develop some strong feelings about them.

You might be familiar with college students complaining about difficulties understanding foreign TAs, but it seems we can trace the seeds of this same-accent bias all the way back to kindergarten. Looking at how accents played into social judgments for a group of five-year-olds, psychologists discovered that they preferred teachers who shared their same accent and also believed they would make better teachers than those with foreign or even just nonlocal accents. These preferences also translate into who they want to hang around with: a large number of studies in both the United States and elsewhere find that five- and six-year-old kids are more attracted to friends who sound like they do. A similar pattern has also been found in terms of race, but it turns out that accent is an even more influential buddy determiner. Kids of a different race but with a similar accent were preferred over those of the same race who sounded different.

One might surmise this simply means kids are drawn to familiar-sounding people over strange people, i.e., the "stranger danger" we instill in them with great regularity, but that doesn't appear to be all that is at work here. First of all, even kids with multilingual exposure show this same social preference despite having more accent experience. Even more compelling evidence that there is more to the story comes by way of another study, which found that kids not only prefer friends who have accents more like their own, but also those whose accents are considered socially prestigious where they live (like Standard English versus Hawaiian Creole English). This tells us that, by the time kids start school, they are already tuned in to, at least at some level, an accent's social currency.

Still, these early language attitudes don't yet mirror those adults hold, in that young kids don't necessarily dislike or devalue other accents, but simply prefer native or high-status ones. It is not until kids are a little older that accents appear to trigger the same cultural stereotypes about speakers as they do for grown-ups. For instance, ideas that Southerners are "nice" while Northerners are "smarter" start to show up in comments kids make around the time they hit upper-elementary ages.

Why do kids hold on to strong allegiance and positive vibes for their own, sometimes less prestigious, accents? Our accents start at birth and are part of our relationship with those who are important to us. Cultural attitudes take years to develop and depend on your perspective, so kids' accents are well established by the time they fully understand how the adult world views them. By then, kids also have bonds to the identities and people that their accents represent. What we find is that cognitive, articulatory, and social factors early in life are extremely powerful influences on the way we talk and how we perceive others. This might seem like a bust rather than a boon, especially to those who wish they could learn to pronounce "th" sounds, but, as we will come to see in the next chapter, it is very likely the way nature intended.

FROM BABBLES TO BABEL

Before we move on to accents as we adults experience them, we have to explore one last linguistic contribution from babies: the beginning of language itself.

Have you ever noticed how many languages around the world have similar words for what kids call their mothers and fathers? Think American English *mama* and *dada*, French *maman* and *papa*, Armenian *mam* and *pap*, Italian *mamma* and *babbo*, Latvian *māma* and *paps*, Spanish *mamá* and *papá*, Slovak *mama* and *tato*, Welsh *mam* and *tad*. You might, very reasonably, conjecture that these languages inherited them from the same ancestral source, like Latin or Greek, easily explaining this prevalence of mamas and papas. While that makes sense for languages like French and Spanish, which descended from the same source (Latin), it doesn't hold up to deeper scrutiny because we find words like *papa*, *dada*, *tata*, *baba,* or *abba* as well as *mama* and *nana* across all sorts of unrelated languages: Tamil *amma* and *appaa*, Chinese *mama* and *baba*, Arabic *māmā* and *bābā*, Swahili *mama* and *baba,* Tagalog *nanay* and *tatay*.

Even more intriguing, the form and meaning of these terms shows remarkable resilience to change: over thousands of years and across many languages, mothers have answered to the call of "mama" by children the world round. This consistency in meaning doesn't tend to hold true for other words that get handed down or borrowed, a process that usually includes shifting senses as words move across lands and speakers. Just consider the semantic distance between the English word *dish* and the German word *tisch* (meaning "table"), which both descended from the same source (Greek *diskos*/Latin *discus*). Likewise, sounds constantly change over time, giving us hard-to-see-at-first relatives like English *tea* and Hindi *chai,* both from the same hypothesized ancient root *lra.* In contrast, baby words for our mamas and papas haven't strayed very far from their phoneme flock. What gives?

A lot, so make sure you are strapped in. Let's revisit our earlier discussion of baby babble. Remember how we said that babbling starts around four to six months and often involves a simple combo of a consonant and a vowel forming a basic syllable? Remember also that those consonants and vowels tend to be drawn from the same limited set of options, which results in common early babbles like "da," "ta," "na," "ma," or "pa." Not to mention that babies tend to be boringly repetitive, à la "mamama" or "papapa," a big reason why they don't make particularly scintillating conversational partners, at least not to those of us who like to banter over a dirty martini instead of a dirty diaper.

But parents, on the other hand, are mightily transfixed by whatever mumblings emanate from their precious offspring and respond with their own baby talk variants, building off those they hear. Since *mama* and *papa* are words extant in many languages—and since the role of mom and dad is primary in most of them—it is not surprising that babies, though actually oblivious, are assumed to be naming their mamas and papas rather than simply performing routine articulatory exercises in advance of the hard linguistic work yet to come. In part due to vanity, and in part due to our job as elder statespeople for language transmission, we parents pick up on and reinforce an association between specific patterns of baby babbles and the words that refer to us. In short, we are teaching our babies sound-meaning correspondences, i.e., the link between specific sound combos and the things they have come to represent.

This parent-child linguistic collaboration is why these words tend to not vary much across time and space—the child provides the building blocks from universal early babbling patterns, while parents provide the glue, namely putting those babbles together with a universal concept, i.e., the presence of a parent. The concepts and sounds are therefore the same with every generation, leading to words resistant to the changes that less elemental words encounter, in large part because young babies can't make other sounds yet.

This, of course, is a beautiful example of how the most fundamental form of social relationship—that of parent and child—drove the collaborative creation of the words we use to refer to mothers and fathers across languages that otherwise might seem quite distant. Some theorists propose that the universality and stability over time of these terms, along with the process of parents' linking babbles to meaning, make a good case that these were the first words ever conceived by ancient *Homo sapiens*, well before true language abilities developed. These words, spawned from the social centrality of kinship ties in hunter-gatherer societies and the obvious fact that mothers and fathers had to have been there since the beginning, could have been passed on as languages diverged, one of the few, if any, surviving descendants of the primordial language from which they evolved. Other theorists instead believe these words have simply sprung anew in each successive language family because of these same tendencies in universal babbling and parents' desires to be recognized and named. The key here in either case is that the patterns from our childhood leave a long and lasting trace not just on our development as we become adults but also on the path of language over time, the very topic that we take up next.

TWO

OUR ORIGIN STORY

There is no doubt among language scientists that nary a one of the seven thousand or so languages we now speak was the original language from which our *mama* and *papa* might derive.* But knowing anything for certain about that language is harder. We can't even be absolutely sure that the advent of language was a singular event in our prehistory, since the earliest *Homo sapiens* didn't leave any physical evidence of language behind. The monogenetic (or one time) theory of language is most probable given the fundamental linguistic and genetic similarities we find across humans, suggesting an original source and its subsequent migratory dispersal gave rise to the range of languages we have today.

Though *Homo sapiens* might have been wandering around as

* The tabulation of languages is a more complex task than it may at first appear, given the fact that the criteria for what counts as a language are not easy to establish. This rough figure comes from the well-respected language catalog *Ethnologue.*

far back as three hundred thousand years ago, it has only been within the last fifty to one hundred thousand years in which we see consistent evidence of intentional artistic, technological, and cultural behaviors that suggest humans had developed the symbolic thinking necessary for language. But while bones, pottery, and tool fragments might help us trace the culture and evolution of these early humans, the fossils of speech lie in the languages that have developed since. Considering the diversity of languages that exist today, there is no denying that language has changed a lot and many times over the course of its history. The question is how and why.

DON'T BE A DING-DONG

The origin of language was the subject of great curiosity to linguists and philosophers in the eighteenth and nineteenth centuries, seeding a number of theories on how human speech originated, including the entertainingly titled bow-wow, pooh-pooh, and yo-he-ho theories. These labels were the brainchild of German philologist Max Müller, who liked to poke a little fun at some prominent theorists, particularly anyone named Darwin. Müller was not a big fan of the idea of the first language developing via the chatter of apelike ancestors, believing language the "Rubicon which divides man from beast." But Darwin, continuing a line of thinking of some earlier German philosophers, thought that language evolved from these ancestors' imitation of sounds in nature (like animal noises or ocean waves), which were then used referentially for those things, spurring more complex symbolic thinking alongside.

The seminal example, of course, is using *bow wow* to mean a dog and not just to imitate a dog's barking, providing the impetus for the theory's moniker. In a somewhat similar vein, the pooh-pooh theory hypothesized that language evolved from the interjections (ah!) and emotional cries humans made, like the primordial grunt that still escapes when you painfully stub your toe. A somewhat different approach is taken by the yo-he-ho theory, which presumes that social interaction drove the instigation of language, as in uttering "yo-heave-ho" to coordinate the physical efforts of multiple people. Müller's own idea, which in a bit of fair play became known as the ding-dong theory, was that sounds themselves carried intrinsic meaning, like a low-pitched sound giving off a sense of something big, i.e., as in a *blob* (low vowel) compared to the smaller sounding *bleeb* (high vowel).

This might seem a bit far fetched, perhaps making Müller sound like the ding-dong, but later research does suggest there is something to it. In a well-known experiment performed early in the twentieth century, individuals tended to match the made-up word *mil* with a small object, while the likewise made-up word *mal* was matched with a large one. Why would this be? Because the /i/ vowel, pronounced "ee," involves a high pitch and a more closed mouth, while the /a/ vowel, as in "ahh," has a low pitch and a more open (larger) mouth. A recent and more famous study also discovered that when participants heard the word *bouba,* they were more likely to assign it to smooth or round objects, presumably because of the lip rounding involved in saying the "ou" vowel. Sounds with sharper "popping" qualities, like the "k" in *kiki*, in contrast, tended to be associated with spiky or sharp objects. This became known as the *bouba-kiki effect* or, using another similar experiment's sample words, the *maluma/takete effect*. In these cases, the sounds themselves conveyed something about the object they described, a theory now known as *sound symbolism*.

This particular theory has taken on more credibility as modern studies have shown that words in many languages do show evidence of such patterning, like words meaning "round" across different languages often including an "r" sound, as it is a sound made with rounded lips. Certainly, this rings true for English's *round*, and, since I mentioned it, for the round-shape-describing word *ring* too. Despite the zany names, all these theories do make a good go at imagining how human proto-language emerged, but because of the largely speculative and unprovable nature of such ideas, continued discussion of the topic was banned in the nineteenth century by European linguistic societies, which deemed it the stuff of philosophy rather than the stuff of science.

GETTING BACK TO OUR ROOTS

While perhaps going back to the very beginning was a bit of an overreach, substantial new insight into how sounds have changed over time came when, in 1786, Sir William Jones, a British judge posted in India, revealed striking similarities across the languages of Europe and the classical language of India, Sanskrit. Most Europeans had never heard of Sanskrit, of course, and his publicizing of its existence—and its unexpected similarity to languages like Latin and Greek—led to a significant expansion in thought about those languages' prehistory. Prior to this discovery, the European line of thinking was that Hebrew was the original language, though locating any identifiable relationship between Hebrew and European languages had proven a bit of a puzzle. In contrast, comparing words across Sanskrit and European languages, Jones and his contemporaries were stunned by what appeared to be systematic correspondences not just in a word or two, but in many many words.

To get a sense of this, compare words for "two" across Latin (*duo*), Greek (*duo*), and Sanskrit (*dvo*). Now let's look at the words for "foot" across these languages too, as in *ped* (Latin), *pód* (Greek), and *pád* (Sanskrit). Finally, we can't forget someone so important that his name is virtually identical no matter the language, namely our dear father, as in *pater* (Latin), *patḗr* (Greek), and *pitár* (Sanskrit).* Though the "pa" might be from the mouths of babes, there is a surprising similarity in the kinship suffix (*ter/tar*) used across these languages, also found when all three describe their mothers (*mater/mētēr/mātār*) and brothers (*frater/phratér/bhrātár*).

Taken together, these shared forms, known as *cognate* words, seemed an impossible coincidence, particularly before the advent of cell phones or airplanes, unless these languages had developed

* In Hebrew, by comparison, "two" is *shenaim,* "foot" is *regel,* and "father" is *av* or *ab.*

from the same original source, a hypothesized language known as Proto-Indo-European. Unsurprisingly, this new twist to the origin story was not at first universally embraced by Eurocentric scholars, who were none too happy to have their version of linguistic antiquity blown up.

So how did one ancient tongue become such disparate languages? Scholars hypothesize that a single Indo-European people spread across much of Eurasia in different waves starting some eight thousand or so years ago following the advent of agriculture and the domestication of horses. As migrating groups became isolated from one another, changes started to occur, driven by our inherent propensities (like ease of articulation and perception) and the tendency we have to talk more like those with whom we hang out—our own tribe. At first, minor changes would simply have been the equivalent of dialects emerging as distance developed among groups, giving rise to the first regionally distributed accents. Over time linguistic variation increased to the point where these speaker groups no longer understood one another, essentially creating new languages—the precursors of the Indo-European languages we have today.

Modern non-Indo-European languages likewise came about via the dispersal of other ancient tongues as humans spread across the world. These now extinct languages included ones like Proto-Afroasiatic, Proto-Sino-Tibetan, and Proto-Austronesian, which eventually gave rise to modern languages such as Hebrew, Chinese, and Tagalog as changes, both social and linguistic, worked their magic. Tracing all these proto-languages for which we have no records back to any shared common ancestor, though, becomes a lot more dicey.

SOUNDING A BIT GRIMM

Beyond revising the origin story, a most influential finding emerging from Jones's discovery (and the subsequent revolution in linguistic thinking it inspired) was that sound change was both quite common in the historical record and extremely principled rather than chaotic or arbitrary.

By comparing the Indo-European languages now known to be related, a group of scholars going by the catchy title "Neogrammarians" found that the sound changes that had happened over time were so systematic that they decided to refer to them as "sound laws." The most famous of these sound laws was Grimm's law, which explains how a number of consonants changed into new sounds as one group of ancient Indo-European speakers went off on their merry way about three thousand years ago.

Their Indo-European dialect became a language known as Proto-Germanic, which was the common Germanic language that existed before splitting into subsequent languages like German, Danish, English, and the long-gone Gothic. Latin, Greek, and Sanskrit, on the other hand, descend from different lines of ancient Indo-Europeans, namely the Romance, Hellenic, and Indo-Iranian groups, respectively. Though these sound changes affecting only the Germanic line had first been noticed by a Danish philologist with the remarkably alliterative name of Rasmus Rask, the credit for the discovery landed with Jacob Grimm. Yup, one of the very same brothers Grimm of fairy-tale fame, who wrote about it in his German grammar book and got all the glory. Guess being a folk-tale celebrity cum linguist makes one a bit more memorable than being just a language historian.

To get a sense of what Grimm's law was, let's take a gander at the "p" sound mentioned earlier as we find in words for *father* and *foot* across Latin (*pater*, *pes*), Greek (*patḗr*, *pód*), and Sanskrit (*pitár*, *pád*). Since all the oldest known Indo-European languages also had "p" beginning these words, it was assumed that this was the original sound inherited from their Indo-European source. For instance, scholars reconstructing the hypothesized ancient root from which our *father* sprung suggest it was something along the lines of *phtḗr*.

Now, if you look at words descended from this same Indo-European root in the Germanic line of languages, instead of "p," these words all start with an "f" sound, giving us modern *father*, *foot* (English), *Vater*, *Fuß*, said as "fater" and "foos" (German), *far*, *fot* (Swedish), and *vader*, *voet* (Dutch), also pronounced as "f" even if written with a "v." This tells us that, as Proto-Germanic speakers were separated from other Indo-Europeans, their "p" sounds slowly shifted into "f" sounds, and this had to have happened before Proto-Germanic itself morphed into separate languages like German, English, Swedish, and so on.

Around the same time, Germanic languages also changed Indo-European "k" into "h" sounds, giving us *hound* (English) and *Hund* (German) for dog, where Latin has *canus* and Ancient Greek has *kúōn*. The word *canine* came into English later from French, providing both its "k" sound and swanky Latin pedigree, which is why using "canine" ups the price of dog food by at least twenty bucks a bag. And what of *dog*? Well, in Old English, the generic word for dog was *hund*, not *dog*, a word that instead seems to have at that time referred only to a specific breed of hund. Nowadays all dogs are dogs and only a specific type of dog is a hound, so go figure, and, while you're at it, stop complaining that "literally" now means its opposite.

As a quick aside, this dog/hund switch up is an example of meaning change called *semantic broadening* (in the case of *dog* moving from a specific to a more general term) and *semantic narrowing* (in the case of *hund/hound* becoming more specific). While it might seem an odd process, it is far from unusual. For instance, *meat* used to refer to food in general but narrowed to mean food from animal flesh around the thirteenth century. In terms of meaning becoming broader, a recent example is how the word *Kleenex*, originally a specific brand name, has become our go-to word when talking about any tissue, as in "Can you hand me a kleenex?"

But, getting back to the effects of Grimm's law, by the time Proto-Germanic split off into its daughter languages, sound changes had made not just Indo-European "p" into "f" and "k" into "h," but also changed Indo-European "t" into "th," and this is how English ultimately came to have this unusual sound. Now, you might wonder how it is that English still has "p," "t," and "k" today, but these sounds made their return to Germanic languages via other processes, only now they exist side by side with the new "f," "h" and "th" sounds they spawned. Whew, right?

These sound changes all happened before English was even a glint in her Germanic ancestor's eye, but many more regular sound changes arrived in English after she split from her Germanic siblings. Examples of these include some "k" sounds becoming what we now know as the "ch" sound, giving us *chin* from *kinn* and *church* from *kirk*. Germanic "sk" clusters also changed into the "sh" sound, morphing *skirt* into *shirt*. English later borrowed the older form of *skirt* back via the Old Norse spoken by the Vikings who settled nearby, nicely providing a bottom to go with those tops. It is during this period as well when the "w" sound began to be deleted after "s," but only before certain vowels. This is why words like *sword* and *answer* are spelled with a "w," which we never pronounce, while we still say *and* spell it in *sweet* and *swish*.

Just to keep things interesting, English also added a new sound or two, as hip and powerful Anglo-French society made "v" and "z" sounds all the rage after the Norman invasion. Today these sounds create a meaning distinction, as in making "fans" different from "vans," but they didn't before French phonology rubbed off on English. It was contact with Norman French, and their words using a "v" sound for meaning differences (as in "fine" versus "vine") that gradually made English speakers start to be aware of and use the distinction. Before that "v" was just an alternate pronunciation for an "f" in certain word positions. In fact, this is the reason we have "f"/"v" pairs in *wife/wives* and *knife/knives* today; this old pronunciation pattern is still reflected in the spelling despite the loss of the final vowels that caused the alternation in the first place. The bigger point being that all of these changes just mentioned came into our speech due to the same type of natural linguistic processes we discussed previously. Whine all you want about people who change "th" sounds into "t" or "f," but know you are the pot calling the kettle black.

It is true that the differences we notice around us at any one moment seem much less obviously patterned—but only because we don't know how to look for the method behind what seems to be madness. The sound differences that looked so regular and systematic to the Neogrammarians were already in the rearview of history by the time anyone thought to talk about them. Since today's variations are not consistently used by everyone, it makes it appear that they follow no "rules." But the piece of the puzzle left unsolved by these early scholars was why these sound changes ever got started in Germanic speech and no one else's in the first place. It turns out the key to understanding the variations arising in both modern and ancient speech rests not in comparing cognate words, but in understanding the social power of sounding different.

THE SOCIAL LIFE OF LANGUAGE CHANGE

Until the 1960s, language change was something that only seemed apparent in hindsight: once everybody started using a new sound instead of the old one and talked about how weird it was that people once said "pater" for *father*. Even those who studied language for a living had not considered how variation occurring simultaneously in the same language (like "shtring" versus "string") might fit into the bigger picture of linguistic evolution.

It took the groundbreaking work of linguist Bill Labov, whom we met briefly in the introduction when he got Paul Prinzivalli off the hook for airline sabotage, to figure out how to look for regular patterns in what felt simply like linguistic chaos around us. Labov was able to show that even the most seemingly haphazard variations in modern speech followed regular linguistic rules and made perfect sense, but only if you took the time to see that speakers were really the main movers and shakers, and natural linguistic tendencies simply their sandbox. As people become socially closer or distant, so goes their language.

This is because it is the group of people you interact with the most who have the greatest impact on the way you speak. This means that our age, our ethnicity, our class, or simply our neck of the woods puts us together in unique ways, and it is the nature of those relationships—beneficial or not, intimate or formal, antagonistic or amicable—that moves us closer or further apart in the way we speak and predicts the variants we use.

As we talked about in the introduction, language variation exists all around us, but we only notice it when it aligns with a social divide our society has deemed important—and about which we, and others we spend time with, have positive or negative views. It's a good bet that when ancient Germanic types chitchatted about their feet and their fathers, there was a period when some segment of that society pronounced it as "poos" and "pater" and bitched about that unsavory group across the horse tracks who sounded like they had marbles in their mouths, saying "foos"* and "fater." But maybe over the years that group had more bountiful crops or more fashion-forward animal pelts, and lo and behold, the new pronunciation became the hip one to know. Soon, everyone was all "foos" and no "poos." By the time English came into being, no one even remembered the social dynamics or alternative pronunciations that had once existed.

What is most germane here to our understanding of today's accents is that the diversification of language is not just a linguistic occurrence, it is a fundamentally social one. While there are natural biases built into the language system that shape the direction of change (guided by the ease of articulation and perception we discussed earlier), the fact that they do not do so in the same ways and at a constant rate tells us that something else is afoot.

A key question is, if such changes follow the same underlying processes, why would similar sound changes not have happened in non-Germanic branches, like the Romance line that produced French, Spanish, and Italian, as well? What made those Proto-Germans so special? Not much, except for the fact that a small articulatory bias toward pronouncing "p" sounds as "f" must have become magnified as part of a process of cultural transmission and in-group affiliation. Since the articulatory bent that morphed "p" into "f" was slight and competition from other linguistic biases prevalent, speakers outside this group would be much less likely to

* For simplicity here, I just use a modified reflex of the modern German word for foot, but, in reality, the "s" we find pronounced at the end of modern German *Fuß* reflects a later (unrelated) sound change of a "t" into an "s."

show evidence of that specific sound change instead of myriad others.

While the way our brains and mouths work predisposes us toward some types of sound changes more than others, specific ones catch on because social pressures of various types made that particular change advantageous or attractive in some socially symbolic way to other speakers who identify with them. Accents are not just accidental by-products of linguistic evolution; they are useful in the same way that dressing like a goth or a jock helps establish one's clique membership in high school. Social divides make for linguistic divides in the same way as miles and mountains, and, once separated, small differences in the way some members of a group pronounce things start to become big things in the way they see themselves and how others categorize them.

ANCIENT ACCENT DIVIDES

There is plenty of evidence that all societies, modern and ancient, have pretty strong feelings about the way people talk. As far back as the fourth century BCE, the Sanskrit grammarian Pāṇini wrote of noticing regional variation in his impressive book of Sanskrit rules, mentioning that some forms were preferred and some more marginal. Though he tended not to be very judgy, those who came after were a bit less accepting. Educated Greeks, in the first few centuries of the Christian era, got pretty worked up about the use of everyday "street" Greek, otherwise known as Koine, instead of the hoity-toity classical Attic dialect, not to mention being none too happy about the increasing use of Latin after those Romans took over. And speaking of Romans, there was certainly no shortage of linguistic snobbery in ancient Rome. Cicero, the famous orator, warns his readers to avoid what he refers to as "rustic" and "outlandish" regional pronunciations, likely reflecting his own desire, as someone with a provincial upbringing, to attain the "proper" accent of elite Roman society.

In perhaps the ultimate example of ancient accent discrimination, the Old Testament relays the story of how the "wrong" pronunciation of a single word became a fatal litmus test, as described in the Book of Judges. As the story goes, there were two warring Semitic tribes, the Gileadites and the Ephraimites. After a great battle, the Gileadites smote the Ephraimites, forcing the survivors to retreat. Unfortunately for the Ephraimites, the Gileadites were also a bit quicker on their feet, making it back to the folds along the River Jordan faster than you can say "shibboleth,"* which is exactly what the Gileadites required all those seeking passage to pronounce.

This turned out to be a quite a problem for the fleeing Ephraimites, because it just so happened that it was about like asking a German to say the English word *squirrel*, a pronunciation one British TV host recently (and jokingly) suggested should be used to weed out German spies. Of course, the biblical stakes were a bit higher than the resulting "Watch Germans say 'squirrel'" videos on YouTube, in that the Ephraimites, who had an "s" sound in

* Thought to mean "stream" in ancient Hebrew. Some have suggested instead it meant "ear of corn," although that seems less likely in this scenario.

their dialect but no "sh" sound, were slain as soon as "sibboleth" instead of "shibboleth" left their lips.

The modern usage of the word *shibboleth*, meaning a pronunciation that pinpoints someone's identity or group membership, derives from this story in the Old Testament. But this biblical account is far from the only example of life-or-death pronunciation passwords, and strangely enough, such shibboleths tend to center around names for foodstuffs. In 1282, the Sicilian word for chickpea, *ciciri*, was used to root out French citizens in Sicily during an uprising against French occupation (known as the Sicilian Vespers) and the Sardinian pronunciation of chickpea (*cixiri*) helped to out unwanted and differently accented Piedmontese officials in 1794. In both cases, those beans really did turn out to be heart healthy—but only for the locals. In 1937, during a horrific period in the Dominican Republic's history, dictator Rafael Trujillo used the pronunciation of the Spanish word for parsley, *perejil*, as a way to recognize (and kill) Haitian Creole–speaking immigrants. They stood out when saying this word because they didn't use the local Dominican "r" pronunciation, resulting in the slaughter of thousands in what has become known as the Parsley Massacre.

Fortunately, not all shibboleths end in death and destruction. In my adopted home state of Nevada, mistakenly saying the state name with the "ah" vowel (Ne-vah-da, as in "pod") instead of the "aa" vowel (Ne-va-da, as in "pad") only invites trouble if you persist after being corrected or you are a national politician who should know better from the get-go. I will admit that not messing up the state name loomed large in my psyche when I first arrived for my campus job interview, especially after the first five people I met schooled me on its proper pronunciation. You might similarly find yourself escorted across state lines if you mess up some names in Kentucky, where the local pronunciation of Louisville is most definitely "Loo-uh-vul" and not "Lou-is-vil." Beyond geography, we also find shibboleths associated with ethnicity, such as saying "aks" for *ask* in African American English or pronouncing "z" as "s" for some speakers of Jewish/Yiddish background, i.e., "is" instead of "iz."

What shibboleths like these tell us is that accent features throughout history have been used as shortcuts for group identification, which might make us wonder whether this might just be by linguistic design.

THE EVOLUTION OF ACCENT

If we look at accents from the standpoint of evolutionary psychology, they provide an important group referencing purpose, allowing members of the same tribe to quickly identify one another while also making outsiders stand out. It has been hypothesized that having accents trigger social categorization is a "design feature" we are endowed with as humans, likely because of this group signaling advantage it conferred. In other words, we are "hardwired" to notice accents.

Looking to test this idea, one study had American participants listen to both American English speakers and British English speakers making neutral statements while they were being shown a photo of each speaker. When, in a pop quiz later on, they were asked to match each photo with that speaker's specific statements, participants made a lot of errors (who wouldn't!), but there was a pattern to these errors: listeners confused speakers within each accent but not so much between them. In essence, they could remember only that some British-sounding guy said that, but not which specific one. Here, listeners appeared to unconsciously be relying on accent type, not other things the speakers shared, like a hair color, coughing, or similar clothing, to remember and group speakers.

In a final study using two different non-native English accents, listeners showed the same pattern of confusing speakers within the same accent but not so much across different ones, meaning, again, that listeners zoomed in on their specific accents as way of sorting speakers. Clearly, accents are powerful tools that help us quickly identify others in terms of the groups to which they belong.

This social categorizing we do today on the basis of accent probably evolved from our early ancestors' need to rapidly assess one another and the potential for cooperation or threat. Since cooperation is more expected when we have shared backgrounds and knowledge, we also evolved to have a social preference for accents more like our own. Even very young babies with no understanding of their larger social world have been found to show a preference for speakers with native accents as opposed to foreign ones. These findings tell us that we are uniquely attuned to the social distinctions signaled by an accent even before we have any capacity to understand what they mean. As linguist Jack Chambers put it, "So persistent and pervasive are the social judgments of language use that they must be embedded in human nature."

This hardwiring doesn't give us an evolutionary excuse to be judgmental. Instead, it just tells us that paying attention to accents is not inherently a bad thing. The key is the perspective we take—accents can highlight our fundamental similarities as humans more than they do our differences. The variation in sounds that we hear as "good" or "bad"—or even just as markers that someone comes from somewhere else—are all sown by the underlying predispositions we share as speakers with mouths and minds constantly adjusting for economy and clarity. Sounds like the "p" that turned into "f" or the "sh" pronounced as "s" simply started as one of many such adjustments, but ones that became enmeshed with aspects of place and identity, like being Germanic or Ephraimite. We will see over these pages, as we trace the path of accents past and present, that issues don't really start to come up until nation, power, and status get added in the mix.

SOUND BITE

Hate Moist? *Join the Club.*

Nineteenth-century philologists are far from the only ones who have spent time pondering the great mysteries that drive our speech. Everyday folks think about language-related questions all the time. They might not be tackling the big ones like its ancient beginnings or how Latin "p"s relate to English "f"s, but a lot of people would be satisfied resolving more minor linguistic concerns, like how to stop the word *moist* from making our ears bleed. In the public's interest, I feel compelled to take a brief detour off the accent trail for just a minute to delve a bit deeper into this most pressing question.

If you are not among the estimated 20 percent of the population that despises hearing the world *moist*, consider yourself lucky. *Moist* aversion is so intense it often ranks first in various surveys of words that should be excised from the English language. Jokes about *moist*—and the repulsion it inspires—have become a comedy staple. *Tonight Show* host Jimmy Fallon, for one, declared it the worst word in the English language. The popular Amazon Prime show *The Marvelous Mrs. Maisel* jokingly listed it as one of the words mental asylum visitors were prohibited to say in front of a mentally fragile patient. And ad execs representing Dove's Deep Moisture Body Wash leaned into some "moist" humor in a commercial with the new marketing tagline "So moist!" making a hilariously big fail in a faux focus group.

Still, there are those who rally around *moist*'s softer side (like making baked goods delicious) and they might hold out hope that the right kind of publicity could reframe its image. But, as pointed out on *Epicurious*, the go-to website for foodies, the word elicits substantial reader backlash even when employed to describe chicken and cakes. The real outstanding linguistic mystery is why we hate the word *moist* so much. After all, if linguists have been able to explain the first sounds we utter and the complexities of how they change over time, why can't we explain why we have such a visceral reaction to the sound of a simple little word? It turns out we can—and it has a surprising connection to a theory on the origins of language our German friend Max Müller came up with well over a century ago.

THE MOISTNESS OF OUR PAST

Moist didn't always inhabit such a precarious position in our psyche. The word certainly had an innocent enough beginning. It was during the medieval period when our modern *moist* was borrowed into English by the Anglo-Normans from Middle French *moiste*, which, according to the *Oxford English Dictionary*, had the meaning of "slightly wet or damp." Used in fairly neutral or even positive contexts, it was regularly called upon to describe something fresh, as opposed to stale. This might explain why Chaucer was much fonder of the word than we are today, using it several times to describe a hearty drink, as in "A draghte of moyste and corny ale" from "The Pardoner's Tale." And if good beer and Chaucer are involved, surely it can't be all bad.

Yet even before it was a pariah at dinner parties, *moist* was poised for problems because it became more and more intertwined with our bodily functions. In its least offensive early physical references, it was sometimes used to describe eyes filling with tears, as by Shakespeare in *Henry IV* when he writes, "Haue you not a moist eie." More often, the word was used in scientific and medical writings in reference to other bodily fluids, i.e., to describe blood as "hoot and moyst" in a text from 1475, or to discuss the body's production of wet by-products like pus.

This is, of course, where the ick factor starts to come in, with medical descriptions like "Scabies, the itch: 'Tis of two sorts, moist and dry," or to elucidate the properties of "moist gangrene." Still, in what might come as a surprise to most *moist* haters out there, it's not until the 1950s that an association with women's vaginas and sexual arousal comes into play. And, of course, once it started to appear in descriptions of panties, it was a bridge too far.

WORD AVERSION

In the world of language, there are certain trends in terms of words that frequently co-occur in phrases or sentences together, something called *collocation*. This can be fun and common pairings like *cake and ice cream*, *salt and pepper*, or *good and evil* (known in the linguistic biz as *frozen binomials* because they are rarely reversed in the order they appear). Even more subtle examples are nouns like, say, *immigrant*, and the adjectives that we often use to describe them (e.g., *illegal*) that may become linked—to negative or positive effect—in our minds. As a result, we can become conditioned to react a certain way to that word more generally based on its memorable collocating word friends. When it comes to words that seem like they should be neutral at worst, our disgust toward them might stem from how we have been trained to associate that word with something we don't like (like gangrene and underwear) rather than something we do (like beer).

Science backs up this idea that our feelings about *moist* stem from a place of semantic uneasiness. In a series of experiments trying to get at what, exactly, characterized the disdain for *moist*, psychologist Paul Thibodeau discovered that people found *moist* more aversive when it was preceded by sexual words (like the f-word) and less aversive after food-related words (e.g., *chicken*). Association with an unrelated positive word (like *paradise*) or negative word (like *murderer*) also seemed to influence how people felt about *moist*, rating it more unpleasant when following a positive word but less so when following a word associated with something negative, likely due to being contrasted with those words' positive or negative senses. The researchers also found that being young, female, and well educated increased the odds that someone would be *moist* averse, as did being disgusted more generally by bodily functions.

Moist may be the seminal example, but there are certainly other words that people get grossed out by. Many words that have to do with our bodies or the things emitted by them, e.g., anus, vomit, pus, or phlegm, don't get a lot of love. Indeed, in the same study, the researchers found that the more related to bodily functions a word was—or the more similar in meaning to *moist* a word was (say, *wet* or *damp*)—the more likely it also was rated high on aversive scales by the same people who found *moist* unpleasant.

Our problem, it appears, is really in how such words relate to cultural beliefs and social taboos about body parts and their associated by-products. These words then take on guilt by association because of the things we have been socialized to find unpleasant, uncomfortable, or disgusting. For *moist* at least, a long history as a word associated with bodily discharge coupled with its more recent use as a sexualized word positioned it as one that makes young modern women squirm more than men.

THE SOUND OF DISGUST

While *moist*'s related meanings certainly might drive our dislike, Max Müller's ding-dong theory, known now as *sound symbolism*, provides an alternative, suggesting it instead (or also) might have something to do with the specific sounds that are in the word. Maybe just hearing the sounds that make up "m-o-i-s-t" annoys us, sort of like phonetic nails on a chalkboard.

As we already know, sound symbolism posits that the relationship between sound and meaning is not always arbitrary. Instead, sounds themselves can help convey meaning, an idea so old we find it discussed in Greek antiquity (as naturalism in Plato's *Cratylus*) and one that we all embrace when we use words like *meow*, *pitter-patter*, or *thump*. Unlike onomatopoeia, where words mimic the sound of things they describe, the idea more broadly is that isolated speech sounds sometimes carry inherent meaning because of the way they are articulated (for instance, with rounded lips as in English "oo") or owing to other properties like their pitch or length (e.g., saying "soooo loooong" with drawn-out vowels when asked how long one's been waiting). The essence is that the sound resembles a concept in some way.

This leads us to the question of how sound symbolism might help explain the heebie-jeebies we get around our not-too-popular friend, *moist*. To answer this, we need to consider the vowels and consonants that make up that word.

Vowel sounds are made by the position of the tongue in either the front of the mouth (as in words like *he* or *hay*) or the back of the mouth (as in *boat*, *boot*, or, as it happens, *moist*). A substantial amount of sound-symbolism research suggests that front vowels appear more often in words that evoke concepts like happy or small, such as *glee* or *teensy*, while back vowels evoke sadness or largeness (e.g., *mope*, *humongous*). Since the main sound in the "oy" vowel in the word *moist* is a back vowel, we might be predisposed to have it conjure up something sad or less pleasant.

And the reason we might have developed this happy versus sad vowel association in the first place? It has been hypothesized that back vowels use the same muscle that we use to frown (the orbicularis oris muscle), while front vowels contract the opposite muscle (zygomaticus major), the one involved in smiling, and, as a result, we embody these emotions. Not surprisingly, this smile-like countenance is the reason we say *cheese* rather than *moist* when we pose for a picture, especially if a look of disgust was not our hoped-for photo vibe.

Another sound-meaning correspondence frequently noted is that certain sounds appear more often in basic word categories, like those associated with body parts, even across unrelated languages. For instance, nasal sounds (linguist speak for sounds like "m" and "n" made with air flow through the nose) tend to appear in words for nose more often than other consonants across languages—e.g., *nose* in English, *nez* in French, and *hana* in Japanese. Since both "m" and "n" definitionally involve the nose in how they are made, it's easy to see how a sound-concept mapping might develop from this shared proboscis property. Likewise, when babies nurse at a mother's breast, they tend to make bilabial (two-lipped) smacking sounds, a sound-symbolic association that seems to explain the preponderance of bilabial consonants like "m" or "b" in words for a breast and its secretions around the world. In English, we have the primordial *mama*, of course, but also *mammary*, *mammals*, and *milk*, as well as *breast*, *bosom*, and *boob*, which all start with a similarly bilabial "b."

The gist here being that these types of recurring sound-body correlations may spur or reinforce the associations of *moist* with bodily functions that have developed over time—potentially increasing the yuck factor. This would also explain why other words like *hoist* or *joist* that sound similar to *moist* don't make us cringe to the same extent. They may involve back vowels, but not paired with the nasal consonant—or the culturally acquired semantic baggage—that makes anyone saying *moist* such a tremendous hit at parties.

As a caveat, though, it is important to note that sound symbolism is generally a statistical tendency across languages, rather than something speakers of a particular language would consciously notice. Sound symbolic tendencies are also not necessarily consistent within a single language's vocabulary (and, in fact, English is not as iconic a language as, say, Japanese). Even still, the rising tide of research recently devoted to the topic does find it is turning out to be, as my teen would say, "lowkey a thing."

CAN MOIST CAKE BRING US AROUND?

So, in the end, it looks like *moist* has been the victim of both its phonemic constitution and its robust use to describe disease states and bodily fluids over several centuries. Given this, the bigger question is why the word hasn't been shunned by the remaining 80 percent of us.

Probably because a lot of both sound symbolism and socio-semantic training takes place when we are young and impressionable. Sound symbolism has been posited as a tool in language and word acquisition for children, who start with more of a blank slate. Sound symbolic connections might help kids or non-native speakers "guess" at meaning in ways that are not completely arbitrary, but the more exposure one has to additional semantic assists (like a word's contexts of use, or other known words that it co-occurs with) the more we might shift toward using those clues instead to fine-tune our understanding.

It also seems there is some variation across individuals in levels of squeamishness, since the more we have developed an aversion to bodily functions, the more *moist* use disturbs us. Those of us less compelled to hate the word might simply have been exposed to *moist* in more positive contexts or heard it used more often to describe cake rather than pus. The benefits, one might hazard, of having a good cook versus a medical professional for a parent or of having gone to a high school where the dampness of undergarments was not the stuff of locker room banter. But, for the other 20 percent who cringe at its every mention, learning to reimagine their relationship with *moist* might be a big ask, though *People* magazine was on to something when they created a "sexy men saying 'moist'" video. Can picturing a shirtless Ryan Reynolds sultrily saying "moist" in front of a luscious piece of cake turn things around? I, for one, am certainly willing to give it a try.

THREE

LINGUISTIC (R)-EVOLUTIONARY

Despite the valiant efforts of Noah Webster to set the record straight, Americans have long been accused of leading the English language astray. Pronouncing *schedule* as "sked-yule," not "shed-yule," eating "tomay-toes" instead of "tomah-toes," and, strangest of all, using bathrooms instead of toilets, even without a bath involved. To the British, and to many Americans who still extoll the accent of the nation's former motherland, the differences on this side of the pond have not generally been improvements.

The big surprise is that one of our most noticeable differences is not an American innovation but instead the preservation of an earlier British form, namely, the way we say words like *mother* and *father* compared to British "mothuh" and "fahthuh." You see, if we venture back to seventeenth-century Britain, the "r"s that seem so infrequent in the king's English were actually pretty common. Today, of course, anyone linguistically savvy knows that "fa" is only a long long way to run when you're from Southern England, while, for most speakers living in North America, it is simply the note that follows "mi."

This difference in our "r" is quite possibly one of the most striking examples of how the flexibility of language over time is intimately tied to watershed shifts in the social, linguistic, and cultural fabric in which they emerge. To see how, though, we have to go back in time to understand why it's easy to lose "r"s like many did in England, as the "r" sound has long been hard to define and even harder to say. As a bonus, we will also finally come to understand what separates the *fur* from the *fir* and why the way we write *Mary*, *merry*, and *marry* is not just somebody's idea of a cruel joke.

WHO R YOU?

As a first step to getting to know "r" history better, let's first figure out a little about you and your rhoticity, or, more simply, the way you pronounce your "r." Since you are reading this book in English, you probably have at your disposal some sort of "r" sound, or *rhotic*. And you probably would anyway, as about three-quarters of languages have some type of "r" sound. If you are wondering why we use the word *rhotic* to talk about "r" sounds, it comes from the letter "rho" in the Greek alphabet that stood for an "r" sound and was written as "P." Making "r" sounds requires complex articulatory gymnastics, which is why children often have so much trouble learning to pronounce them (think "twee" for *tree*) and why speakers of different English dialects can vary greatly in how and when they say it. So let's start off with a little diagnostic test to figure out which type of "r" speaker you might be.

To establish this, say the following words out loud and notice whether you pronounce the "r" sounds in all cases where it appears in the spelling form.

Heart

Car

Farther

Rope

Trip

If you heard yourself fully articulate the "r" in all of these words, you are what we call a rhotic (or "r-ful") speaker, meaning you pronounce "r" when it occurs in any context in a word, namely:

At the beginning of a word (rope)

Before a vowel sound (trip, rope)

After a vowel/before a consonant* (heart, farther)

At the end of a word (car, farther)

But, if any of these "r" sounds were mysteriously missing, you are probably what we refer to as a non-rhotic, or "r"-less, speaker.

* Linguists refer to these two contexts for "r" (those occurring before a consonant/at the end of a word) as a *post-vocalic position*, as in these cases (e.g., cart, heart, cheer, far), the "r" always follows a vowel. This ends up being an important factor in how our "r" changes over time.

Non-rhotic speakers essentially say the "r" sound only when it occurs *before* a vowel sound, but not when it occurs *after* a vowel. Using the examples above, you would pronounce the "r" in *rope* or *trip* but not in a word like *car* or *heart*, which would sound more like "cah" and "hot." The word *farther*, likewise, would be absent both of its "r" sounds, since neither happens to come before a vowel, giving us a pronunciation akin to the upper-crust Southern-British-English-sounding "fah-thuh." This, of course, leads to the overlap in how one pronounces the distance remaining on a road trip whenever an impatient child inquires how much longer and the call sign of the exasperated patrilineal inhabitant of the front seat.

Fortunately, most Brits don't suffer negative social consequences when they use "r"-less pronunciations, because being non-rhotic in this way is classically associated with a posh English accent. But when one hears an American say "fahthuh" when referring to dear old dad, it somehow comes across as less King Charles and more street-smart New Yorker. What we have here is an example of exactly the same linguistic feature across varied dialects ("r"-lessness), but with a completely different social evaluation. The less elite air given off by many of those we find still exhibiting the loss of "r" in America (notably in Boston and New York) carries vestiges of the humble beginnings for the loss of "r" centuries ago in Britain, where it slowly made its way up the social ladder until it became an indelible mark of being "proper." But before we get to that part of our story, we have to first understand what makes our "r" sounds so special.

WHAT'S R'S PROBLEM?

At the time the "r" began to disappear in earnest from trendy London speech in the late eighteenth century, America was a fledgling nation—one that was often called out for its unique accent and novel word coinage. But those who had risked it all to settle this new land had already brought "r" with them a century before, and their descendants fully intended to keep it.

Still, the "r" that was so omnipresent on American lips was already different from the "r" that came with the Angles, Saxons, and Jutes when they decided to set up shop on the British Isles around the fifth century. The arrival of these tribes and their subsequent conversating about who should rule over whom ushered in the Old English period (circa 449 to 1150), and this earliest form of English inherited its "r" sound from the Germanic tongues these tribes brought with them. Based on the ubiquity of "r" sounds in more distantly related languages, the Germanic languages also likely inherited their "r" sound from a much earlier source language, that reconstructed language we previously discussed known as Proto-Indo-European, which died out about six thousand years ago. Based on studies tracing back historical sound changes, scholars conjecture that these older "r" sounds were probably something like the robust trilled or rolling ones found in Scots and southern German, rather than the softer "r" sounds found in most modern English varieties.

In Scotland, for instance, we find an "r" sound that, like English, is made near the alveolar ridge (that hard ridge sitting right behind your teeth) but with a vibrating tongue gesture, sometimes referred to as the Scottish burr. To try this, make a "ruh" sound, only try to vibrate the tip of your tongue quickly as you do, getting more of a "rrrrruh" sound. This rolling sound, so Scottish sounding it almost wears a kilt, was likely similar to the original "r" sound inherited into Old English from our Indo-European ancestor (which is why we find a similar sound in other Indo-European-derived languages like Spanish and Italian). Still, despite its stereotypical association with Scottish identity, fewer and fewer modern Scots make the sound this way. Today, younger speakers use more of just a single flick or tap of the tongue tip when making their "r" sound, especially when it occurs at the ends of words, sounding a bit similar to the American "r."

Comparatively, the American "r" has strayed much further from English's earlier rolling roots. In American English, we use what is called a "retroflex r," an impressive way of saying that you slightly curl the tip of your tongue behind that little hard ridge (the alveolar ridge) to make your "r" sound. Go ahead—point the tip of your tongue right at the spot you tend to burn with pizza and say "ruh." If you are a native American English speaker, you probably notice that your tongue doesn't quite make contact with that protruding ridge, but the tip curls back or bunches up slightly behind it as you push air across it to make an "r" sound. Nor does your tongue tip vibrate in the process, making your "r" decidedly more mellow than the trilled or rolled "r" from which it descended.

So why do Americans have this less rollicking "r" sound? And why are younger Scots also shifting away from the trilled "r" redolent with Scottish identity?

Well, this is where linguistic predispositions and principles enter the fray. Unlike consonant sounds like "k" or "t," which involve the tongue completely obstructing or closing off airflow for a second to make that sound come out right, "r" sounds have instead a fairly open style of articulation, with air continuing to flow through the mouth. Say the "t" sound and compare that to how you say "r" and you can feel the air pop for the "t" but pass unheeded around the tongue through the mouth for the "r" sound. This type of more fluid airflow is something also characteristic of vowels—try saying "ee" and feel how it is more like the way you say "r" compared to "t." This means that "r" sounds have a bit more in common with vowels from an articulatory perspective than most other consonants.*

This may make one wonder why we even keep "r" on our consonant list, but it is because "r" lacks a defining quality of a vowel: the ability to form syllables. What this means is that when you say a word with one vowel, like *pat*, and then ask a bunch of first graders to clap out the syllables, they would clap once. But if you add on another vowel, like an "ee" vowel (as in the word *patty*, remembering that the letter "y" here denotes a vowel, not a consonant as in *you*) that's twice, since we've now created a word with two

* The "l" sound (as in *like* or *dull*) is another sound that is similar to "r" in terms of how it is articulated and, lo and behold, it is also a sound that is often deleted in dialects (e.g., "hep" for *help* or historically the "l" in the word *talk* or *walk*). Kinda makes you wonder if there might just be some sort of underlying linguistic pattern at work here, hmm?

syllables. But "r" sounds, as with consonant friends like "p," "t," or "g," don't make new syllables on their own, they need a vowel to co-occur to do so: the word *peer* pronounced with a vowel plus an "r" sound forms just one syllable. This is not absolutely always true, as the vowel-leaning qualities of "r" allow it to form syllables when no vowel is to be found in languages like Czech and Slovak, such as in the Slovak tongue twister *strč prst skrz krk.* But such syllabic "r" examples are pretty rare across languages, and "r" is, at heart, a consonant.

"R"s more freewheeling articulatory traits also give it greater susceptibility to a process that linguists refer to as *weakening* (or *lenition*). Weakening simply means that a sound tends to become less complex (or more vowel-like) in terms of how it's made in the mouth, and this is why trilled "r"s, like those of our young Scottish friends, have started to sound more like the American "r" over time. This tendency for "r" to weaken is also what set the stage for perhaps the most recognizable accent divide to have developed over the centuries and across the Atlantic—a beautiful example of how the linguistic tendencies we all share don't always end up affecting us the same way when social distance enters the fray.

MIND YOUR ARSE

Haven't you ever wondered why Americans have an *ass* while the English have an *arse*? After all, we have all our "r" sounds while they don't, so how the heck did they get to keep the "r" in their *arse*? Because when the English say *arse* without its "r," it often sounds more like *ass*, and so who can blame colonists who also just called it an *ass*, despite the fact that *arse* was the original pronunciation?

Spelling at that time was very far from uniform, so as also happened with words like *bust* from *burst*, *cuss* from *curse*, and the occasional *hoss* from *horse*, we've immortalized the process of "r" weakening in how we sometimes wrote these words. Though at the time the first wave of settlers made it to America, English dialects were all still rhotic, the key exception was a fledgling tendency to weaken or entirely drop "r" sounds before "s" (in words like those just mentioned). This trend had started as early as the fifteenth century and well before the *Mayflower* set sail. Since literacy and spelling standards were hardly tops on anybody's list, especially when it came to spelling indelicate words, *ass* stuck around in America but its "r" stayed in England.

In the South of England, though, this early "r" dropping was just the tip of the non-rhotic ("r" dropping) iceberg. We see the same small hints that "r" sounds got dropped here and there in the fifteenth and sixteenth centuries, especially before "s" sounds in informal writing (e.g., *fust* for *first* or *passel* for *parcel*). Without widespread spelling conventions in this early period, writers wrote more like they spoke. This is a boon to modern linguists as such misspellings give us a hint into when the earliest types of "r" deletion (i.e., before "s" sounds) likely began.

Once we hit the seventeenth century, this weakening of "r" sounds began expanding to more and more types of words—and only then do we start to see it really get noticed. Writing in 1640, famed dramatist Ben Jonson described the changes he heard in the "r" sounds around him this way: "R . . . is sounded firme in the beginning of the words, and more liquid in the middle, and ends." By liquid, scholars think he was suggesting that "r" was becoming less clear and separate when it followed vowels (as in *far* or *cart*) in contrast to when it occurred at the beginning of words (as in *rat* or *rope*), where it sounded more like a harder consonant.

All of this suggests that a weaker-sounding "r" was becoming more and more common in London until, by the eighteenth century, we find language authorities such as well-regarded British elocutionist John Walker remarking that many "r" sounds were not just less "firm" but often completely missing. As he put it, R "is often too feebly sounded in England, and particularly in London where it is sometimes completely sunk." This quote hints at its early reception, which was that it was a mispronunciation that should be avoided. Even into the early nineteenth century, we find "r" droppers characterized as low-class, as articulation expert Benjamin Smart tells us in his 1836 pronunciation guide, *Walker Remodelled*: "The extreme amongst the vulgar in London doubtlessly is, to omit the *r* altogether—to convert far into fah, hard into hahd, cord into cawd."

Why this association with vulgarity? Based on a comparison of texts versus diaries and letters, "r" dropping was at first most common in lower-status folks' and women's colloquial writing, likely because formal literacy tended to reinforce the "r" more for those educated in spelling norms, meaning upper-class men. But, as anyone with teenagers can tell you, even if one might know what is considered proper, it doesn't mean it sounds cool to say it. And since people tend not to speak as they write, and the underlying pressures toward "r" loss had already gained a significant foothold, by the nineteenth century, even the rhotic holdouts in London had given up the battle.

Crucially, though, this deletion of "r" was not happening everywhere—primarily it affected speech in the southeastern part of Britain, an area encompassing London, which had become the economic and cultural center by the early modern period (after the fifteenth century). Northern British dialects, on the other hand, were still fully rhotic, as were the West Country dialects, in places like Devon and Cornwall, which allowed speakers in this area famed as a pirates' nest to keep their "ARRRR"s intact. But, as the center of economic, artistic, and royal life, the power and prestige of London made it a model of what was fashionable, in language as well as dress, and what is fashionable often involves some innovation, and generally by those recognized as socially relevant, which seems to be how "r" dropping moved from being stigmatized to stylish over the centuries.

As has happened often in the history of English, the logical tendency to follow intrinsic linguistic pressures that make what we say more compatible with cognitive and articulatory principles led the way, and those who spent more time talking and less time stressing about whether they sounded appropriately posh followed. Importantly, at the time when the early reflexes of such changes were first gently percolating in the sixteenth and seventeenth centuries, there really was not the strong focus on "good" and "bad" that came to dominate the discussion of "r" in the eighteenth century. Instead, the larger conversation about English was on its growing stature as a literary and learned language in the shadow of Latin, French, and Greek and arguments over what its norms *should be* rather than norm enforcement.

Against this backdrop of English coming up from being a less esteemed vernacular language, regional and class differences in speech doubtless would have been noticed, but they were not policed the same way they would be a couple centuries later. By the time later "proper" speech pundits like Walker and Smart are putting what not to do down into grammar and elocution manuals (like not forgetting to put one's "r"s in all the right places), it is because the change has already become widespread enough to notice and try to stamp out.

But if enough "r"-dropping riffraff (i.e., the rest of us) make it to the top or hang out with those already up there often enough, even the nay-saying of linguistic curmudgeons can't do much to stem the tides of change. Not to mention that, with the growth of industrialization and the massive in-migration into London, there simply were a lot more of those common-speaking folks than aristocratic ones, and the rise in the wealth and status of a new middle class gave non-highborn sorts more social clout alongside those who once tightly held the reins. With this softening of class divides and extensive comingling with middle-class "r" droppers, by the nineteenth century even courtly types seemed to have come full circle.

This is not to say that the upper class did not also exert strong language pressure on the lower classes. In fact, many pronunciation guides, dictionaries, and grammar books of the eighteenth century were precisely directed at those seeking upward social mobility. The key was that certain features, like dropping one's "h" sounds (as in "'enry 'iggins" for Henry Higgins) were shibboleths of being lower-class, something painfully clear to poor Eliza Doolittle in the George Bernard Shaw classic *Pygmalion*.

"R" dropping, though frowned upon by language gurus, seemed to already have gained social currency and become fashionably hip among high-class speakers by the time people started to remark on its absence. The golden age of "r" in Britain was a thing of the past—and "r"-less speech not only became prominent in culturally powerful parts of Britain but also spread to Australia and New Zealand, since most of their English settlement took place after the postvocalic "r" had already gone the way of the dodo.

MERRY, MARRY, MARY CHRISTMAS

But it was not just the "r" itself that seemed to be changing. Before full-fledged "r" dropping was a thing, the vowels before "r" sounds started to sound more and more alike, even though they were originally distinct vowel sounds (e.g., in words like *fern*, *fir*, and *fur*). Why? Apparently, the "r" made them do it. Because of how they are created in the mouth, "r" sounds at the end of syllables seem to basically dampen or muffle some of the contrasts in the vowels that precede them.

We get a sense that this overlap in how vowels were said started happening well before "r" got dropped based on frequent written forms like "clark" for *clerk* and "sarve" for *serve* in letters and diaries as far back as the fifteenth century. Such mixed spellings suggest that many speakers were no longer maintaining differences in how these vowels were pronounced. By the 1800s, we see that this merging together of vowels before "r" starts getting brought up in commentary on English pronunciation, as when an early language observer noted that "vergin, virgin and vurgin would be pronounced alike." We may never know what the heck vergins and vurgins are, but at least we know how to pronounce them. This pressure that pushed vowels to sound alike before "r" sounds was something that did follow many settlers to the New World, leaving us to scratch our heads over confusing contemporary homophones like *horse* and *hoarse* and *poor* and *pour.*

But despite the fact that no one likes to dwell on what they have lost, there is a bright side to knowing why you have fewer vowel contrasts than you should—especially for those of us who have endlessly pondered why the heck we spell *merry*, *marry*, and *Mary* differently when they all sound the same.* Many modern English speakers merge all three of these historically distinct vowels because of the same forces instigated by the troublemaking "r" sound.

For the speakers who still maintain these distinctions (you

* For those who are in the more-is-better camp when it comes to language, the effects that "r" has historically had on vowels also includes the introduction of some new vowel forms (namely, certain diphthongs, i.e., two-part vowels) in non-rhotic varieties of English. This development, though, was quite phonetically complex and is best left a stone unturned here.

know who you are), *marry* has the "aa" vowel that is used in a word like *mat*, while *merry* would have more of an "eh"-like vowel (as in the word *met*). Finally, *Mary* has a vowel more like the word *may*. According to what can be gleaned from the *Linguistic Atlas of New England*, Northeasterners often had this distinction until the mid-twentieth century but have generally fallen in with the rest of the non-distinctive American lot in the twenty-first century. One place you might yet hear a difference is in a city that doesn't tend to give up linguistic distinctiveness easily: New York. Though dying out in younger New Yorkers' speech, you can hear old-school New Yorkers still making the differences between their *marry*s, *merry*s, and *Mary*s count. This difference can also be heard in some Bostonians' and Southerners' speech, particularly older speakers. And, always keen to shake things up a bit, some Philadelphians have their own take, merging *merry* with *Murray*—all while still maintaining a three-way distinction among *merry*, *Mary*, and *marry*.

Our general fondness for vowel mergers before "r" sounds is also the reason why *fur* and *fir* look like they should absolutely sound different but don't (they used to!), and also why pairs like *horse/hoarse* and *morning/mourning* now generally sound identical. So, next time you think to poke fun at anyone who says *pin* and *pen* the same way, you should probably just keep your merged mouth shut.

But how did this merger in vowel sounds lead to the dropping of "r" sounds altogether for large swaths of English speakers? Well, that is a bit of a complex tale, but, as mentioned earlier, "r" sounds by their nature tend to become more vowel-like over time. The "r" sound as it was pronounced in London in the early modern period was not the trilled "r" but already a weaker version, meaning it had become less articulatorily complex and more vowel-like over the history of English. As well, the presence of "r" in a word like *bird* or *serve* influenced the preceding vowel sound as just discussed, and also made the vowel take on a smidge of an "r"-like quality, something referred to as a vowel becoming *rhotacized* or *"r" colored.* To get a sense of this, slowly pronounce *far* versus *father* and notice the difference even just in how you position your lips in anticipation of the "r" sound when you say the vowel in *far.*

Eventually, it seems, some speakers stopped bothering to make the tongue gesture that formed the separate "r" sound when it came after vowels, probably because the "r"-influenced vowel sound hinted at its underlying presence anyway. And, in the same fashion as saying things like "wok" for what was once "walk" with an "l" sound, speakers simply started to just leave off the "r" for a more harmonious and pronounceable syllable. This didn't happen across all dialects, of course. The strong trilled "r" sound that is associated with the Scottish burr was less likely to blend into the quality of the vowel before it, probably because of its more robust tongue movement, which is why we still find words like *fur*, *fir*, and *fern* with distinct vowels there.

A RHOTIC NEW WORLD

Given all the "r" deleting happening elsewhere, how was it that most Americans managed to hang on to all their "r"s? Mainly by virtue of the fact that America was a rhotic ship that had already sailed. At the time of the British settlement of the earliest colonies in the seventeenth century, rhoticity was still the fashion in most of England. So, bringing their home dialects with them, most colonists were "r" speakers, though there was most likely, as in England, a tendency among a number of colonists to drop an "r" here or there (especially when discussing their arses). Yet the vast majority of speakers brought their "r" along with their plucky can-do spirit.

As non-rhotic dialects started to emerge in Southern England in the late eighteenth century, travelers from those parts brought over their trendy speech style along with the latest in London fashion—spending time in lovely little spots like eastern New England, the central Atlantic Coast, and the South. Many of the elite inhabitants of coastal cities, like those living in New York, Boston, Savannah, and Charleston, still retained strong cultural ties with London throughout this period, and they looked toward increasingly "r"-less London speech as the prestige model. Many, particularly in the South, also sent their children back to England for education, providing even more exposure to recent developments in Old World upper-class English. This sustained contact with those who were using the new London norm created pockets of non-rhotic speech in those areas that still persist (though in far fewer number) today.

"R" dropping is also a feature of some modern African American English (AAE) varieties, emerging from linguistic mixing between the African languages brought into the colonies by enslaved people and Southern White American dialects. Outside of these groups, most other settlers, whose "r" arrived with them, kept their "r"s and passed them down to their descendants. Though at that time these rhotic areas tended to hold less cultural and economic sway than eastern New England, there were vastly more speakers in these parts who were removed from regular contact or concern with those back in Europe. Most had left their homeland to escape various forms of persecution or economic hardship and, unlike the elites in parts of New England and the South, had less access to trendy London speech and much less interest in keeping these ties alive.

Thus, whatever social appeal dropping "r" was gaining in London did not carry over to vast swaths of the heartland outside of those areas, like Boston and Charleston, that still looked to London as a cultural homeland. And if there is one thing linguists have learned, it is that social triggers are the crucial force behind language change.

The same underlying linguistic pressures (like "r" weakening) exist over the centuries and across languages, but the specific way they affect speech depends on the social and cultural contexts in which they are embedded and the social meaning they come to represent in different communities. While the underlying linguistic pressures that these speakers shared did make vowel mergers before "r" commonplace in our speech more generally, rhoticity became a symbol of what it was to sound like an American, particularly as the influence of the British Empire waned in the twentieth century. I think it is safe to say that our differences with England did not just involve a tea party, but an "r" parting as well.

A LITTLE BIT INTRUSIVE

Now, while the weakening of "r" over the course of our history might go far in explaining why "r" gets dropped altogether, it doesn't explain why, in some odd circumstances, "r" magically reappears where we least expect it: for instance, when we "warsh" our clothes or watch one of the seemingly endless episodes available of *Lawr & Order*. In fact, one of my favorite jokes is precisely about the phenomenon to which I here refer, so let's see how well your linguistic sense of humor has developed:

Question: "What do you call a deer with one eye?"

Answer: "One idea."

Now, if that fell completely flat, it is not because you lack a sense of humor, and certainly not because I can't tell a joke. It's because you don't pronounce the word *idea* with what has been termed, in linguistic lingo, an *intrusive "r."* To be more precise, you lack "idears," something that a number of Southern Brits and anyone related to the Kennedys have plenty of. If you are still pondering what the heck that has to do with a myopic deer, just try saying "one i-dear" and think about it for a minute. See, I knew you'd catch up.

Intrusive "r" is a phenomenon where "r" sounds that are not historically part of a word get inserted anyway—"law" becomes "lawr" or "Obama" become "Obamer," as several British newscasters used to say. It might seem that such "r" additions are random and simply wrong, since none of these words had an "r" originally, but that would be a rather hasty assumption. What's fascinating about intrusive "r" is that it is actually the result of the overapplication of a linguistic rule rather than "r" gone rogue. You see, in dialects where "r" sounds get deleted in the pattern we described earlier—namely before consonant sounds—they are still present for those speakers before vowel sounds. That means a word like *cart* would always be pronounced like "caht," but *car* only loses its "r" in non-rhotic dialects if the word that follows begins with a consonant. However, if a word with a vowel follows, the "r" is pronounced, something more specifically known as a *linking "r."* So, *car* ***p****ark* becomes "cah park," because a consonant follows the "r," but *car* ***e****ngine* keeps its "r" since a vowel follows.

This might seem complicated, but it is an automatic rule that applies for speakers of non-rhotic dialects, just like you don't think about pronouncing "s" as a "z" sound when you pluralize words ending in "b," "d," or "g" (as in *tubs*, *lids,* or *dogs*); it just always happens because you know your linguistic rules so well. Since it is so automatic, the "r"-adding rule sometimes get overapplied to words that seemingly might fit the bill—i.e., words that end in a vowel, like *soda* or *Obama* or *law*—when they are followed by another vowel.* Voilà, we end up with "Obamar administration" and *Lawr and Order*, remembering that the word *law* is actually pronounced "la" with a final vowel and not a "w" consonant.

---

* For those of you on your linguistic toes, you would notice this means we can actually only have "idears," as in the joke above, if *idea* is followed by a vowel.

But how about those of us who "warsh" our hair, live in "Warshington," and like to eat "squarsh"? Well, that too is an example of intrusive "r," meaning an "r" where it doesn't historically belong, but, in a bit of a twist, it is usually not r-dropping speakers who use it, and why it happens is a bit more of a mystery as it doesn't follow the same pre-vowel rule. In the United States, we find this pronunciation mainly among speakers in the U.S. Midland, an area stretching west from Pennsylvania (particularly Pittsburgh) to Kansas, especially those with more old-fashioned dialects.

All of these "warsh"-type words have one thing in common: they all occur with an "ah" vowel, which in colonial English days had a pronunciation with a bit more lip rounding. Particularly before "sh" sounds, this lip-rounded vowel can come off a bit "r"-like, giving rise to what might have sounded more like "warsh" and "squarsh." This bonus "r" got picked up since nobody was too keen on spelling in those days, and this pronunciation spread with these early settlers. A few have suggested that this was particularly prevalent among the Scots Irish, a group of Scottish speakers who had lived in the Ulster region of Ireland before settling in the Delaware Valley starting in the early 1700s, and that it was their influence—and fearless frontier busting—that spread this pronunciation through the American Midwest. While it is unclear how much, if any, "warshing" the Scots Irish are really responsible for, coming up next, we will discover that they were pretty dang important to establishing what would end up as some of the most recognizable accents of American speech.

FOUR

THE DIVIDED TONGUE OF A DIVIDED NATION

George Bernard Shaw has often been quoted as saying, "England and America are two countries separated by a common language" and, surely, the fact that an American should never discuss their fanny pack in polite British company is proof of that. But the colonists who made a home on American shores had much more than a new take on their arses and a grudge against imported tea; they also arrived with a geographic, religious, and economic diversity that laid the foundation for the varied American dialects we have today. While *y'all*, *yu'uns*, and *you guys* are the icing on the regional American dialect cake, it's the pronunciation differences that developed over time that remind us that a new nation was forged from a fragile and delicate union of regions that had become, and still often remain, economically, politically, and linguistically divided.

This push and pull toward and away from a cohesive national identity began shaping our speech as far back as the 1600s and, by the 1700s, writers often noted that colonial accents had started to take on a distinctly—and unexpectedly uniform—American sound. One commentator from the period notes, "The language of the immediate descendants of such a promiscuous ancestry is perfectly uniform, and unadulterated; nor has it borrowed any provincial, or national accent, from its British or foreign parentage." That a linguistic separation would grow between Britain and this new world comes as no surprise because, in the mouths of the young and far removed from their motherland, language always has a way of finding new forms and fashions. This new linguistic frontier is the fascinating story we move to now, where we find early settlers' scrappy pursuit of economic and religious freedom first uniting then ultimately dividing this new American tongue.

PLAYING BY THE NUMBERS

Before we get to how British colonists hitting the shores of Massachusetts and Virginia set the American accent stage, the first question we should really be asking is why English even became the language of the land. Many other tongues were spoken early on in the Americas, starting with the Indigenous languages of the original inhabitants like Algonquian and Iroquoian, as well as the European languages spoken by other early colonizers like the Dutch, French, Swedish, and Spanish.

In truth, it was mainly a numbers game. English became dominant through sheer linguistic swamping, as the majority of early European settlers were British, and, with an intention to set up permanent digs rather than trading posts, they were willing to flex some muscle. When the Dutch didn't make much of a fuss, the British took over their settlement in the Hudson Valley in 1664, renaming it New York after the Duke of York, but kept handy Dutch terms such as *cookie, boss, Santa Claus,* and *cruller.*

More notably, the colonists also displaced or killed many Native inhabitants whose linguistic influence mainly survives in the loanwords English took on to describe new places and new things encountered in a new world, i.e., places like Connecticut, Massachusetts, and Kennebunkport and things such as raccoons, chipmunks, squash, barbecues, and persimmons. Beyond vocabulary, little trace of other early colonial-era or Indigenous languages remained in what was to become American English. In fact, substantive non-English influence on New World speech did not really get going until the eighteenth century. But before we complicate our linguistic picture too much, let's go back to the earliest influences that forged what would become American English.

FOUNDING FOOTPRINTS

The first British colonists to permanently call the New World home were, strictly speaking, Southerners, at least in terms of where they came from and the spot along the coast they landed. Jamestown was first settled in 1607 in Tidewater Virginia, with many of its inhabitants coming from southern and western areas of Britain. Their more celebrated counterparts, the Pilgrims, did not hit upon Plymouth Rock until 1620, well after the arrival of the original Jamestown colonists (who mostly died of starvation) and following that of the first enslaved Africans in 1619 to work the tobacco fields of Virginia.

The Pilgrims were the settlers who specifically arrived on the *Mayflower*, though they are often conflated with other, slightly later Puritan arrivals who settled the Boston area, a number of whom hailed from East Anglia in Southeastern England. But, as in Jamestown, a good array of major dialect areas of Britain were represented, a fact that ended up being central to the modern dialect story of America. What would later also turn out to be very important about this early pattern of settlement was that these two very different colonies created what are known as *founder's effects*, i.e., cultural and linguistic areas that persisted through time.

It was what they had in common, though, that first forged an American sound divergent from the British ones left behind. In both spots, we had a similar convergence of people who had risked everything to start a new life in this new world. Seeking a place to live out their moral, religious, and economic dreams, the settlers who called New England home typically arrived in cohesive groups, bound by either kinship, friendship, or as followers of particular religious leaders. Many worked as farmers, artisans, or tradesmen and, as the Puritans valued education, most were literate.

The commercial interests that drove the Virginia colony attracted a different sort of settler, but like Massachusetts, most were not of noble birth. It's true that some were what we might call "spares," as in they were second or third sons of landed gentry, sort of like Prince Harry, seeking grants of land they couldn't get back home. But aristocratic settlers found themselves in the company of many indentured servants and former convicts who came to labor on the tobacco farms in hopes of earning their freedom and a little piece of New World land to call their own.* It was this unique mix of people who would give rise to an American tongue very different from that left behind.

In part, those in the colonies were bound to start sounding different precisely because most of the fanciest folks stayed back in Britain. For sure, the well-heeled set invested heavily in the New World, but to actually move there and give up everything? Yeah, no. That they left mainly to those who were young, hungry for change, and foolishly optimistic. As a result, features that would have been stigmatized as common or lower-status in Britain—like saying "yit" for *yet*, "dafter" for *daughter*, "Sary" for *Sarah*, "bes" for *best*, or "wrastle" for *wrestle*—would have been heard regularly, even among many of those with some power in colonial political and social life. We see plenty of evidence of such pronunciations from speakers of both upper and lower stations via varied spellings in records and trial transcripts, of which a number exist, in particular, from the New England colonies.

On top of this folk-speak influence, the need for collaboration and community was vital to the establishment and continuity of each colony, bringing together people of diverse education and class who would not have interacted the same way back in their

* Now, I know it's typically Australia that has a reputation as having been Britain's penal colony, but that is only because, after 1780, America would take their criminals no more.

mother country. Whether a gentleman, a tradesman, or a servant, everyone's future success rested entirely on the ability to collectively work together with other colonists, regardless of stature, to build a new society.

This increased contact among those from all walks of life dampened any strong regional accents that created barriers to communication while increasing the use of shared features—something linguists refer to as *linguistic leveling.* As J. L. Dillard writes in his *A History of American English*, "Individuals among the early American colonists varied their pronunciations, perhaps even more than the average speaker of a language, in order to adjust to their multidialectal environment." In each colony, a blending of the original dialects gave rise to new accents using the ashes of the old, particularly as babies acquired these leveled features as part of their native speech. Since both Massachusetts and Virginia had settlers from all over the dialect map, with a higher concentration from the South of England, the amalgamation of these various accents would have made the speech in both areas fairly similar at the outset.

LOST IN TRANSLATION

Damned by the lack of smartphones and YouTube, we don't really have sources other than written ones from the 1600s, which makes it somewhat difficult to ascertain what these first colonial accents would have sounded like. It would have been somewhat Shakespearean, as the Bard was also a speaker of Elizabethan English and, like many of the New England and Virginia colonists, was also from the South of England. We can reconstruct it to some degree based on what we do know from rhymes and nonstandard spellings: words such as *nature* and *creature* would still have been pronounced with a "t" not "ch" as in modern times, giving us "na-ter" and "crea-ter,"* *raisins* and *reasons* and *whole* and *hull* were still homophones (pronounced as "raisins" and "hull," respectively), the vowels in word pairs like *father/bother* and *hoarse/horse* did not rhyme, the vowel in *lot* and *cot* sounded more like "auw" (pronounced with rounded lips), and all "t" sounds remained intact, meaning they drank "wa-ter," not "wa-der." So, translating a phrase such as "a whole lot of reasons for a hoarse horse to drink water" into colonial English comes out as "a hull lawt o' raisons far a who-erse harse to drink wauw-ter."

As you can hear, the first American accents would not have sounded very American (or very British either), at least to modern ears. Of course, all of this would end up changing to sound like the speech we now recognize, but not for another century or two—and any claims of today's American English still being similar to Shakespeare's English are a hull lawt o' harseshet, or, according to Google Colonial Translate, a whole lot of horseshit. A few features might remain from that era in today's American English, but no more than we could find in modern British varieties because, as we know, language changes as groups separate and their dialects develop in different ways.

* From which we get the colloquial *critter*.

It is in fact exactly such separation—in both geographic and social space—that eventually gave rise to what would become noticeably distinct Northern versus Southern accents. The seeds for these regional dialects came from some substantial differences existing between these early colonies, starting with what had brought them to the New World in the first place, namely, religion in Massachusetts and private enterprise in Virginia. While Puritan values of self-discipline, hard work, and devotion helped the New England colonies thrive and grow, the Virginia colonies struggled with disease but also with malaise, as the colony lacked the strong community outlook and bonds found in Massachusetts.

Some of the difficulties Virginians faced arose because of the contrasting styles of governance between the two. Though they excluded women, the Massachusetts colonies followed a model that required the consent of those governed, and membership in the church, rather than pedigree, allowed such participation. Leaders were typically elected, not appointed. The Virginia colonies, on the other hand, reflected more the aristocratic model of England, where rank—and appointment—determined who was at the top. Their focus on intellectual life was also distinct. The Puritans strongly promoted education, founding the first colonial college (Harvard College) in 1636, and believed everyone should become literate so that they would be able to read the Bible. Providing access to education was of less central import in the Virginia colonies, particularly for those who worked the land rather than owned it.

To put it starkly, the Virginians focused on building a profit while the Puritans focused on building a home. As we will soon see, these differences in religion, person, and purpose would have a huge impact on the way American regional speech would eventually develop by establishing distinct cultural hearths, but early on, they did not make most of these colonists sound all that much different.

MIDWESTERNESE? YOU BETCHA.

The origins of what we know and love as the Midwestern accent were a bit different from those found for the Massachusetts and Virginia colonies. It started in the Mid-Atlantic, when the Quakers, led by William Penn, settled Pennsylvania around 1681. Unlike those to their north and south, many Quakers came from North or North Midland dialect areas in England, where there had been more Scandinavian and Scottish settlement. They also counted a number of Welsh and Irish among them.

What would these middle colony speakers have sounded like? Written records show similar variations in spelling as found elsewhere, i.e., *git* for *get*, *ax* for *ask*, and *sarve* for *serve*, suggesting pronunciations that would have sounded much like those of other colonists and like what modern speakers might hear as rustic country speech. Still, a few differences would have called out their Northern British roots such as having "roofs" and "rooms" rather than "rufs" and "rums" (as heard in New England), the pronunciation of words like *off*, *drop*, and *crop* a bit more like "aff," "drap," and "crap," as noted by Noah Webster,* and a strong dedication to preserving the distinction between *thou* and *you*.

But what turned out to be most pivotal to what would become known as the General American accent was the willingness of the Quakers to share the New World with others from the outset. Early on, the Quakers settled the Delaware Valley alongside a community of Swedes and Finns, who had been part of the New Sweden colony, which had been captured by the Dutch and absorbed into the New Netherland colony. That colony, in turn, ended up being taken over by the British in 1664, who also stuck a "new" moniker (as in New York) on their recently acquired piece of New World heaven.

As settlement of the middle colonies hit its full stride, the diversity of new arrivals and the contact among them appears to have led to a leveling of features to an even greater degree than that occurring elsewhere. Why? Brotherly love, my friend. Unlike the Puritans, who were pretty picky about who settled amongst them, and the Virginians, who were pretty picky about who deserved grants of land, the Quakers were welcoming to all—and come all they did.

In particular, two groups, the Ulster Scots (Scots Irish) and the Palatine Germans coming from the Rhine Valley, started to arrive in large numbers after 1720. These immigrants, who first settled

* If you have ever heard others (or yourself) say "awff" versus "ahff," you can see how variable the pronunciation of this vowel is. Historically, we find a lot of alternation in the pronunciations of the vowel we often write with "o" (as in *off*, *drop*, *frog*, or *dog*), and this variation likely relates to where the colonists originally hailed from.

the backcountry of Pennsylvania before pushing farther to the western and southern frontier, brought with them a cultural and linguistic separateness that had an immense impact on the speech of the American heartland.

For instance, from the Scots Irish, we get the now disappearing but once prevalent pronoun form "hit" instead of "it" and a very strong dedication to all their "r" sounds. The Scots also contributed to the tendency to make "ow" endings sound more like "er," as in "feller" for *fellow* or "winder" for *window*, along with other traits, like leaning heavily on the "in" pronunciation of the progressive "ing" ending ("goin'," "huntin'"). And those folk pronunciations comedians play for cheap laughs when imitating so-called rednecks like "thar" for *there* or "nekkid" for *naked*? Not mistakes at all—simply older Scots Irish pronunciations retained but stigmatized owing to the less than glowing reputation they attracted and probably not helped by circulating stories of blood feuds like that which later developed between the Hatfield and McCoy clans.

Even more than their accent, the grammatical contributions the Scots left behind are some we still most recognize today. The Scots gave us phrasing like "the clothes need washed" and a fun desire to stick "uns," from Scots *ane*, meaning *one*, on the back of words as in *big'uns* and *young'uns*. They also gifted us the more logical *quarter 'til* in place of *quarter to*. Much of this influence played a role in what would become the dialect of the South more generally as Scots Irish settlers and their descendants spread into the backcountry of the Upper and, a bit later, the Lowland South.

On the other hand, the Midland states attracted more German

settlement, especially in what became known as the German Belt, an area including upper Ohio, Illinois, Wisconsin, and Minnesota.* Because of this pattern of upper German/lower Scots settlement, Midland states like Ohio and Illinois are still often noted as having distinct accents associated with their southern and northern sections.

In the Great Lakes region, German mixed with Scandinavian influence from Finnish, Norwegian, and Swedish settlers, and this mix is responsible for the *Fargo*-famous Minnesota accent and the "d" for "th" substituting tendency when rooting for "da" bears in Chicago. And my Ohio-based mother-in-law's curious habit of saying she brought home "bakery" when referring to the actual cookies and pastries she gets from a bakery (the place), a usage my dialect simply can't make work? Ja, ein Geschenk (a present) from the Germans! We find a similar meaning as an option for *Bäckerei* in some dialects of German. Finally, if you've ever asked someone if "they want to come with," this comes from a common German structure in which a prepositional particle (like *with*) teams up with a verb.

The influence of the Scots Irish and the Germans should not be underestimated: by 1790, about 6 percent of the total White population was Ulster in origin, with much of it concentrated in certain states like Pennsylvania, where they were about 30 percent

* Though they didn't contribute to the Midwestern accent, Texas also had extensive German immigration in the nineteenth century. Descendants of these immigrants developed a unique version of German known as Texas German, though its use is greatly dwindling.

of the population. The Germans too came in substantial numbers, making up around 9 percent of the population—and another third of Pennsylvania's residents—by that same date.

As non-English immigrants' numbers ticked up, Ben Franklin and other notables of the era openly fretted that such linguistic diversity was a threat to the "American" language and the new nation's identity. In the end, with the exception of the self-isolated German communities that gave rise to Pennsylvania Dutch, a misnomer based on the word *Deutsch*, which meant "German," German simply became part of the American dialect landscape.

What Franklin was unaware of was something that modern linguists now know: children learn the language of their peers—no matter what language their parents speak. This means linguistic trouble, but only for their parents' native tongue. As today with Spanish and English, when one language has higher status, the second generation typically becomes bilingual and, by the third generation, the family loses the heritage language in favor of the new, something known as the *three-generation pattern*. So it is safe to say that worries about English's certain death from high degrees of foreign immigration are greatly overstated, both in Franklin's time and our own.

BREAKING UP IS HARD TO DO

Now, going back a bit to the pre-Revolutionary period, we don't see a lot of evidence that strong regional differences had yet to emerge, but that didn't mean a distinctive colonial manner of speaking had not. Around 1720, we find mention of the striking uniformity of colonial accents across people of all places and ranks in sharp contrast to the myriad dialect differences in the motherland. Hugh Jones, English-language reformer and professor at the College of William and Mary, was one of the earliest to write of this development, expressing his happy surprise that, in contrast to the "linguistic 'confusion'" back in Britain with its "abuses and corruptions" of correct English, the colonists "generally talk good English without idiom or tone," regardless of background or economic status. What might be surprising is that, in these accent accolades, he included speakers both White and Black, though using terms I would not want to repeat. It seems it was the lack of strongly stigmatized features in provincial British speech that had been erased in the speech of those in the New World.

Later writers made similar claims about the difficulty of identifying an American's origin from their speech. In his 1828 travelogue *Notions of the Americans*, James Fenimore Cooper tells us, "The people of the United States, with the exception of a few of German and French descent, speak, as a body, an incomparably better English than the people of the Mother country. There is not probably a man of English descent born in this country, who would not be perfectly intelligible to all whom he should meet in the streets of London, though a vast number of those he met in the streets of London would be nearly unintelligible to him." Such commentary suggests that the shared challenge of and greater collaboration in this new world had leveled the linguistic field, at least compared to the British dialect situations.

Also contributing to this less "corrupted" English was the fact that the colonial elite used the emerging London standard as a model, spreading the prestige associated with this one specific variety more generally in the colonies. This type of adherence to homeland cultural models is quite commonly found in colonial contexts, and the New World had no hardened provincial patterns to block the way. As this type of linguistic reworking occurred, settlers' own dialects no doubt would have shaped the relative value of different forms—what was kept, what faded away, and, while there would have still been some pronunciation differences across the early colonies, they were a lot less noticeable than in England. Of course, the unifying pressures of pioneer hardship didn't last forever, and, as colonies expanded their territory and spheres of influence westward, incipient social and linguistic differences traveled with them too. As we witnessed with our ancient Indo-European tongue as its speakers were separated by land and sea, linguistic and social stuff continually reshapes our speech, driven by natural language tendencies such as assimilation, deletion, weakening, or sound change triggered by contact with other languages.

With a pretty big pond separating the colonies from Britain and each colony's autonomous nature, it is no surprise that this isolation, tossed with a bit of regional rivalry, led to increasing regional speech distinctions over time. By the late eighteenth century, and especially into the nineteenth, we find comments alluding to these regional speech divides. One frequent comment about the New England accent was that it had a grating cadence to it, oft described as a nasal twang. This so-called New England whine might stem from New England's East Anglian roots, where we also find written reference to a similarly distinctive Norfolk or Suffolk "whine."

Even with a whiny twang, or perhaps in part because of it, the Puritans had a reputation of being a tad elitist and snobby, and New England was in many ways the linguistic and intellectual touchstone of the colonial world. Puritan influence spread far outside Massachusetts as a number of families splintered from the original colony, dissatisfied with aspects of the rigid order, to establish settlements farther inland and west, in areas of Connecticut, New Jersey, and New York. About a hundred years later, their descendants moved into the Great Lakes region, spreading New England's social and linguistic clout across the upper North.

One key factor that influenced what would become our modern New England accent was the fact that many in high society there remained culturally in sync with England. As discussed in the last chapter, that meant that they viewed London as a beacon of style. So, when new linguistic fashions, like "r" dropping and a preference for the "ah" sound, took off there, New England's posh elite snapped up these new features like hotcakes—making "vahses" a bit higher brow than regular vases. By the early nineteenth century, the highly recognizable "pahk the cah at Hahvahd Yahd" accent had arrived, and Southern British influence would remain a powerful force on speech there for the next century.

Though New England's prestige radiated pretty far, the Southern colonies had their own thing going on, not to mention a disdain for Puritans and their way of life. The heart of Lowland Southern society really rested in Richmond and in Charleston, led in large part by the aristocrats who came to the colonies, especially those who found themselves on the wrong side of the English Civil War. Many such so-called Cavaliers (or Royalists), meaning those loyal to King Charles I, settled in Virginia and South Carolina, which is the origin of the name *Charleston*, originally *Charles Town*. The plantation culture they spawned spread down the Southern coast and eventually west to Texas (which was part of Mexico until 1845), establishing a way of life and a way of speech that diverged from that in other regions.

This pre-Revolutionary South was also a place of immense linguistic diversity. The Southern settler mix included the Dutch, a smattering of French Huguenots, and a large number of Barbadians who relocated to Virginia and the Carolinas after sugarcane replaced tobacco cultivation in Barbados. It also included many speakers of West African languages. This African influence was significant: by the early 1700s, Charleston had three times more Black speakers than White, and White speakers, particularly women and children, spent a lot of time around enslaved Black speakers who were the house servants, nannies, and cooks. By the mid-1800s, we find commentary about the tendency for Southerners to co-opt African American speech patterns, with women in particular called out for this habit.

Let's think for a moment about all the speech features that have come into American speech lately, i.e., the *like*s, the non-literal *literallys*, the vocal fry. Who is associated most with such new trends? Old White dudes? Um, no: the young and the female. From the Elizabethan tendency to replace *ye* with *you* to the very modern bent of vocal fry as heard from the Kardashians, impressive numbers of sociolinguistic studies have shown that women and kids are the ones most likely to pick up and spread novel features. Couple that with the long-standing appeal of African American linguistic innovations, from *cool* to *finna* to *rizz*, and you have yourself a sizzling linguistic hot pot. If these words are unfamiliar, *finna* is an amalgamation of *fixing to*, which first developed in the South but became prevalent in African American dialects more widely. *Rizz* captures someone who has a particularly irresistible charm and was made popular by African American Twitch streamer Kai Cenat. Both of these words have found an eager audience falling well outside their originating groups.

In the 1700s, frequent interaction among women, children, and enslaved laborers and that era's lack of formal education for women created a perfect situation for a similar type of linguistic blending. Thus, it is no surprise that the intermixing of West African languages with British English has been widely suggested to have been a formative force on what was to become the Southern accent. One interesting hypothesis is that the development of "r" dropping in Southern speech was furthered by this close daily contact with non-rhotic West African languages rather than being based solely on the "r"-deleting pattern gaining a foothold back in Southwestern Britain.

WHY THE DRAWL WAS LATE TO THE PARTY

Archetypal Southern speech traits are ones that many even outside the South are familiar with; it includes things like merging *pins* and *pens*, shortening words like *bye* and *fire* to "bah" and "far," and the famous Southern drawl. Much research has been devoted to the question of where, exactly, these features originated, but, in what may come as a surprise, it has been hard to find any direct links to colonial speechways. For instance, in a study looking at Tennessee Civil War veteran questionnaires and linguistic atlas data, Vivian Brown found that the *pin/pen* merger was rare before 1875, but rapidly increased in the subsequent decades where we see *pins* increasingly confused with *pens*, *since* mixed up with *sense*, and *again* increasingly pronounced as "agin." Likewise, linguist Erik Thomas suggests the so-called /ay/ monophthongization we find in "bah" (*bye*) and "far" (*fire*) is also a relatively new feature, appearing predominantly after the Civil War.

And how about that most hyped of Southern features, the laid-back *y'all* that competes with expressions like *you guys* or *youse*? Well, research by linguist Edgar Schneider examining a collection of letters from antebellum overseers found this too was a later innovation in Southern speech, uncommon before 1875. Complementing this body of research is evidence from a unique Brazilian English variety spoken by descendants of the Confederados, the twenty thousand or so disgruntled American Southerners who fled to Brazil after the Civil War. Because their relocated English community was so isolated, linguists Michael Montgomery and Cecil Melo called it a "time capsule" for preserving nineteenth-century Southern English. As found with the Civil War questionnaires and overseers' letters, the features most associated with today's classic Southern accent—from "bah bah" to a singsongy drawl—are absent in their English as well.

Why this wellspring of Southern linguistic creativity after 1875? Two key things happened around that time: One, the South lost the Civil War but not its Southern spirit and, in fact, postwar animosity toward the North fostered greater Southern social and cultural unity. Two, urbanization rapidly increased in the South during the Reconstruction era owing to the expansion of industry (labor and land in the South were cheap) and greater railroad access. As small towns blossomed, often centered around country stores and railroad lines, so did the sense of shared regional identity, allowing local speech norms to arise and coalesce. Some of the South's "new" features built on incipient tendencies in British dialects, like /ay/ monophthongization found here and there in Southwestern England or the close *pin/pen* vowels in Scots Irish English, suggesting they may have been present in some degree, but simply not prevalent or socially meaningful as regional features prior to this era.

Of course, the Civil War was not the first war to have a significant linguistic impact on those it brought together. The Revolutionary War had been pivotal in making the otherwise splintered colonies start to see themselves as united and separate from the British. Sounding American became a celebrated part of this national identity. This is why, in the late eighteenth century, when regional differences started gaining more notice, many of the Founding Fathers—including George Washington, John Adams, and Ben Franklin, as well as their pal and American speech expert extraordinaire Noah Webster—were concerned that regional dialects would threaten the already fragile federal union among the highly divided states.

Franklin and Webster, in particular, were extremely vocal about the need for a national language and in objecting to giving any status to non-English languages like German or French or being soft on "provincial" pronunciations. One of Webster's main goals in writing his dictionary and his "Blue Back" speller textbook was to codify American speech forms and to establish an American standard, using as the model what he referred to as the New England "yeoman" class.

These early ideas about the democratization of English—that "good" English should be available and the goal of everyone, not just the upper class—has had a profound influence on the long-held prescriptive views of most Americans and their firm belief that, somewhere out there, exists "proper" English. But no Founding Father or wordsmith could stop the emergence of local regional and social dialects. As linguist Edgar Schneider sums up nicely, "No doubt the national identity of Americans is a strong and unifying force. In addition, however, most Americans regard themselves as members of sub-national groups which are important for their lives and their identities." So, as regional self-interests increased and the Western frontiersman and his wild and colloquial tongue became part of the American story, we also discovered the freedom to sound American in many different ways.

HEADING WEST

While today's recognizable Northern, Southern, and Midland accents were already part of the picture in the nineteenth century, the Western accent was just getting started. I hear the naysayers out there who might argue that there is really no such thing, since Western English seems devoid of remarkable features, but I beg to differ. Much of what we comment on as youthful speech habits, from vocal fry to uptalk to the tendency to say *biking* as "bik-ene," *that* as "thot," and *kitten* as "ki'in" are actually features more associated with the West. Despite not being a strongly marked accent, there most certainly is one.

The development of what would eventually turn into this Western accent happened much later and was quite distinct from that of the original colonies, as forging a new path across wild punishing terrain was not for the faint of heart or very popular when East Coast land was going cheap. Another key difference was that the West's formative accents, arriving on the heels of the Gold Rush, would have already sounded American.

In the mid-1800s, when the Western frontier really started to heat up, the main migratory routes kept Northern, Middle, and Southern settler streams fairly separate. Northerners also tended to head west earlier, particularly to California. For instance, considering both historical records and archival speech recordings, my research found that Northern-dialect speakers made up the heaviest influx into nineteenth-century San Francisco and northern Nevada, while Midland and Southern speakers arrived later and had a larger presence in the southern half of each state. Once there, though, these later settlers became part of the dialect scene. Non-English-language contact was also extensive—from Indigenous Salishan and Uto-Aztecan languages to Spanish, German, and Chinese.

This extensive dialect mixture, along with the strong need for collaboration, led to a second American linguistic leveling. Highly regional features, like the dropped "r" of New England, were filtered out during the acquisition process by pioneers' children. A more generalized accent then emerged—one which embraced the features most common in the input accents. The formation of this more homogenized Western accent was helped along by the birth of public schools in the West in the mid- to late 1800s, which brought young'uns of varied backgrounds and dialects together. As anyone who has a child or has met one knows, it is kids' main goal in life to be nothing like their parents but everything like their peers, a fact that forges a linguistic world in which young people get on with it, even if older folks don't.

As distinct social and regional identities formed within the West, subregional accents followed. These often took the form of a retention of some noticeable pronunciation features found in feeder dialects or in novel features that developed over time. In looking at the history of speech in the San Francisco Bay Area, linguist Lauren Hall-Lew found that the classic Mission Brogue associated with old-time White San Franciscans harkens back to the late-nineteenth-century influence of Irish and Jewish immigrants who came by way of New York and Boston. Though this accent is dying out, you can find echoes in certain multigenerational-descended San Franciscans, like the traces heard in former California governor Jerry Brown's speech.

Likewise, some Southern influence is still heard in California's Central Valley after large numbers of Oklahomans arrived during the Dust Bowl migration in the 1930s, bringing along their *pin/pen* merger and slightly longer vowels. In the Southwest, a long history of Spanish influenced the English spoken there, making, for instance, "v" sounds at the ends of words sound more like "f," as in "fayf" for *five*. At the same time, new features came into play as well. In Utah, linguist Joey Stanley found a change in the pronunciation of words like *mountain* or *button* away from "moun'n" and "bu'n" (with a sort of catch in the throat in the middle) to a pronunciation like "moun'in" or "bu'in," with a more prominent second vowel. Ironically, Stanley also found a hyperarticulate "moun-TEN" pronunciation growing in popularity after "moun'in" gained notice and took on some stigma as a nonstandard pronunciation.

HELLA NEW

A lot of the accent examples we've talked about might have a sort of quaint quality about them—you know the kind of accents we hear in old movies or from Gramps. Nowadays, especially with TV and social media, it feels like no one has an accent anymore. Or do they?

In the eighteenth century, British accents were the benchmark, and they were so richly varied that the differences among colonists paled in comparison. But surely, in reality, New Englanders and Virginians were not often confused about who was local, even if highly salient differences from back home had leveled out. Today, regional dialects are still around, though the strong regional markers that had developed by the late nineteenth century—e.g., the traditional New England and Southern accents—have indeed started to disappear. Instead, novel differences, predominantly in the form of vowel shifts, have come to characterize regional speech.

Around the mid-twentieth century, speakers in the Great Lakes region were affected by something called the Northern Cities Shift, a series of vowel changes that, if you've ever seen the "Super Fans" skit on *Saturday Night Live*, or happen to know anyone from Wisconsin or Michigan, should sound familiar. In the Northern Cities Shift, which affects cities stretching from Buffalo, New York, to Chicago, Illinois, the vowel in words like *bad* or *that* sounds more like "bed" or "thee-at." Words with vowels pronounced more in the back of the mouth, like *socks* or *job*, are said with the tongue a bit more to the front, like "sacks" or "jyab." And that "melk" pronunciation for *milk* that drives everyone else crazy? Yup, blame it on vowel shifts. To be completely fair, the vowel shift responsible for "melk" is thought to be Canadian in origin—from a shift not surprisingly called the Canadian Vowel Shift. So don't be surprised if you hear a similar "melk" pronunciation in Toronto.

The West Coast is also rife with shifty vowels, spawning that recognizable SoCal accent that gets played hard for laughs on *SNL*'s "The Californians." In what's known by the mouthful Low-Back-Merger Shift, words like *bad* or *that* in California (and other parts of the West) are now pronounced more like "bod" and "thot," while *I did it* comes across more like "I dead et." The coup de grâce of this Western accent is the merger happening in word pairs like *cot* and *caught* or *hock* and *hawk,* leaving them as homophones. Let's just say if you're from the West,* it's hard to tell whether the sizzle in your "wahk" refers to your cooking or your runway sashay. Not to be left out, in the South, in places ranging from Texas to North Carolina, we find something called the Southern Vowel Shift creating a situation where words like *said* and *sit* sound more like "say-ud" and "see-it." On the other hand, these same Southerners know how to keep *wok* and *walk* in their own lanes. Anyone who believes regional accents have completely disappeared has clearly not been listening—or at least not listening to people from the right generation.

Riffing off the famous words of Tina Turner, you might ask, "What's age got to do with it?" It turns out that many of these seemingly recent vowel shifts—all of which only became widely

* The so-called cot/caught merger is also prevalent in eastern New England and in Pennsylvania, where it seems to have developed because of leveling caused by contact among speakers from different language and dialect backgrounds with highly variable ways of saying the vowels.

noticed by linguists in the latter half of the twentieth century—are already starting to fade away in younger generations. Not only are these relatively new vowel changes going bye-bye, but so are the more classic accent features: the "d" to "th" substituting tendency of Chicagoans, the *pin/pen* merging of Southerners, the Pittsburgh "dahntahn" accent, and the "r" deleting tendencies of New York and Boston.

Research measuring the extent of many of these traditional features across different age groups has discovered that, starting with Generation X, born between roughly 1965 and 1980, speakers have been moving away from using them so consistently that by the time we get to Gen Z, they are pretty much out the door. In other words, regional accents seem so last century. But what was the dividing line between the baby boomer generation when these accents were thriving and the subsequent generations where they've started to fade?

According to exciting new work by a number of scholars focused on this very question, the basic answer is that between baby boomers and Generation X, major post–World War II demographic and economic changes came into play. One significant change was suburbanization. After World War II, we find parents hightailing it to the burbs and away from urban centers, taking their boomer babies away from the greater linguistic diversity found there.

In the 1970s, the Northern industrial powerhouse, so vital to our war efforts in the first half of the twentieth century, began to restructure, cutting costs and jobs and/or relocating to areas with lower wages and fewer environmental regulations. This corporate greed—uh, I mean, reorganization—spurred population movement out of Rust Belt cities toward warmer Sunbelt climes, which tended to be more business friendly. Lower costs also brought more and more companies to the South, a region that had previously experienced more people leaving than coming in during the first half of the century. In cities like Raleigh, North Carolina; Atlanta, Georgia; and Memphis, Tennessee, which experienced explosive corporate growth in the latter half of the twentieth century, this meant a lot of non-Southerners started moving in—and their kids started going to school and hanging out with Southern children.

Now, none of this might seem like a big deal, especially when compared to two world wars and a Great Depression in the first half of the century, but economic and population changes like these alter who we come into contact with and the types of social interactions we have—all of which impact language.

For instance, it has been suggested that much of the post–World War II push toward suburbanization was led by Whites effecting a de facto segregation under the guise of seeking better education and safer streets, something often referred to as White flight. Since urban centers were more ethnically diverse than suburbs, linguistic and social interaction between European Americans and African Americans, particularly in the North, decreased. It is around this same time we see the Northern Cities Shift really take hold among White baby boomers in these Northern cities, a linguistic White flight of sorts. However, as racial tension decreased and younger generations had less opportunity in local industries due to outsourcing and a move toward external hiring practices, young White speakers shifted away from accents that strongly symbolized local and ethnic identity.

In the South, Northern in-migration and the stigma of Southern accent features outside the South not only led to a decrease in Southern accents, but also turned young Southerners toward the model of the West's vowel shift and its *cot/caught* merging. What appears to have happened is that, for many born after the boomer generation, and particularly middle-class speakers in cities and suburbs, these migratory, economic, and social changes altered their sense of rootedness to any specific place or local group compared to their parents. In its place arose a more pan-national or external focus, precipitating the movement away from highly regional sounding speech, beginning with the first generation after such population and economic changes came into play,* Generation X. It is also Gen X who grew up with increased awareness of social issues like women's rights, civil rights, and gay liberation, and, importantly, they were also the first generation to start the transition to digital technology.

What potential role could television, the internet, and social media play in shifting people away from localized features? Linguists have long known that it takes more than just plopping a kid in front of a TV screen to make much of a linguistic dent. Despite Peppa Pig's reputation as the British accent whisperer who had American tots calling for their "mummies," studies on the role of

* This is not found to the same degree in rural areas, where rootedness often exists in greater measure.

television's influence suggest the effects on accent acquisition are fairly limited. In cases like Peppa Pig, it is simply individual instances of accented words or phrases being picked up, the same way that it's hard to resist saying "blimey!" with British flair.

The most important ingredient in picking up an accent is an (often unconscious) motivation to sound more like people who you have some relationship with and engage with in real life. Television, given its unidirectionality and generally scripted nature, just doesn't offer that sort of opportunity. But things like TikTok, Twitch, Instagram, and Zoom have changed the way we engage in very colloquial and casual—even intimate—ways with people we otherwise would never have a chance to know. What's more, the appeal of social media to one particular linguistically fashion-aware audience, i.e., teenagers, makes it more likely to spread novel speech features within that group.

Such geographic boundary-bending connecting has absolutely helped spread new slang like wildfire; just consider the stunning and somewhat inexplicable trajectory of *skibidi*, a nonsensical word picked up from the YouTube show *Skibidi Toilet.* Before the internet, slang was previously shared mainly via high school cliques and bathroom walls, a much slower way to get the word (literally) out. Now, not only can a word go viral overnight, but we also find social influencers picking up linguistic trends from one another, as found with what has been tagged the "TikTok accent," featuring commonalities like uptalk, vocal fry, and, among non-Americans, a more American-style accent. It is much less clear, though, that full regional accents could travel through this form of relatively limited exposure and be picked up by non–social influencers/everyday people.

What is most likely is that, starting with the millennial population, children who were digital natives, i.e., practically born with a phone in their hand, have become avid consumers of linguistic norms that originate far beyond their local communities. This increased exposure to more global or pan-American accents has had the effect of not only spreading slang much faster and farther than ever before, but it has also eroded the attraction to highly localized features, a trend particularly true with the very digitally oriented Gen Z population. As a result, we are not moving toward a specific accent as much as moving away from our noticeably regional ones.*

Does this mean regional dialects are gone for good? Not completely, as even with this leveling out of strongly regional features, some more subtle habits are hard to break, like the Southern deletion of "t" sounds in words like *internet* "innernet" and *Atlanta* "Atlanna," the West Coast's more tongue-backed pronunciation of the "aa" vowel as in "thot" (*that*) or "moth" (*math*), and the Upper Midwestern tendency to say some vowel sounds before "-g," like in *bag* or *tag*, closer to "bayg" or "tayg." But, as in the colonial days, the leveling of regional accent features has made it much harder to easily pinpoint where someone hails from, since most of these features are matters of degree rather than exclusive to any one region.

* Social media has also increased young non-Black speakers exposure to and adoption of African American speech forms, a topic we will revisit in a later chapter.

Still, don't be lulled into thinking that we are all moving toward some sort of linguistic kumbaya where we buy the world a Coke over a soda or pop, as all self-respecting Southerners know it should be, because such harmony only exists in marketing campaigns. Even as regional accents have started to fade into the background, dialect diversity is far from dead. As just one example, preliminary research suggests that regional vowel shifts may now be more about ideological and political divides than geographic ones; recent analysis of vowels, voting patterns, and views revealed that Southerners professing more conservative politics and voting habits used more Southern vowels and, in the North, those leaning left used more Northern-shifted vowels. What has become clear is that the accents of the twenty-first century are less about where we live and much more about how we see ourselves—a linguistic space where class, ethnicity, and even political orientation have become more important than, or are often intertwined with, region. In short, stay tuned.

SOUND BITE

A Lost Colony and a Lost Language

Okay, I might have fudged just a smidge when talking about who were the "first" British settlers to set upon American shores. The truth is, decades before our accent-forging colonists landed at Plymouth or Jamestown, a little baby girl named Virginia made her mark as the first British New World baby, born near the Outer Banks of what is now known as North Carolina. Sure, the greater historical glory went to those who came later, but only because, not long after her birth, she along with over one hundred others vanished into thin air, leaving an enduring mystery—and an unusual linguistic legacy—in their wake.

While many of us might have heard this story of the so-called Lost Colony in elementary school, fewer are likely familiar with how this tale is interwoven with the mystery of a Native American people known as the Lumbee, who have no name for or memory of their ancestral language, a language that also disappeared not long after these early colonists went missing. As we move from exploring the impact of geography on shaping our accents toward dynamic factors like power, class, and ethnicity, it seems like the perfect time to again veer slightly off course to explore how an early colonial mystery links to a much more modern tale of how a language lost—and accent found—has featured prominently in one group's search for identity.

LOOKING FOR A LOST COLONY

Before we jump ahead to the story of the lost language of the Lumbee Indians,* let's go back in time for a minute to the ill-fated settlers who had hoped to be the first of the English to make a successful home on New World shores.

In 1584, British adventurer, sailor, and, on many days, privateer, Sir Walter Raleigh received a charter from Queen Elizabeth granting him the right to colonize areas in the New World. After several scouting expeditions and a few embarrassing failed settlement attempts, in 1587 Raleigh sent a group of British settlers, led by an artist named John White, to establish an agricultural colony in the Chesapeake Bay area. Unfortunately, after what was supposed to be a brief stop to pick up a few sailors left behind on a previous ship's voyage to Roanoke Island a bit south of the Chesapeake, the ship's captain refused to sail on, and the island ended up their de facto new home.

Within a few months, food and provisions became scarce, and John White, who was serving as the colony's governor, was forced to return to England for a resupply, intending a quick return. His daughter, Eleanor Dare, who also happened to be baby Virginia's

* The Lumbee refer to themselves as Indians rather than Native Americans, and so I adopt their preference here.

mama, remained behind with her family and the rest of the settlers. White made it back to England, but, unfortunately for those left in Roanoke, the relationship between the British and Spanish had become increasingly tense, and Sir Walter's priority turned to defeating the Spanish Armada rather than feeding his band of not so merry colonists a world away. Unable to quickly secure a ship sufficiently defensible against pirates and the Armada, White did not return with the needed supplies for nearly three years, far longer than the three months he had anticipated at the outset. When he finally made it back to Roanoke Island, the colonists, including his daughter and her baby, had all gone missing.

Numerous theories have emerged over the years about these colonists' fate and, in most of this conjecturing, their story interlinks with that of local Native American tribes in some form or fashion, be it as the recipients of aid and kindness, as vectors of a deadly influenza outbreak, or as the targets of retribution for attacks they and others had led. And it is also here, in the evolving mythology surrounding the Lost Colony, that the story of the Lumbees' lost language starts to take shape.

GETTING THE LAY OF THE LAND

At the time of Raleigh's colonial aspirations, three main Native American language groups were present in what is now North Carolina: Siouan, Iroquoian, and Algonquian. We can't know for sure which tribal nations the settlers had most contact with—or even the degree of friendship or antagonism between them. But what we do know is that, on earlier missions to the area, the English explorers sent by Raleigh became allied with one particular Algonquian man, Manteo, a member of the Croatan tribe (also known as the Hatteras). He would end up being the pivotal connection in our story between the early colonial settlers, the modern Lumbee, and the language they would end up sharing.

After having spent some time in England, Manteo accompanied John White and the other colonists on that fateful voyage back to his homeland in 1587. He was to serve as an interpreter and a facilitator in what White hoped would be the re-establishment of friendly relations with the local tribes, which had been imperiled by a bloody massacre led by the earlier explorers. In his historical account of the Lost Colony in 1888, North Carolina legislator and local historian Hamilton McMillan suggests that, upon Manteo's return alongside the English, he became the leader of the Croatan Indians, who at that time resided on Croatan Island, south of Cape Hatteras.

This is important because, according to McMillan, when John White returned to Roanoke, he noted in his journal that he had found a clue that reassured him about the colonists' fate: carved in one of the trees within the colony's boundaries was the word CROATOAN.* An additional hopeful sign, at least as White saw it, was the fact that there had been no cross symbol carved on any of the trees, a previously agreed upon signal of distress, nor was there

* *Croatoan* and *Croatan* are alternate names for the same people.

evidence of any bodies or recent graves. All of this led White to believe that his daughter and the rest of the settlers might have removed with Manteo to Croatan Island to survive the intervening years.

Unfortunately, weather and other events precluded White from making it over to the island to check on their fate, and some later Jamestown colonists who delved further into the matter likewise discovered no proof of the survival of the Roanoke settlers (or of their death). To this day, there has been little evidence found that can definitively tell us whether they ever made it to Croatan, and, if they did, what happened afterward.

Tree-ring data examined from centuries-old trees in the area suggest the year the settlers went missing was one of extreme drought, meaning they would have almost certainly perished without some form of external help. But, even if we will never know for certain what fate befell them, by the time we get to McMillan's era in the late 1800s, the Croatan come back into our story in a second role: as the hypothesized ancestors of today's Lumbee Indians.

LINKING THE COLONISTS AND THE CROATAN

In his journal, which was published in 1709, North Carolina surveyor general John Lawson writes of encountering some striking grey-eyed tribal members on Hatteras Island (formerly known as Croatan) who used English and spoke of White ancestors who "talked in a book." Lawson conjectured they were descendants of the colonists who had taken refuge with Manteo and his people over a century before. Likewise, in the 1730s, Europeans settlers spoke of meeting Indians near the Lumbee River who spoke English, used European farming methods, and owned slaves.

All of this supported historian Hamilton McMillan's theory that the Indians now living near the Lumbee River in Robeson County, North Carolina, were the blended descendants of these Indians and the Roanoke colonists. This would also help explain why the tribal members in McMillan's time spoke English rather than any Siouan, Iroquoian, or Algonquian language. Supplementing this evidence, McMillan pointed to the prevalence of British surnames such as Berry, Brooks, and Sampson common to the Lumbee that were also found among the Roanoke colonists.*

Such extreme acculturation to European speech and names, though not unusual in situations of colonization, is surprising in that it happened quite a bit earlier than for most other tribes, who can still point to specific native languages (though often also extinct or nearly so) and tribal ancestry. The ability of the Lumbee to withstand the European incursion into their homeland was in many ways precisely due to their skillful and rapid adaptation to their new reality at a time when other tribes instead were wiped out. And, as we know, whenever languages encounter other languages that are more powerful and dominant in an area, what results is a typical three-generation pattern of language loss, as found

* Though it's true that these surnames were common among the lost colonists, they were very common surnames in general and are found across the non-Lumbee population there as well.

with German in prior centuries and as is currently happening with Spanish in the United States today. Following this pattern, the loss of the Lumbees' ancestral language likely happened over two centuries ago, given the reports of English-speaking Indians in North Carolina in the early 1700s. This unusually early language loss explains why today's members no longer even remember what that language was and from which language family (or families) it came.

UNIQUELY LUMBEE

This lack of a specific heritage language has proven problematic to the Lumbee in establishing straightforward tribal identity and gaining official recognition and entitlements, but, at the same time, their unique cultural and linguistic situation has led to the development of a very distinctive Lumbee English. Sociolinguistic research over the past three decades done in Robeson County indicates that the Lumbee absolutely sound quite different from others who live there. As one tribal member put it, "If we're anywhere in the country and hear ourselves speak, we know exactly who we are."

For those living outside the South, Lumbee English might sound similar to Appalachian varieties, but to anyone in Robeson County, there is no confusion about what it sounds like. A study run by linguist and North Carolina language expert Walt Wolfram had county residents listen to recorded speech samples and found that listeners could correctly identify a speaker as Lumbee over 80 percent of the time, a percentage that topped even their identification of a speaker as White. This linguistic uniqueness was also explicitly noted in the act that granted federal acknowledgment (but not full recognition) to the tribe, stating they had a "distinctive appearance and manner of speech."

Much of this distinctiveness comes from the way in which this dialect combines relic forms, like "a" prefixing ("I'm a-going") and older uses of the verb *to be*, as in "He bes late" and "I'm been there," unique vocabulary items like *juvember* (slingshot) and *ellick* (cup of coffee), and innovative twists on traditional Southern pronunciations, like pronouncing the /ay/ vowel in *time* more like "toym" (versus more traditionally Southern "tahm"). Some of these forms, like the "a" prefixing and *to be* usages, can be traced to earlier features brought over with English colonists and the Scots Irish, now faded from use in most other American varieties. But one pronunciation feature in particular has been heralded as evidence of some lingering traces of an ancestral Native American language on Lumbee English: the extensive dropping of final consonants in words like *old* or *most* found among Lumbee speakers.

Of course, deleting consonants is a very common process in general and is also found in early White varieties, as amply evidenced in early spelling by colonial settlers. Even today, pretty much every English speaker deletes consonants when three of them occur in a row: Quickly say "fi**sts**" or "be**st m**an" and see if you pronounce that "t." If so, you are weirdly hyperarticulate, but, hey, I'm not here to judge.

What's different in Lumbee English, as well as in other English varieties strongly influenced by transfer from a second language like Spanish or Vietnamese, is that a phrase like *that desk on my left* might sound more like "that des' on my lef." This second-consonant deletion pattern contrasts with the more common English pattern of deleting a sound only when three consonants occur together (as in ***desks*** or ***left side***). Though subtle, this specific two-consonant pattern appears to be particularly characteristic of cases where an English dialect bears the residual influence of languages with limited or no consonant clusters—exactly like those Siouan or Iroquoian languages hypothesized as the most likely to have been spoken by the Lumbee's ancestors.

Even more interesting is that this pattern of deletion was found to be about five times greater in Lumbee speakers born before 1910—those who had been educated in the Lumbee-exclusive schools that existed at the time—than in modern (and more integrated) speakers. This cross-generational pattern suggests that the lingering influence of an ancestral language is being leveled out as each subsequent generation is further removed from that language influence. But even as younger speakers have become more similar to other speakers in their consonant-dropping pattern, their attachment to Lumbee English and Lumbee identity appears to be far from fading either linguistically or culturally.

In following the trail left behind by linguistic clues, both of unexpected English-speaking Indians as noted by early Europeans and of the almost undetectable hints of a language long lost, we are again reminded of how pivotal language can be in unraveling the mystery of who we are. Whether it's Proto-Germanic, Sioux, or

Elizabethan English, as our original tongues disappear, there are parts of our past and identity that remain in how we say what we say. In this way, our accents are much more than simply a map of the places we come from or the geographic distances that have grown between us; they tell the story of the social spaces that we inhabit and the unique histories that brought us there.

FIVE

CLASSING IT UP

This might come as a bit of a shock, but I wasn't exactly a pillar of popularity as a young child. Having parents from a different country on top of being awkward and gangly was the death knell of cool in my Southern hometown. Yet I persevered in my attempts to make friends and impress people. One day in kindergarten, when it was my turn to share something, I was certain I had the golden ticket. I was going to tell everyone about the most amazing present I received for my birthday—a giant teddy bear that I had been begging my parents for all year.

I started off confidently describing my new friend Stuffy: he had white fur, a cute little black nose, and, most impressively, he was seriously huge—standing about three feet tall. I was prepared for the looks of shock and awe, but what I wasn't prepared for was that it would be about how I pronounced "huge" rather than about the clearly remarkable toy I had in my possession. With her head a bit cocked to the side, one little linguistic smarty-pants immediately said, "Why did you say 'huge' that way?" Her little sidekick topped it off with "You sound funny!" Certainly not the reaction I was hoping for.

What they had noticed was that, without my realizing it, I had picked up some aspects of my parents' accent. Namely, the fact that French speakers don't pronounce "h" sounds, so my *huge* came out as "youge" rather than a breathy "hhhhuge." I spent the rest of that year so aggressively pronouncing my "h" wherever I thought it should go that I became known as the girl with the spitting habit.

What I wasn't aware of then is that being called out for my "h" sounds—or more rightly my lack of them—put me in very good company. Even back in the day of Cicero, dropping an "h" was a bit of a sore subject. Cicero writes with disdain on the then new-fangled habit of pronouncing "h" sounds in Latin (otherwise known as *aspiration*), even while begrudgingly admitting to having succumbed to the habit himself as it became fashionable among swanky Roman types. There is also a poem by a contemporary of Cicero, the famed Catullus, that pokes fun at a rustic Roman bumpkin, Arrius, who has a tendency to put his aitches in all the wrong places. So, if I am going to be the subject of aspiratory shaming, it seems like it's been a few thousand years in the making.

Maybe I should have pointed out to my young "h"-articulating friends that it has been argued, by Cicero and others, that speakers of Latin did not pronounce the "h" sound in everyday speech either but that its trendy reemergence was based on Ancient Greek—a language and culture that Romans aspired to in much the way we look to Latin today. The Latin language we are familiar with now, especially when sitting through long incomprehensible religious sermons, is not the Latin that was spoken by the masses living under the rule of the Roman emperors. Instead, the language spoken on the streets was known as Vulgar Latin, using the term *vulgar* in the sense of "common."

This vernacular Latin differed quite extensively from what we recognize as the esteemed classical language of today, but it is this everyday spoken form that brought us the modern Romance languages. Many a Latin lover whispered their sweet nothings with no "h" in sight, inspiring the same in later French, Italian, and Spanish lovers, who inherited this lack of "h" from the get-go. This leads directly back, of course, to how I got to be dropping my aitches in the first place, and I squarely put the blame on my parents. It was, after all, its historic lack in French that ultimately led me to this traumatizing early childhood "h"-dropping experience.

But, while perhaps a bit painful at the time, this experience taught me two very important lessons: one, kindergarteners are a tough crowd, and two, getting noticed for the way you sound often doesn't feel like much of a good thing.

A LIL BI' SLOPPY

The reality is that we have all dropped a few consonants, even those of us who believe we have perfect elocution. If you doubt me, I have just a few words for you: *loud*, *nut*, and *what*. These words, along with numerous other words like *ring*, *honest*, *honor*, *hour*, *it*, *whale*, and *bought*, have all lost sounds over time to get to how we present-day speakers say them—and not just any sound. The very same sound little mini-me struggled with in kindergarten. Some words, like *hour*, *what*, and *honest*, retain that no-longer-spoken "h" in spelling. Many others, like *ring* and *it* (originally *hring* and *hit*), dropped any pretense of aspiration, spelling or otherwise, long ago. But what hasn't changed over the centuries is both the reason our "h"s drop out of sight and the fact that we often look down our haughty noses at those who dare drop their consonants in front of us.

Our tendency to characterize some speakers' way of pronouncing things as sloppy errors, rather than rule-governed differences, rests on the attention we pay to the social differences that divide us and the relative status that develops between us. In other words, one's class and social standing matter. Over time, those with more of these qualities become viewed as intrinsically better, rather than just socially lucky, and this tendency to assign the rich and well positioned more social value rubs off on the way we view their speech. The deletions and substitutions associated with the speech of those less esteemed in society—like the "h" dropping that destined fair lady Eliza Doolittle to a life selling flowers on the street as well as crushed my dreams in kindergarten—are heard not as accents but as bastardizations of the "right" sounds. By virtue of this firm belief in the superiority of one version, these pronunciations come to be seen as evidence a speaker is less worthy and intelligent.

A lot of modern sociolinguistic research has focused on how and why certain accents are heard as less educated and less prestigious and what linguistic pressures gave rise to them in the first place. What studies all find is that to delete and change is human, but that it is the social worth we associate with those uttering them that ultimately determines how we view these differences in the end—as either lazy and sloppy or articulate and clear.

WOULD YOU LIKE SOME "T"?

Take, for example, the tendency for some speakers to delete "t" sounds altogether in words like *winter*, *twenty*, *center*, or *internet*, coming out instead as "winner," "twenni," "cenner," or "innernet." Commentary on the way locals say "Torono" or "Sacramenno" (in lieu of "Toronto" and "Sacramento") shows up in a surprisingly large number of TikTok videos. I can't tell you how many times someone has emailed me to ask why some people drop their "t" sounds in these words, generally with the intention of calling attention to the lazy uneducated speech that seems to be endemic around them these days. But let's see whether there is a method to the madness before we determine whether or not these speakers deserve to go to the linguistic gallows for their slovenly ways.

Take a minute to examine the words just mentioned—do you see a pattern in the structure of the words in terms of the sounds next to the "t" sound in question? If you were paying attention, you might notice that in the cases just mentioned, the "t" being deleted is immediately following an "n" sound—think *winter* or *twenty*—while also occurring right before an *unstressed* syllable. In contrast, these very same "t"-deleting speakers don't say "inend" for *intend* or "con-ain" for *contain*, cases where the "t" sound follows "n" but appears at the start of a *stressed* syllable. As a linguist, this tells me that what some hear as an error is more accurately a systematic and highly patterned variation that is simply the result of hanging with a different crowd, one that allowed a natural linguistic process to progress while another group of speakers didn't and instead felt compelled to write to me about it.

So why exactly does this happen? Basically, "n" and "t" are both what we call *alveolar* sounds, meaning they are made with the tongue tip placed on that hard ridge behind your teeth. The only difference between them is that "n" is a nose sound, while "t" is a mouth sound. Essentially, they are made with exactly the same articulatory gestures, where the air builds up behind the tongue tip but is released through either the nose to make what linguists refer to as a *nasal sound* ("n") or the mouth to make what is called an *oral sound* ("t").

Now if you make a "t" sound in isolation, you will notice that the building up air part is actually silent—it is not until you let the tongue go and release the air that you hear the pop that is what we hear as a "t" sound. But when an "n" and "t" are said rapidly back to back, especially when the "t" occurs at the beginning of a shorter unstressed syllable, some speakers simply don't release the pop of the "t" so they can get their tongue straightaway into position for the upcoming vowel sound. This fact, coupled with the similarity in mouth position for the "n" and "t," makes the "n" sound the dominant one we hear. In contrast, in words like "intend," the longer stressed syllable allows more time for the "t" to get in its full articulatory groove, so it sticks around to do its popping thing.

Does this make "win-ner" speakers sloppy? Not from a linguistic perspective, since they are just streamlining their speech gestures in the very same way that we all are when we delete the "d" in *handsome* or the "t" in *moisten*. These words involve deletions that were driven by a similar economy of effort but caught on as the "right" pronunciations before any of us were around to complain about it.

The reason pronunciations like "winner" and "innernet" get our goat today is because we notice that certain speakers—typically less socially prestigious speakers or ones with less well-regarded accents like Southerners—show this pattern more than others, leading to its association with "uneducated" or sloppy speech. In fact, I am guilty of this type of "t" deletion myself, likely a result of my Southern upbringing, but I didn't realize it in my own speech until some helpful gentleman decided to write to me to let me know of my transgression after listening to a video lecture series of mine. In particular, my pronunciation of "sennence" seems to have struck an irritating chord for him.

As with this gentleman, the naysayers who call out this deletion pattern generally cite reasons of intelligibility for their complaints. Those who do not include the "t" in these words are slurring their speech and can't be properly understood by those, like themselves, for whom all consonants are clearly enunciated. This brings up the question of how they knew which words the speakers were aiming for, given that the complainant generally provides the "proper" pronunciation alongside the deviant one, e.g., asking why people say "innernet" for *internet*. It also flies in the face of research on how our brains deal with reduced speech forms, which suggests that we subconsciously get the regular patterns behind reduced forms (like the consistent "nt" contexts described above), which helps us reconstruct the intended target word (i.e., *internet*).

This research also generally suggests that the more frequently we hear these forms used around us, the better we are at arriving at the right word, and that a closer match with how a word is written (its canonical form) can also speed up our processing. What this means is that we can be good at understanding both reduced forms like "cenner" and ones that more closely reflect their written forms like "center" without too much trouble as long as they follow a regular pattern, and particularly the more routinely we hear them around us.

Often, as with my own experience as a "t" dropper, speakers aren't aware that what they say is different from people outside their group because most of their exposure is with people talking just like they do. This underlying familiarity makes it easier to match those reduced forms with the right target word (i.e., *center*). It also explains why the alternative form ("cenner") is more noticeable and less easily processed for those not as used to hearing it. Of course, context also plays a big role in disambiguating our speech more generally, and certainly "winters" and "winners" don't tend to be discussed much in like circumstances. One additional interesting finding of research on this topic is that the more disfluent a speaker is (e.g., uttering "um"s or repetitions), the *less* likely they are to delete a nearby "t" sound, probably because hesitations slow down a speaker's speech rate, which has also been shown to decrease deletion rates.

Despite the systematic nature of this dropped "t" pattern, another reason we consider deletions like this to be a "mistake" is related to our valorization of spelling and our relatively recent view that the written word is the authority for how words should be said. The problem with this view is that many very influential languages have come and gone without ever being written (i.e., Proto-Germanic and Indo-European) and most modern languages, like English, were spoken long before writing them down became popular. And this means that, despite today's widely held belief that pronunciations should reflect spellings, it's really the other way around: it's the oral forms that mostly inspired the written forms.

Take, for instance, the wide variation in spelling we talked about earlier in the colonists' written records, with forms like *bust* based on pronunciation, written side by side with *burst*. Over time, various written forms became unified toward a "correctly" spelled version usually determined by who was using that spelling and the sway they held in society. As literacy increased and access to formal education became more widespread in the nineteenth and twentieth centuries in England and America, the expectation that our speech should conform to spelling drove much of what we perceived as "incorrect" or "lazy" speech forms. This conviction hangs around despite the fact that many of our spelled words contain sounds we also never pronounce even when we're speaking "properly," e.g., *coup*, *knight*, *walk*, and *sword*, which leads us directly to the question of how it was decided whose pronunciation should be the one written down for the ages.

SOUNDING BOUGIE

The impetus for what we think of as standard speech and spelling started back when London was developing into a cultural and economic center in the seventeenth and eighteenth centuries. Prior to this point, social mobility was not really something people spent much time worrying about, mainly because it wasn't an option. One's position was fixed through a rigid system of rank based on land, title, and standing. You were either a member of the gentry or a commoner and, if you were of humble birth, there was little reason to hope that your circumstances might change.

Differences in how people sounded were certainly part of this earlier social separation—we see mention of "vulgarisms" or "provincialisms" alluding to common or folk speech in texts from this time—but people using such speech were not assigned strongly negative social traits like being ignorant, lazy, or sloppy because of them. Of course, the aristocracy surely saw themselves as more educated (they were) and more socially advantaged (also true), but since the commoners were not a threat, there was little reason to need language as a gatekeeping device to keep the masses off the well-manicured grasses. After all, who else would keep the rosebushes pruned?

But, by the eighteenth century, massive urban industrial and economic growth made London the place to be, attracting a flood of people from other parts of Britain (and Europe) into the city to take advantage of the new opportunities it afforded. Of course, this was not limited to Britain—the same forces contributed to the increased wealth and power of other European urban centers like Paris. These forces also spurred the traditional social hierarchy based on rank to break down as industrialization created a need for a professional class, i.e., manufacturers, bankers, lawyers, accountants, and retailers. As a result, many without rank increasingly found themselves at the helm of booming businesses.

These changes precipitated a shift away from a social system determined by birth to a more flexible one based on socioeconomic status, allowing the possibility of upward mobility. There was only one problem—wealth and property alone could no longer be counted on as a metric of social standing, as the "nouveau riche" came charging up the ranks once reserved for those who had done the very exhausting work of being born there. Just one thing stood between them and full respectability—an accent. While pronunciation differences had developed for centuries because of the social and economic separation among these speakers that had once been etched in stone, now these variations in how things were said became one of the last ways to determine someone's standing—or more importantly, how they came by it.

By the nineteenth century, the newly rich and the old aristocratic elite were increasingly mixing, but there was still a social barrier to full cultural acceptance among those whose speech retained traces of where they had come from. Certain pronunciations like "h" dropping at the beginning of words or deleting the "t" in *bottle* ("bah'ul") had become marks of ill breeding. In her book on the rise of prescriptivism in English, scholar Lynda Mugglestone relays the story of nineteenth-century shipping magnate Charles

Booth, whose provincial accent was held as a strong mark against his character by his old-money in-laws. Ironically, Mr. Booth's legacy far outlasted anything his snobby in-laws left behind: he was a deeply influential social reformer whose research on poverty helped set the stage for the government pensions and free school lunch programs of today.

Mr. Booth was not alone in being seen as lacking somehow because of his accent. The likelihood that you'd be judged based on the way you spoke inspired a cottage industry of speech manuals and elocution lessons aiming to help people lose their provincial ways of talking and sound more like the wealthy London elite. Gradually, as what was valued in society became more and more linked to particulars of pronunciation, the higher-class model became not just a means to success but symbols of morality, intelligence, and purity, while lower-class pronunciations were viewed as ignorant mistakes. So, dropping your "r" while never forgetting to articulate your "h" and "t" became the order of the day.

The coinciding rise in literacy and the increased interest in codifying usage in grammar books and dictionaries helped cement these upper-class pronunciations and spellings as the norm,* while the deletions and "mispronunciations" of unsavory sorts were called out by the growing use of eye dialect (colloquially inspired spellings like "mawl" for *mouth*) and apostrophes (*so 'appy, swimmin'*). Crucially, these standards were not enforced through any sort of legislation or

* In particular, Samuel Johnson's *A Dictionary of the English Language* and Lindley Murray's *English Grammar* held a lot of sway from the time they were first published.

edict, but through everyday people's awareness of their social standing and desire for acceptance and respect. Our modern complaint culture has grown out of these deeply classist ideas of "good" versus "bad" speech, shaping not only how we speak but how we listen.

GETTING YOUR BEER LEGS

There is no doubt that listeners are quite sensitive to how class plays a role in forming accents—even to the point that we hear the same sounds differently depending on what class we think someone inhabits. One study looked at a fairly new vowel merger happening in New Zealand English, where the vowel in words like *air*, *fair*, or *bare* has started to sound exactly like the vowel used in words like *ear*, *fear*, or *beer*. The result is that *airfare* sounds like "ear fear" and *bare legs* like "beer legs." Of course, this adds to the confusion of hapless travelers already scratching their heads over why Kiwis seem to say "sex" all the time when really they probably just intended "six," due to a different vowel change. Pro tip: You should probably confirm any lewd-sounding propositions from Kiwis before jumping to conclusions.

In the study just mentioned, researchers had people listen to recordings while being shown a photograph of the speaker and then asked them to identify which word they had heard from two choices (e.g., *bare* or *beer*). The researchers found that listeners tended to be more accurate when they were shown photos of people who appeared white-collar or professional—for instance, when wearing a blue blazer in front of an office building compared to wearing a T-shirt in front of fast loan/check-cashing shop.

When shown photos of people who looked more working-class, listeners heard the words less accurately (i.e., reporting "beer" for *bare*), suggesting they expected a lower-class speaker might have merged the vowels. Of course, all listeners heard exactly the same stimuli—the only thing the researchers changed was the photos. But these listeners' sense that social class would affect how a speaker pronounced the word was based on the fact that in their everyday experience, socioeconomic status was a good predictor of whether or not people would merge these two historically separate vowels.

Confirming listeners' intuitions, studies of this *bare/beer* merger in New Zealand find that younger speakers and those of lower socioeconomic status actually do tend to produce this merger more than older and higher-status people. Such staggered adoption by class is not uncommon, as, in the early stages of language change, lower-class speakers often take the lead. Eventually, higher-class speakers catch up, as long as the change is something that doesn't get stigmatized as "bad" before it makes the leap to everybody's speech. Most of the regional vowel changes in twentieth-century U.S. English we discussed in an earlier chapter followed a similar class pattern before becoming widespread among boomers.

The takeaway from such experiments is not that being young and lower-class makes you difficult to understand, but, instead, that our tendency to make quick class assessments leads us to certain expectations about how certain people will sound—to the point that we are biased to "hear" them a certain way regardless of how they actually sound. The key, though, is that in real life—no matter how you say them—*bare* and *beer* and *air* and *ear* are rarely easily confused, since our conversations with one another are grounded in topically relevant contexts, like throwing a kegger or taking a trip to Bali.

Interestingly, we do this kind of accent projection not just with class but with other social characteristics as well. One fun study switched up the nationality listed for a stimuli speaker from American (Michigan) to Canadian on the response sheet given to participants. Lo and behold, those listeners started to report hearing words in line with more Canadian vowels than those who thought the speaker was American, like hearing *bed* pronounced more like "bad."

Another study looking specifically at how class affects linguistic perception discovered that listeners tended to be faster and more accurate in understanding what others said when they were the same class as that speaker, a result attributed to the fact that people tend to have the most exposure to the speech of those most like themselves. This means that blue-collar speakers have more working-class speech experience to use to interpret what they hear—but they are also likely to have a lot of exposure to middle-class speech from teachers, supervisors, media, and the like. However, the reverse is not necessarily true in that middle-class speakers may not have a similar range of exposure to lower-class speech given the way the world works, meaning that their teachers, bosses, and news anchors sound a lot like they do. It is easy to see how this might lead to some linguistic trouble across class divides, particularly for those whose speech is deemed less upwardly mobile and, as a result, less "correct."

Hollywood, for one, has certainly embraced class accents as a shortcut way to establish character types and ensure audiences get the "right" impression off the bat. Think about Julia Roberts's Erin Brockovich, Jodie Foster's Clarice Starling, Marlon Brando's Terry Malloy, or Sally Field's Norma Rae, all characters whose working-class accents help to establish down-on-their-luck but salt-of-the-earth personality types. We might like them, but we don't tend to see them as head honchos in the CEO's office, which makes their fight to rise above their allotted station all the more impressive. I mean, if you've ever seen the movie *Good Will Hunting* about the wicked "smaht" Boston local who works as a janitor at MIT and can't help but solve the impossibly difficult math problem left on a professor's whiteboard overnight, you know that his working-class Boston accent is a key part of the way we get the drift that no one ever expected that much from him.

Both empirical evidence and such recurrent rags-to-riches themes in popular entertainment remind us that we do use speech cues to judge one another's social standing quite readily. Even more, we go on to use that evaluation to determine things as important as whether that person has the ability to be successful at math problems, legal battles, or desk jobs—only, in real life, we generally don't root for the underdog with the lower-class accent.

THE ACCENT OF EMPLOYABILITY

Most studies looking at our reactions to accents over the last fifty years have converged on the same finding: we attribute a lot of good and bad qualities to people based on hearing very short snippets of their speech. How short? Try three words on for size—at least according to recent research that focused on how listeners assessed deviations from "proper" or standard-sounding speech when hearing words spoken in various American accents.

Not only does it not take much speech exposure to get a sense of class, but the same study found that people in hiring positions relied on these types of class-signaling cues when hearing potential job applicants answer a pre-interview warm-up question, using such cues as a way to assess competence and fit for a job, despite having no résumé or other evidence of ability. Higher-class-sounding applicants not only were favored for the jobs but were also offered higher signing bonuses and salaries.* Ouch. That means that simply asking where the bathroom is (four words!) could derail your career prospects before you even start the actual job interview. Some advice? Plan to find the facilities beforehand.

One issue in the United States is that we tend to attribute lower class standing to any accent that is perceived as varying from what we consider an "accentless" norm, a tendency that particularly singles out accents associated with non-Whiteness or rurality. As well, the regional accents we most notice—like a Southern, New York, or Philly accent—are often heard not simply as locational pointers as to where someone grew up, but also as provincialisms tied in with being lower-class. These kinds of accent prejudices can

* While the evaluators were people with previous hiring experience (themselves of varied class backgrounds), these were mock interview situations.

make for serious trouble for such speakers hoping to climb the corporate ladder.

In fact, one acquaintance asked if I could coach her on getting rid of her Philly accent because, as she got to the upper echelons of management, she worried it was hurting her prospects for higher advancement despite stellar credentials; she got the sense that people just didn't think she sounded smart enough to play in the big leagues. At the same time, Americans still harbor a latent sense of the superiority for one quite recognizable accent—proper British. One very well-known high achiever once confided in me that he had asked a standard-speaking British friend to record his voicemail message because he was self-conscious about how his slight Hawaiian accent came across.

These two accented speakers were probably not wrong. A meta-analysis (looking at all the comparable studies researchers could find that had been done on the topic) found an extremely robust result emerging from the work they reviewed: nonstandard-accented speakers were almost always much more negatively evaluated on traits like intelligence, status, and dynamism. Standard accents, like those associated with network news anchors, were much more favorably viewed, which means Will Hunting, as well as my Philly friend, had a tall mountain to climb to get past the gatekeepers and into the classroom and boardroom.

If you think sounding lower-class in America is rough, you're definitely not any be'er off in Britain, where classism is more entrenched and more overt than in the United States. A recent project led by several prominent sociolinguists examined how having an urban working-class accent like that from West Yorkshire or Liverpool (i.e., Scouse) affects judgments about professional suitability for "elite" jobs. Features from these accents tend to be highly salient, for example, saying *luck* with a vowel more like "look," dropping "h"s ("'ouse" for *house*), and changing up "th"s (e.g., "den" for *then*). In the experiment, the researchers had actors use different accents in a mock interview for a position at a law firm. Lawyers had helped prepare the answers to the mock questions posed, so that the content of the responses were of reasonable quality. These answers were then recorded in each accent and played for non-experts, who evaluated them as to their suitability for an entry-level legal position.

As expected, the standard British accent (Received Pronunciation) received the highest score for hireability, while the regional urban accents ranked lower. But most interesting, for younger raters, the accent difference did not seem to affect their evaluation of the candidate very much. Those over age forty-five, though, were much more inclined to hire the standard speaker than the lower-class-accented speakers, even with them giving answers of the same quality. This might make it appear that younger speakers are just fabulously unbiased and dedicated to making the world a beautifully democratic place, but this pattern echoes that discovered in separate but similar research studies done in 1970 and 2007, where the youngsters of each time period were similarly less judgy than older people.

Why? Because younger folks are more open to diverse accents at their stage of life and gradually become more biased toward conventional standard language norms as they enter later life stages where they have become more embedded in the labor market. In short, they become more conforming to workplace ideals about the types of accents that culturally "fit" different types of work. Since it is this same older group that makes many of the hiring decisions in organizations, accents (and the people they grace) that don't fit the right vibe tend to be shown the door.

The good news is that when the "candidates" (as voiced by actors) appeared to be highly knowledgeable about legal topics, it seemed to counter the triggering of accent stereotypes for listeners, meaning that being qualified and showing it in an interview can land you a job even when your accent isn't posh. The researchers also found that when those who were evaluating the candidates scored high on tests that showed they were motivated to try to avoid appearing prejudiced, they tended to be fairer in rating accents the equivalent in hireability. What all this suggests, luckily, is that people's attitudes are not set in stone. Everyone comes to language with learned beliefs and biases that may influence reactions to others, but our desire to come across as fair and nonprejudicial (regardless of any actual prejudice), as well as our ability to pay attention to what people say and not just how they say it, can offset our stereotypic inclinations.

TALKIN' UP OR DOWN

These studies might make us wonder why anyone would continue to use accent features that seem to announce a lack of refinement and education. It's for the same reason that leather jackets have stood the test of time—because those features give off a particular social vibe, even if it isn't the one that CEOs and teachers value. Accents that give us an edge by helping us sound tough, friendly, hip, or simply like a local can offer as much in the way of reward as using "proper" speech. After all, not everyone can or wants to wear the linguistic equivalent of a constraining three-piece suit.

Linguistically speaking, we are rather arbitrary in which deletions or substitutions we make a fuss about, so how we pronounce something itself has no intrinsic value. After all, the very same "r" dropping is held as a marker of posh speech in Britain but mostly looked down upon in U.S. accents like those of Boston and New York City. As we discussed, the vast majority of variation in speech arises simply because language inherently tends to change, and when groups of speakers are separated by geographic or social distance, it changes differently among different people. Since most of those we chat with talk the same way we do—whether this means in our country, our town, our neighborhood, or the school we attend—most of us don't even realize we have an accent until someone from outside our group remarks on it. The key here is that, as kids, we adopt a particular linguistic style based on our family's, friends', and neighbors' way of talking well before we are really aware that we talk in any particular way.

But over time specific features of accents begin to take on positive or negative social associations depending on who uses them most often. Sometimes this means that features in wide use by those with standing and privilege become valued as "better" or "correct," but it can also end up that features used by those with less privilege become symbols of class consciousness and solidarity, since one's accent is deeply tied to one's identity and self-worth.

In linguistics, we refer to the attraction toward standard speech features as one of *overt prestige* (the type of prestige associated with those holding social, institutional, and economic power), in contrast to that of *covert prestige*, an alternative type of cachet based on a harder to capture type of social influence, one tied to particular qualities of or membership in a group. Why would covert prestige even be a thing? Well, duh. Who wants to hang out with uptight Sandy from *Grease* when way more appealing Rizzo is the option? More importantly, not everyone gets the same benefit from adopting standard speech.

When we look to sociological research on social networks, we find an interesting pattern: working-class communities tend to have tighter-knit and more multifaceted social ties than middle-class communities. Because standard forms are used widely in formal and impersonal contexts like offices and classrooms, the features that typify middle-class speech come across as stiffer and more distant than nonstandard forms, which promote closeness and insider status among speakers. Even if learning to change one's accent was easy (it isn't!), most people with working-class accents would not find it of much interest in daily life since their professional, social, and romantic opportunities are typically found in their local networks. Not to mention that quacking like a duck doesn't necessary grant you access to the pond where the fancier ducks reside, if you even wanted it.

It is also the case that the physically demanding work and hardship traditionally associated with working-class life give off a sense of trustworthiness and authenticity or of toughness and swagger, and these characteristics have become associated with working-class speech features. Just think of how Donald Trump's colloquial New York accent helps him connect with the average Joe or Jane and come across as relatable. And how other politicians change their speech depending on what audiences they're addressing—sometimes even taking on class or regional accents that aren't native to them.

The attraction to working-class features by those who might not themselves actually be lower-class comes by way of their desire to project a rugged salt-of-the-earth image—and benefit from the chumminess it can represent. On the flip side, these features' ties to nonstandardness also fuel an association with laziness and ignorance. The reality is that these associations are simply classist stereotypes—but they do seem to influence how we behave.

We see this dynamic at work in a very creative study using a computer game involving two made-up competing species, the Wiwos and the Burls. For the study, linguists Betsy Sneller and Gareth Roberts taught players a few features of each species' dialect of an "alien" language (which the researchers had invented) to use during the game. When one of the species, the Burls, were characterized as tougher than the Wiwos, players assigned to the

Wiwos group were more likely to borrow Burls language features because they wanted to be perceived as more physically powerful when facing off with another player. But, when the alien language was instead simply described as "Burl talk" with no mention of toughness, the rate of borrowing of Burl features dropped. This tells us that speakers see the value of features differently depending on what they believe they will achieve by using them and that sounding standard is not always the order of the day.

To this end, a number of recent studies have found that urban vernacular features have become increasingly popular in large cities (both here and in Europe) particularly among younger speakers. For instance, witness the growing popularity of Multicultural London English (MLE) in London, Citétaal in Flanders, Cockney in Glasgow, the "new" Toronto accent in Canada, Miami English in the United States, and Kobenhavensk in Denmark. These were all originally stigmatized and predominantly ethnic and lower-class varieties that have had greater and greater uptake among young adults who were not original users. And what makes them so attractive? Their charismatic, non-posh, forceful, and cool associations, in contrast to the staid, stodgy, and weak character often ascribed to higher-class "educated" speech forms.

While there are many upsides to a working-class accent, such as invoking authenticity and solidarity, the most serious downside is that it is a trigger for negative judgment about intellect, ability, and confidence. As mentioned previously, much research suggests that accents are used to infer a speaker's status and capabilities, particularly when we know little about the person that might counteract these biases. As well, ideas about cultural "fit" can often come into play, even when applicants or employees have the requisite skills. Part of this idea about "fit" is a sense that somehow those in lower classes just don't have the same beliefs or are internally unmotivated.

For example, in one experiment, listeners heard a fictional background story about a speaker that included information about whether they succeeded or failed at things like getting a promotion. When listeners had been told that the speaker was lower- instead of middle-class, they were more likely to attribute the failure to an intrinsic cause like low ability rather than some external cause like bad luck. Since just hearing an accent often provides class cues, this means that such views about someone's abilities might become activated even when their class status is not made explicit, as it was in the study.

These classist beliefs get embedded early and deep, just like our preferences for in- versus out-group accents. In studies with both elementary- and preschool-aged children, researchers found that children who were perceived as wealthier were more likely to be liked and preferred as friends than children perceived as poorer. Not only that, but kids associated with more material possessions (i.e., expensive clothes, nicer houses, etc.) were also seen as more likely to be academically successful and more popular. Though it is improbable that young kids have any understanding of something as abstract as class, what they clue into is the way some things and some people around them are valued by adults and institutions more than others, making them seem "better" and giving them a lot of social and academic clout. At the same time, kids also get vibes about how other types of speech carry an alternative form of social currency, i.e., the covert prestige of nonstandard forms. There is a social power in those forms as well, particularly for those whose identities and communities are represented in their accents.

In the labor market, though, overt prestige often outweighs covert prestige, which is why speaking with a working-class accent can be a barrier for certain types of jobs, regardless of one's education or skill set. We see the negative effects of accent stereotypes everywhere in the workplace, from just getting in the door to getting a promotion. Since, as we learned in an earlier chapter, accents develop very early in life, even those who actively want to change them are not always able to do so effectively. Perception studies show us that even one nonstandard pronunciation like "walkin'" instead of "walking" is enough to impact how well we are professionally perceived, something former British home secretary Priti Patel learned firsthand when Tony Blair's former press secretary remarked, "I don't want a home secretary who can't pronounce a G at the end of a word."

This may seem harsh, but the truth is that many of us do this kind of quick and dirty judging without batting an eye because discrimination on the basis of an accent is not something we tend to legislate or even notice, as we believe the problem lies with the speaker who just didn't put enough effort into learning to speak well. It is true that local accents tend to decrease as speakers become more educated, but they are typically not eradicated, meaning that the speech of highly educated people often still gives up class clues.*

Efforts at eradication are also not without a cost to the speaker, who may be losing connection to an identity tied to their accent, something South African comedian Trevor Noah wrote deftly about in his autobiographical collection of stories *Born a Crime*. To further rub salt on this accent wound, those who reduce or change their accents are often seen as putting on airs or as sounding pretentious—as Meghan Markle discovered when she was accused of adopting a posh, somewhat British speech style. In short, class matters, and the accents that clue us into it matter too, whether it's pronouncing *there* as "dere," talking about the Pittsburgh "Stillers," or droppin' "plenny" of "g"s and "t"s.

This is not to discount the fact that employers might have reasons to find standard speakers more attractive to hire, given the way society associates standard speech with competence, education, and motivation. Where we go wrong is this automatic equating of accent with abilities and attributes. In reality, there is no evidence that, outside of stereotypes, having a working-class accent makes you a worse employment bet for white-collar work, all other things being equal.

For example, though research finds that those in higher classes

* This may be a chicken and egg issue, as research also shows that young people with stronger interest in leaving their communities (i.e., to attend college or work out of state) are less likely to have strong local accent features compared to those planning to remain in the community.

are more likely to end up in positions of leadership, this doesn't mean that they actually make more effective leaders. Rather, because a higher-class upbringing provides a wealth of resources and positive attention (e.g., from teachers and other adults), individuals feel more valued and more assured that their opinions will be well received. This makes those individuals more confident and assertive, qualities that tend to be tapped for leadership, even when their actual abilities might not make them the best choice. On the other hand, those experiencing poverty have fewer resources and are rewarded less for independence and speaking up, making them less likely to make a play for leadership. But this in turn doesn't mean they wouldn't make strong leaders once they got there. In fact, this greater relational awareness of others might actually make them very good at it.

Still, a large number of professional jobs go to those with higher-class speech regardless of other qualifications because of business owners' fear of turning clients and customers off in the face of centuries of linguistic prescriptivism that has taught us that standard speakers are better bets. We all play a part because we too have been brought up with this same sort of standard language ideology, and it is hard to get past it. But instead of shutting the door on the working-class accent because it sounds ignorant, perhaps now that we are a bit linguistically wiser we can understand what it really is—an accent that we come by as children that makes no inherent claim about our intelligence and ability or lack thereof. That doesn't mean that all speakers sporting a working-class accent will turn out to be the right choice for the job, but it really should be qualifications and experience rather than a fancy accent that gets someone through the door.

To that end, research exploring what kind of interventions are most effective at mitigating accent bias in employment settings has pointed to a number of successful strategies. For one, when trained HR professionals are asked to ignore irrelevant information such as accent and focus only on the content and quality of answers during an interview, accent bias decreases. Having a predetermined set of objective criteria going into an interview and being required to justify decisions to others also softened the impact of accent on the hiring process. But the biggest surprise was that the most successful intervention was something shockingly simple: just being made aware of the potential for accent bias had the greatest reduction effect of all. Can't get much more of a mic drop moment than that.

SIX

WHAT COLOR IS YOUR ACCENT?

In the United States, conversations about race are almost always mired in controversy—just look at the many different ways *woke* has been employed by people on both the left and the right of the political spectrum to get a sense of how fraught discussions around the topic can be. And while the politics of race has been part of the national discourse for decades, the language of race has received surprisingly little attention despite the fact that the upsides and downsides of "sounding Black" are quite familiar to many African American speakers.

In part, this lack of conversation around race and accent stems from the worry that even the mere suggestion that ethnic identity can be recovered from auditory cues is itself racist. In the widely watched O. J. Simpson murder trial in the mid-1990s, witness Robert Heidstra said he overheard two voices near the murder scene on the night in question. Critically, the prosecution asked the witness whether one of the voices he overheard sounded Black. Johnnie Cochran, the attorney for the defense, heatedly objected, claiming that it was impossible to glean someone's race from just hearing their voice and that to do so was racist.

The legal standing of this issue—whether laypeople can offer testimony as to the race of the voices they overhear—has not been sufficiently resolved. In fact, the same argument as Cochran's, that you can't tell someone's race just by hearing their voice, is often used to dispute claims of discrimination by prospective employers or landlords accused of doing just that. Yet most of us have, at some point in our lives, very likely assessed a caller's race just from hearing a voice over the phone. Though Judge Lance Ito sustained Cochran's objection, a decent body of research suggests that people often do perform much better than chance when guessing someone's race from the sound of their voice, even from just hearing a short clip.

Is that really a form of racism? No, not really. People are savvy to the features and cadences that typify certain accents, as when we surmise that someone is Southern from the way they sound. That doesn't mean all Southerners talk that way, but simply that there is a distinctive accent associated with some Southerners that we recognize as being from that region. Linguistically speaking, associating an accent with a speaker of a particular ethnicity is no different a process.

However, just as living in the South doesn't mean you have a Southern accent, being Black doesn't make you "sound Black." Education, class, cultural orientation, and who we hang with most of the time all factor into the accent we acquire no matter the color of our skin, since shared heritage, experiences, and culture can bind you in ways that encourage the development of in-group linguistic norms. Recognizing correlations between such accent features and a particular ethnic group's use is in itself not racist. But here lies the real issue: hearing recognizably Black voices doesn't just trigger accent recognition; it also triggers stereotypes about the speakers who own them.

WHITE NOISE

Of course, the very idea of a "White" voice versus a "Black" voice seems to suggest that accents are somehow linked to race in some intrinsic way. In reality, as we have explored in these pages, our specific accents are really sociohistorical inheritances, not biological ones: we sound like those we are surrounded by and care about in the places and social spaces where we grow up. This can mean that we sound like posh speakers from London or working-class speakers from Chicago. But what we so far haven't talked much about is how we've come to link race and accent in the ways we do.

Before we dive in, let me ask you, during the several chapters when we were discussing colonial English, what did the speaker you imagined right at first look like? I am going to hazard a guess that, in addition to their breeches and petticoats, they were probably White. Why? Because most of the time when people think about the development of American accents—those that we don't label in a particular way as being racialized—they are really thinking about the historical journey of White English, not Black English.

Though the colonies had hundreds of thousands of people of African descent, the history of the British/German/Scots Irish settlement behind early colonial dialects is, essentially, the linguistic history of White folks. The pre-Revolutionary linguistic journey of African Americans has pretty much been left in the dust. African American English, throughout its history, has largely been regarded as a deficient form of English, and, not surprisingly, linguistic corruption is not seen as having a historical trajectory. The thing is, research exploring the linguistic traces of those who survived slavery's Middle Passage as well as studies on the isolated dialects of their descendants in enclave communities tell a very different origin story. That origin story starts with the West African tongues spoken by those who were transported on slave ships and ends with today's African American English varieties, varieties we find are becoming *more* divergent from White dialects than perhaps even the English that helped form their ancestral roots.

THE BIRTH OF "BLACK ENGLISH"

Despite its name, African American English (or AAE) is not spoken by every Black person, and many non-Black people speak it too, particularly those who have grown up with strong ties in the Black community. Likewise, some African Americans who grow up in diverse or predominantly White environments don't speak it at all. Many—even speakers of languages other than English—have picked up and use features of this variety, even if not really a speaker of AAE per se, because of the substantial influence that African American language and culture has had more widely.

What most people mean when they talk about African American English is only the vernacular form, sometimes referred to as African American Vernacular English or AAVE. But, just as with American dialects more generally, African American English is a generic label for multiple dialects, ranging from middle-class to regional to working-class varieties. By and large, what gets noticed and disparaged under the rubric of "Black English" is the variety associated with the inner city and street culture, an association reinforced through that specific variety's visibility in movies, rap, and hip-hop.

Many of the most negatively stereotyped features occur to a much higher degree in the vernacular variety and are grammatical rather than pronunciation features. These are things like double negatives ("They don't say nothing"), the habitual be ("I be working all the time"), deletion of the conjugated *be* verb in certain contexts like "they good" for *they're good* (also called *copula deletion*), use of "we was" for *we were*, a lot of "ain't," and no "s" on things like "he go" or "five cent." In terms of the specific sounds that African American English is known for, we find things like "aks" for *ask*, pronouncing "r"s and "l"s more "softly," or more like vowels, as in "mo" and "caw" for *more* and *call*, and leaving off the final consonant in words ending in groups of consonants (so-called *consonant clusters*) like "tol'" and "des'" for *told* and *desk*.

As with other American varieties, these patterns didn't just appear out of nowhere but are driven by the same type of linguistic and social pressures we've been talking about throughout these pages. When one views these as errors rather than dialectal differences, it is under the assumption that today's Standard English was the model at which African American English speakers have always been aiming. The problem is that this ignores the developmental history of a variety that was born hundreds of years ago, forming very much alongside other colonial varieties and before the cementing of most of the prescriptive English norms we have come to know and obsess over.

As with other American dialects, other languages and inter-settler contact were foundational to what was to become modern African American English. Much of what is heard as "incorrect" are actually relics of older forms, ones that have faded away in most predominantly White varieties of American English but were retained, often in slightly shifted form, in African American speech. If people can claim Appalachian English is Shakespeare in the holler, they could just as well say African American Vernacular English is Shakespeare on the street corner. Neither claim is completely correct, since all English dialects have changed a lot since Shakespeare's day, but there is a grain of truth here, since dialects like these two actually do retain some older features, including some we can trace back to Elizabethan times. The sense people are trying to convey—that some unique four-hundred-year-old features still linger on in those dialects—would not be so far off.

In many ways, AAE could be considered a more conservative dialect, if conservatism is measured by the retention of older speechways (though it's also frequently innovative, as we will discover).

Many of the features that get disparaged in this variety today were common among both Black and White speakers in colonial times. For instance, *we was* was used repeatedly in records we have from that period, like in testimony from the Salem witch trials in the late seventeenth century, where it seems to have been—hold on to your bonnets—looked upon as the more prestigious form.

Likewise, using *ain't* was perfectly fine back in the 1600s and early 1700s, when, in its earliest incarnation as *an't*, even fancy ladies and gentlemen could be heard to utter it. It didn't start to get a really bad rap until the later eighteenth century, when grammar-mavening really got its groove on. It wasn't just *ain't* that took on shade at the time—contractions in general were considered uncouth. Why *ain't* became a particular pariah while *isn't*, *won't*, and *can't* managed to cling to respectability is just one of life's many linguistic mysteries, as is the question of which verb combo contracted to create "ain't" in the first place. Some linguists put their money on the combo of *am* plus *not*, or *amn't*, which, given the mouthful it is, morphed into *an't* then *ain't*. Others conjecture that *hain't*, as in *have* plus *not*, started the ball rolling. Regardless of its origin, its descent into ill repute was most likely driven by its growing associations with lower-class and African American usage as time went on.

And as for that little third person singular "-s" that crops up whenever we say things like "he hopes" or "she dreams"? It turns out that when the colonies were first getting settled, that "-s" was a rebellious suffixal upstart, used more by those with less status, while "-eth" was the stately old-school ending. Now, *doth* and *maketh* have long made tracks, while the "-s" ending has persisted as the general third person singular marker on verbs, as in *does* and *makes*. To be fair, neither ending is really necessary, since whatever's in the subject position (the *she* or a noun like *cat* versus *cats*) or the context usually makes it clear how many subjects we're talking about.

Moving on to another feature that gets called out as "incorrect," even Shakespeare would tell you that double negatives were not altogether unfashionable at the outset of the colonial era. In *As You Like It*, we find him putting several negatives to work in "and yet give no thousand crowns neither." And, before the Elizabethan period, when it had not yet started to fall from favor, didn't nobody blink at the inclusion of an additional negative word or two. Just take a glance at Chaucer's impressive negation rate in the famed *Canterbury Tales*, where he doubles down on negatives in single sentences about one-third of the time.

What I am getting at with this dive into our linguistic history is not that they were all a bunch of ignorant fools back in the day, but quite the opposite: many prominent features remarked on as signs of corrupted English in African American varieties were once widespread in everyday colonial English—and these varieties of English were among the language-learning models for enslaved people coming from West African language backgrounds.

WHAT DO BIRDS, WASPS, AND AXES HAVE IN COMMON?

Let's take a moment to consider the strongly marked pronunciation of the word *ask* as "aks" (or "axe") that has become an ethnic shibboleth almost on par with that singling out the Ephraimites crossing the River Jordan. While perhaps not leading to quite as murderous a fate, there's still a good chance saying "aks" might kill some educational and professional opportunities. In his book *Spoken Soul*, linguist John Rickford recalls a *60 Minutes* interview where an African American corporate recruiter was asked what would happen if a job candidate said, "May I aks you a question?" His response? "He won't get to aks that very often."

As a linguist, I can't tell you how many times people have brought up this pronunciation as a perfect illustration of a lack of education and language gone wrong—and not just those who notice it in others but even sometimes those who have used it themselves. On the other hand, no one has ever come up to me and complained about how people pronounce *wasp*, *horse*, *third*, or *bird*. What's the relation? One word: *metathesis*, which, despite its slammin' vibe, is not the name of a new heavy metal band but that of a phonological process long operating in English whereby sounds get switched in the order they are said. So, in Old English, *wasp* was "waps," *horse* was "hros," *third* was "thrida," and *bird* was "brid."

Likewise, in Old English, *ascian*, the verb meaning "to ask," had an alternative metathesized form, namely *acsian*, a.k.a., the original "aks," with both options regularly appearing in texts of the time.* Typically spelled as *axe*, the "aks" form was used by literary giants like the (unknown) author of *Beowulf* as well as Chaucer, and even in several early biblical translations. For instance, "Axe

* Just in case you forgot, the "k" sound is often the pronunciation we mean when we use "c" in English spelling.

the catell, & they shal enfourme the" appears in the Coverdale Bible in 1535. Even earlier, around 1400, we find "Yow loueris axe I now this question" in Chaucer's "The Knight's Tale."

All this suggests that these two forms peacefully coexisted without impacting anyone's job prospects or inviting ridicule through the Middle English period. There did seem to be a dialectal difference. The *ask* version was the more common Northern British form while *aks* was more common in the South. By about the sixteenth century, the Northern form became recognized as the norm more generally, and Shakespeare preferred to *ask* rather than *axe*. Still, that didn't mean everyone woke up and suddenly started uniformly "asking." Many would have still used the Southern form for quite a while longer.

Now, time to connect some dots. Think back to our discussion of which British settlers first set up shop in the New England and Virginia colonies: a decent majority were folks from Southern England. And guess what pronunciation we see appearing in early colonial records from New England and Virginia? Yup, I think you already know: "axe." And, last quiz question, which colony had a huge reliance on enslaved labor to keep their tobacco farms in business? Right again! Virginia. Enslaved workers worked side by side with English-speaking indentured servants, some of whose English would have included the metathesized version of *ask*. As time went on, *ask* became the form associated with prestigious varieties, while *aks* stuck around in some dialects like those spoken in Appalachia and became more of a rural Southern feature, a path that sealed its linguistic destiny. Over time, most White Southerners stopped using the form, and it became not only a marker of class and region but also of Blackness.

But why do we have no conflicted feelings about *birds* and *horses* (I admit to hard feelings about *wasps*) when they too have a similarly metathesized history? Because we no longer use the words *brids* and *hroses* and so we don't have them around as reminders of our social differences and sound-switching ways. They disappeared completely while our *ask/aks* pair instead became associated with high-class/low-class usage. For a while, "waps" too could be heard as a relic folksy form, especially in early African American English, but it also faded away over time.

Still, *ask* and *aks* are not the only examples of older metathesized forms coexisting in modern English: the words *task* and *tax* are actually derived from the same French root *taxa*, which, in one case, i.e., *task*, underwent metathesis. But, over time, *tax* and *task* took on different meanings, with *task* requiring payment through labor and *tax* requiring payment with cold hard cash, so we don't notice their etymological relationship the same way we do *ask* and *aks*. Frankly, if we really want to make the world a better place, let's stop worrying about "aksing" and just get rid of both tasks and taxes.

Getting back to how all this relates to our current topic, the aforementioned examples are important to our origin story in more than one way. First, they make clear that our sense that these forms are somehow linguistically "wrong" can't hold up unless we want to claim Shakespeare, Chaucer, and those translating early English Bibles didn't know how to use English properly (along with most others of their ilk and era). Even more importantly, they help explain how these forms came to be part of African American English in the first place. When large numbers of people from West Africa were brought to the New World, these features were present in the English already spoken there. Many of the features that have become recognizable in today's African American English remain from that early exposure. In fact, in the formative days of what would become African American English, there was probably not a huge difference in the dialect spoken by lower-class Whites and enslaved people born in the colonies, an important fact we'll return to in just a bit.*

OUT OF AFRICA

But there was one huge and glaring difference in their linguistic experiences. Those who were brought to the British colonies involuntarily from Africa would have come with a West African/Niger-Congo language background. This means that first-generation enslaved peoples in the New World would have encountered English as a second language, and, unless we learn a new language when we are young, our first language always affects the way we

* This view of the origins of AAE is a very simplified version of the so-called *Anglicist hypothesis*, which suggests the source for most AAE features lies in early British varieties. The discussion of the view that follows—that there is African substrate in AAE—is known as the *creolist hypothesis*. The debate among linguists as to which theory better explains how AAE began and how it developed is long-standing and heated, but the modern view is generally that both British and West African influences played a role in how the variety ultimately developed. The discussion in this chapter assumes that perspective.

speak our second language, something linguists call *language transfer*. And this type of influence continues into later generations, like when my mother passed along some traces of her accent, namely my aforementioned lack of aitches, as I acquired English as a child.

When a parental or heritage language has a lasting influence on a language learned natively by children, it is known as a *substrate effect*. This is why Minnesotans are often known by their accent—a German and Scandinavian substrate lingers on in the "Minnesooota" vowel sounds they use even if they themselves have only ever spoken English. The difference comes from the fact that the "oo" vowel is what is known as a *diphthong*, or two-part vowel, in English, while in German or Swedish it is a monophthong, meaning that it does not have a tiny little secondary "w"-like sound after the "o" as it does in English. This slight difference in how the vowel is articulated lingers on in subsequent generations despite the fact that few speakers have direct knowledge of these languages anymore. This is also why you can borrow someone your car in Minnesota too: in German, the same word, *borgen*, means both "borrow" and "lend."

Substrate influences are very common in the development of dialects and accents whenever lots of people from closely related language backgrounds settle in a new place but retain some of their linguistic and cultural background. Such influences are especially likely to be maintained when those new arrivals are treated differently, even disdainfully, by the rest of the community (as German immigrants were early on in the United States or as Spanish immigrants are today), because it becomes important to that group's cultural identity. And this brings us back around to the other key to the historical puzzle of African American English: its African substrate.

ESTABLISHING ROOTS

Spain and Portugal were the first European powers that got into the business of capturing and selling people into bondage, but, by the middle of the seventeenth century, Britain came to dominate this transatlantic trade. Without Google Translate around, some sort of basic communication method or lingua franca has to develop in an international trading situation to complete a successful business exchange. Though the languages spoken along the African coast differed a bit, similar forms of pidgin languages developed that used aspects from both African languages and British English.

A pidgin is a simplified form of language that no one speaks natively since it is limited in size and scope and is used only in specific contexts. Typically, the native language of one group serves as the grammatical base upon which words from another language are superimposed, but these words are combined with a simplified version of this grammar, i.e., initially lacking things like case marking or auxiliary verbs, allowing a situationally specific chat to take place.

In the 1600s, pidgin languages were used for trade between Europeans and Africans and also for trade among African speakers of different languages. When enslaved Africans were forced into cargo holds, many did not share a home language, as ship captains purposefully limited the numbers of same-language speakers on any single ship. Why? Because, even with the crew greatly outnumbered, it's a lot harder to plan a successful revolt when people can't communicate easily, never mind being chained and shackled. A similar thing sometimes occurred in the Southern colonies, as many larger plantation owners also tried to disperse slaves who might share the same native language.

While some enslaved Africans were sent directly to the North American colonies, many others were sent to colonies in the Caribbean, where they were in high demand to do grueling work on tobacco and sugar plantations. There, the African English pidgin provided the basics from which languages like Jamaican and Barbadian Creole developed. A creole is not only part of the name of certain languages, it's also a particular type of language—one that has its beginnings in a pidgin language but then gradually develops into a full-fledged new language for use across a wide range of situations, not just trade.

Though calling a language a creole may make it seem exotic, the truth is that some very familiar languages have elements of what we call *creolization* in them. Even English could be considered to have been creolized after the Norman invasion, since at that point the Germanic-based language became so altered by contact with higher-status French that older writings like *Beowulf*, without French influence, became practically impenetrable. The tendency to treat the formation of creole languages as somehow different from the development of European languages has been referred to as *creole exceptionalism* and arose at a time where exoticism was strongly associated with non-White peoples and their languages. But the reality is that whenever we get contact between two languages under conditions where one language is more powerful, be it the English of colonial landowners or the French of William the Conqueror, linguistic transformation follows.

A SHARED SOUTHERN TONGUE

And how does this tie into the African American English that developed in North America? Recall from a previous chapter that the coastal colonies were the heart of Southern plantation culture. These areas were also at the heart of early African American language and culture, as it is the coastal South that had the largest population of enslaved labor brought from the Caribbean. There, the creoles of Caribbean captives alongside White settlers' varieties became the language models for African adults and children learning English. In places like South Carolina and Georgia, where the Black population rivaled or surpassed that of Whites, new creoles were created—for example, Gullah Geechee, which we find still spoken in pockets along the coast today. Studies of Gullah have found a striking similarity between it and the creole language known as Krio spoken by descendants of freed slaves in Sierra Leone, as well as the creoles in places like Jamaica, Barbados, and Guyana. This linguistic likeness points to a similar origin and process underlying all of them, namely early pidgins formed from African languages and English.

In other areas of the South, conditions were less conducive to a new creole developing, as White settlers were a much larger majority. This left British English varieties as a far more pervasive model. Despite the enduring myth of the South as a collection of sprawling vast plantations, smaller family farms with just a few enslaved people per household were very common in much of the Upper and interior South. Such a living situation resulted in White settlers and Black slaves having a relatively high degree of contact, leading more extensively toward assimilation to White speech with the shift to English.

Still, some differences between White and Black varieties existed from the substrate influence carried over from African languages. Linguists have suggested that modern AAE features like the deletion of consonants at the ends of words like "des'" for *desk* or "bes'" for *best* is a residue of this African substrate. In West African languages, final consonant clusters are largely prohibited, just as in the Siouan and Iroquoian languages discussed a few chapters back. As with Lumbee English, this substrate influence is thought to underlie today's African American English pattern of consonant deletion. This is the pattern where final consonants can be deleted not only when there are three consonants in a row, as found in most English varieties, but also just two, as in "des'" for *desk*. But, even though all speakers share the same general tendency toward deletion, the African American pattern was heard as corrupted speech rather than as the result of a lingering African influence, owing to disdain for its speakers.

Likewise, most creoles use substitutions for "th" sounds, as in "dat" (*that*) and "ting" (*thing*), as would newly arrived African speakers, whose languages also lacked the "th" sound, as a great many languages do. This type of substitution stuck around as a substrate influence—again, the possible origin of this tendency in some modern African American English varieties.

Last but not least, the greater frequency of open syllables found in many West African languages primed African American English speakers to join with the "r"-dropping tendencies that were starting to appear in the speech of the British settlers around them, as discussed earlier. With new African and creole speakers arriving for a span of over two hundred years, there was a constant influx of African influence, contributing to the cementing of several of these features that are associated with African American dialects.

On top of this combo of British and African influence, African American English, like Southern dialects more widely, continued to develop in new ways as a result of the changing social, political, and economic landscape brought on by the U.S. Civil War. During Reconstruction, the South's rural economy left many former enslaved people with few options other than to work as tenant farmers. While an improvement over slavery, many found themselves again with a boot on their backs, this time from landowners who forced them to take on high-interest loans for land, seed, and equipment that they struggled to work off or pay back. Within a few decades, White farmers increasingly joined Black farmers in sharecropping, driven to it after incurring their own large debts from a few years of crops gone sideways. As a result, after the Civil

War, socioeconomic circumstances forced Black and White Southerners in close contact still.

This contact played a key role in the development of not just African American English, but Southern English itself. Just as African speakers picked up English from the White settlers of the colonial era, White Southerners in the nineteenth century picked up some of the speech habits of the Black speakers around them. For instance, copula deletion ("he tired"), consonants being deleted in the two-consonant pattern discussed earlier, and "r" dropping are features associated with African and creole speakers that have been located, at lesser frequencies, in vernacular Southern White speech. We know of this bidirectional influence not only from comparisons of written narratives, transcripts, and archival recordings from White and Black Southerners born in the 1800s, but also because of observations of and parodies about White Southerners sounding like their slaves from others of that era.

And, as you might recall from an earlier discussion, it is in this period after Reconstruction that we find Southern speech developing many of the accent features we notice as "Southern" today: features like the *pin/pen* merger, the tendency to make *fire* into "far," and our favorite Southernisms, *y'all* and *fixin' to.* All of these features became part of both White and Black speech not because of any love for each other (far from it!) but because both groups had deep roots in Southern identity and lifeways. Southern culture is something they both built, even in the face of continuing racial tension and hostility.

THE DAWN OF "SOUNDING BLACK"

At the turn of the twentieth century, 90 percent of all African Americans still lived in the South, with the vast majority—over 80 percent—living in rural areas. There was really no comparative Black community in the North, so, if you were a Black American around this time, it generally meant you were a Southerner. Life in the South was incredibly harsh, particularly after the passing of Jim Crow laws in the 1890s, which effectively legalized segregation. Even with the desire to find better opportunities outside the region, it wasn't that easy. The industrial North was not exactly opening its arms wide to Black farmers, and there were few avenues to relocation even if one could escape the cycle of debt most sharecroppers were caught up in. What changed? Put simply, the world went to war.

With the advent of World War I, factories in the North lost a lot of young workers to the draft, opening up, for the first time, employment possibilities for Black tenant farmers. Frustrated with economic and political oppression they faced in the South, many answered the call, moving with their families from the rural South to the urban North. What started as a Northern migratory trickle became a flood by World War II, and from about 1916 to 1970, Black people left the rural South in such great numbers that we refer to this era as the Great Migration. During this period, over 6 million African Americans moved, mainly to Chicago, Detroit, New York, Los Angeles, D.C., and Baltimore. In effect, by 1970, almost half of the Black population of the United States now lived in the North.

It wasn't only people who were relocating, it was also a vibrant culture and a distinctive accent. Features like *pin/pen* mergers, dropped "g"s, "y'all" for *you*, and vowel distinctions like saying "susta" (*sister*) and "whup" (*whip*) as well as "cain't" for *can't*, which started linguistic life as Southern, all became instead linked with Black identity in the North. Likewise, having "ahnts" (for *aunts*), a common pronunciation used instead of "ants," is thought to have traveled with the Great Migration beyond the South. This pronunciation first gained ground in African American speech via its uptake in the speech of some White Southerners as it became the prestige pronunciation in Southern England in the nineteenth century.

This new association of these features with "sounding Black" rather than "sounding Southern" came on because White Northerners did not exactly embrace incoming Southern African Americans as brothers and sisters. Instead, they were met with de facto segregation of housing and employment and relegated to the inner cities. For many, the twentieth century brought with it less consistent interracial contact and greater linguistic separation than experienced in previous centuries. At the same time, tight-knit African American communities blossomed in dense urban areas, creating spaces for the African American culture, music, art, and literature that would end up making African American language and life much more visible and, ironically, increasingly appealing to White kids in the burbs.

Speaking of the burbs, recall that the Great Migration time frame is exactly when we find large numbers of Northern Whites flocking to the suburbs, and this is also when Northern vowels started a-changing among White speakers following the pattern we now call the Northern Cities Shift. The twentieth century is also associated with another vowel change pattern—the Southern Vowel Shift—that begins to show up in the speech of Southerners, though again predominantly in White varieties. And what of African American English vowels?

Historically speaking, vowels have always been something that separated Black and White speakers, since early African American English was heavily influenced by the vowel systems of African languages. Over time many African-influenced vowel sounds, like the monophthongal pronunciations of "fes" and "bot" for *face* and *boat*, disappeared. But much of what makes African American English vowels sound distinct today is the lack of participation in White varieties' vowel shifts alongside avoidance of other recent changes like the Valley Girl sounding "ke-ul" for *cool* and the merging of *cot* and *caught*.

At the same time, the twentieth-century African American system had some innovations of its own, with many of its more recognized features coming into being relatively recently. Studies of recordings of ex-slaves born in the mid-1800s show that many of the most recognizable forms, like the use of habitual be, as in "we be workin' everyday" and the use of "ain't" for *didn't* were absent before the Great Migration.*

Likewise, a study by well-known linguists Walt Wolfram and

* Early use of *ain't* in White and Black speech substituted for *am not/are not* or for *has not/haven't*. The use of *ain't* for the auxiliary *didn't*, as in "No, she ain't see it" is more recent and typically only found in African American Vernacular.

Erik Thomas of how people perceive White and Black speakers in rural, coastal North Carolina found that older African Americans from the area were more likely to be heard as White, by both Black and White listeners, while younger local African Americans were heard overwhelmingly as Black. The researchers suggest that the civil rights era and school integration highlighted racial inequality and injustice, which had the effect of further "intensifying the ethnolinguistic divide" for those born after the mid-twentieth century. What all this means is that the desire to "sound Black" has increased, brought on by greater in-group consciousness, power, and solidarity—and with it, greater freedom to resist assimilation.

TAKING A MORE EXPANSIVE VIEW

Now, for people whose main exposure to African American English comes from watching *Boyz n the Hood* and listening to 50 Cent, it might seem like sounding Black emerges only from gritty urban "gangsta" life, but they would be wrong. Pop culture loves to both critique and covet language "from the hood," and the intense focus on only the vernacular form of African American English has obscured the fact that the twentieth century also provided the opportunity for an expansion of the Black middle class as well as regional varieties of African American English.

Linguist Arthur Spears, an early expert on African American English, found that the twentieth century was pivotal in the development of African American Standard English (AASE), which lacks most stigmatized syntactic features like double negation, but includes African American intonation and pronunciation features. We hear this exemplified in the speech of well-known African Americans such as Malcolm X, Martin Luther King Jr., Toni Morrison, and Jesse Jackson. It is manifested in cadences, pausing, vowels, and rhythm—but also in the ability to use more stereotyped grammatical features in certain situations, to create certain effects, as when Barack Obama connected with a Black cashier who offered him change by replying, "Nah, we straight."

It might even surprise you that we can hear it in the speech of Oprah Winfrey, someone who has expressed strong feelings about the need for Black speakers to adopt Mainstream or Standard English. One study examined her use of the Southern "ay" vowel pronunciation, a vowel that also became associated with AAE after the Great Migration. That study found that when she was introducing or talking about other African Americans, she increased her use of this form, as when pronouncing *time* more like "tahm." Using such forms along with more standard ones carves out a social space distinct from speakers of the working-class vernacular, while, at the same time, still "sounds Black" via more subtle use of African American language features. In short, it allows for what's been dubbed the "double consciousness" that middle-class African Americans must inhabit to be successful both professionally and socially.

As Spears writes, understanding African American Standard English as a variety coexisting with vernacular English allows "our view of the African American community that is not attached in the main to the parade of Black images in the US popular imagination that prioritizes poverty and degradation."

FROM SOUNDING BLACK TO HEARING BLACK

Now let's revisit the topic that led off our discussion of language and race: it's not a big leap to say that people who "sound Black" are often assumed to be Black. Though we shy away from acknowledging it, we make these kinds of implicit associations between race and language all the time—noticing whether someone "sounds Black" or, by the absence of racialized accent features, "sounds White." What's really the surprise here is that we socially categorize those we hear with very little acoustic information to go on. People have been shown to be able to estimate gender after hearing less than 50 milliseconds of exposure to their speech. Racial identification starts in about half a second, i.e., the time it takes to say "Hello."

Of course, we can be (and sometimes are) wrong. We go by past experience and make generalizations about links between voices and social groups, but these links are culturally learned. Exceptions, like a White person speaking AAE or a Black person speaking a dialect commonly associated with White speakers, are very possible. Still, social category and in-group perception are part of being human. After all, noticing language patterns is something we've done since we were wee little ones. But another part of being human is that we love our shortcuts. I mean, who bothers with calculus when simple division will do? And stereotypes are the equivalent of a division shortcut in the world of speech processing because they allow us to make quick assessments about what people are like, without really knowing anything about them.

Not surprisingly, a lot of stereotypical baggage comes with sounding Black because people have a lot of (sometimes conflicting) beliefs about Blackness itself, many of which stem from the long history of oppression and strained race relations we've just discussed. But there is also a lot of self-realization and identity work that gets done through the way we speak, and accents are an incredibly important part of how we create a sense of shared values, experience, and community with others. For Standard English speakers, the accent of home and the accent at school or work is often not that different, but for those who speak AAE, especially vernacular varieties, the divide between the two is much larger and code-switching can feel like, or be judged by others as, a betrayal of heritage and identity.

This is why accents are a double-edged sword, as I doubt anyone will argue that the way one speaks can be separated from the types of opportunities people are given. For those who sound Black, the opportunity costs can extend past the job market into classrooms and courtrooms. When we look at studies of voices that have stigmatized features, such as consonant dropping or certain vowels like saying *said* as "sayd," the speakers to whom they belong are often rated as less competent, less educated, and more questionable in character than Standard speakers.

African Americans usually rate AAVE speakers more positively than White raters, especially on dimensions like authenticity and likability, but their ratings, too, suggest that many have internalized the message that AAVE is nonstandard and less "proper." All this is of course reminiscent of how the nonstandard working-class speakers we got to know in the last chapter were viewed; only, for some African Americans, there is the added layer of not just stereotypes of what it means to be poor, but also what it means to be Black and poor.

Studies looking at the consequences of sounding Black have found that, beyond professional and housing discrimination, African American speakers earn less, are more often associated with weapons and violence, and are more likely to be found guilty in criminal proceedings. Not only that, but they are also heard as less credible even just when serving as witnesses. If you recall the case of George Zimmerman, who was put on trial for the murder of Trayvon Martin in 2013, the prosecution's key witness's testimony was roundly mocked and largely dismissed as incomprehensible and not credible because she spoke with a heavy AAVE accent, despite providing testimony that, had it not been for her accent, potentially might have altered the trial outcome.

This all might seem like awfully good motivation not to use African American Vernacular English, but, even setting aside the important identity piece and the fact that children typically don't "opt into" which dialect they grow up speaking, research suggests that African Americans who don't use stigmatized forms can still be affected by these same negative stereotypes.

Remember when I said that listeners are able to identify ethnicity in as little as the time it takes to say "Hello"? Well, I wasn't kidding. In an experiment designed to test whether listeners were able to make inferences about a speaker's race from just hearing a single word, linguists found that listeners were able to identify whether a speaker was Black, White, or Chicano just based on the pronunciation of the word *hello*.

That means that we attend to accents associated with race very quickly and on the basis of very subtle cues, even without hearing someone use two negatives or delete a copula. Studies have been pretty consistent in finding that using fewer stereotypical features lessens negative attributions, but the social stigma of sounding Black doesn't completely disappear even when speakers don't use recognizably AAE features.

For instance, in a study that explored listener reactions when hearing a bidialectal African American professor, meaning one who spoke African American Vernacular and Standard American English equally well, linguists Sharese King and Charlotte Vaughn and criminologist Adam Dunbar found that, while the professor was heard as more comprehensible when speaking Standard English, he was still not heard as someone with an advanced degree or as economically mobile. Other studies have found that when shown an image of a Black person while listening to a recording of a speaker, study participants tend to report the voice on the recording as being less standard-sounding than when that same voice is paired with a photo of a White person.

These results likely speak to listener expectations about what it typically means socioeconomically and educationally to be Black, with middle-class Black speakers viewed more through the lens of exceptionality outside of the African American community. Such ideas are also what drive the greater tendency to comment on successful Black professionals, athletes, or politicians as "articulate" or "well-spoken," such as when Joe Biden described Barack Obama as "the first mainstream African American who is articulate and bright and clean and a nice-looking guy."

Biden was right that Obama was a bit cuter than Al Sharpton, another former Black presidential candidate, but I am willing to bet that Al did shower every day—as do the many professionals who happen to also be articulate while Black. While it is true that there exist dialect differences that can lead one to sound White or sound Black, how those differences are heard is clearly influenced by the stereotypical leanings we bring to listening.

This brings us to the question of how to think about African American English in the classroom, where there is no denying a persistent Black-White achievement gap. In addition to understanding the history and structure of this variety, linguists have been involved for decades in trying to understand its relationship to reading failure. Studies have found that AAVE-speaking children struggle with literacy more than children who come into the classroom from standard language backgrounds. In large part, this has to do with a greater mismatch in the sound/letter correspondences that nonstandard dialects have, i.e., standard language is what is typically written and therefore shows more similarity between oral and written forms.

But what also appears to be influential on kids' success is the knowledge the teacher brings to the classroom. When teachers come armed with greater understanding of both the background behind African American English and its linguistic structure, we find reading achievement improves because they can be more helpful in pointing to systematic differences while helping African American students, whose culture is often invisible in academic settings, feel seen. Mind you, we are not talking about teaching AAVE, as is often represented in media coverage of such approaches, but rather using compassion and knowledge about its history and structure to help nonstandard-speaking kids bridge the distance between it and Standard English.

For example, using a program designed by linguist Bill Labov—the very same one who saved Paul Prinzivalli's bacon in an earlier chapter—reading test scores of minority children improved in the Pennsylvania and California school districts that adopted it. What stands in the way of more districts adopting this type of approach? Well, of course the eternal question of funding, but also the lingering belief that AAVE is simply a corruption rather than a legitimate language system. If we want to help children acquire Standard English, we need to be willing to work outside the traditional linguistic box and understand how deeply language is tied to one's sense of ethnic and cultural identity.

ONWARD AND UPWARD?

A unique historical journey coupled with increasing ethnic and community pride over the last century fueled many of the differences in White and Black speech we have come to pay so much attention to today. Earlier, Black English was in many ways Southern English. But, once relocated to the North, some Southern dialect features became identified as ethnic rather than regional, and then social separation created the conditions for further differences in varieties of White and Black English to develop.

The South served as the touchstone and linguistic foundation of this variety, even as it spread north and west. Because ghettoization in the inner cities kept Black folks mainly talking to other Black folks, all while still under the oppressive thumb of White folks, it heightened a shared sense of ethnic heritage and identity—and, importantly, reframed cultural and linguistic differences as sites of resistance to being defined by dominant White norms. "Sounding Black" was no longer simply a historical journey, but an important sociocultural one. As part of a flourishing, innovative, and provocative culture, African American language has also become increasingly attractive to speakers far outside this originating group, particularly those, like Gen Z and Gen Alpha, for whom social media has provided greater access than ever before. For those not part of the Black community, the attractiveness of AAE features comes from the chill, tough, or edgy vibes they are heard as giving off because of larger stereotypes around what African American English is and what sounding Black means.

Now that we know its history, a remaining question is why "sounding Black" remains such a key part of Black identity despite the negative stereotypes that can disadvantage its speakers. The answer is that, for all of us, so much of who we are and where we come from is tied up in the way we sound. It speaks to the families and friends who mean something to us, the cultural practices and places we embrace, and the histories that created us and the groups we form. For African Americans, much of that history involved poverty, prejudice, and the denial of formal education, all of which relegated the variety that developed from English and African roots to the linguistic gallows in the eyes and ears of many. But, as we have learned through these pages, African American English offers much more than gritty street vibes. Sounding Black can be the vernacular voice of hip-hop and rap, but it can just as easily be the squarely upper-class cadence of professors, poets, and presidents. Because of the antagonistic forces that forged AAE for much of its history, for many people, sounding Black is an expression of cultural pride and assimilatory resistance, a strong incentive to maintain its covert prestige in the face of intense pressure from Standard English.

SEVEN

STRANGERS WITHIN THE LINGUISTIC GATES

Most of us are too young to remember the urban legend in the 1960s claiming that Paul McCartney of Beatles fame had died and been replaced with a clone-like impostor. Fueling this myth (heartily denied by the band, including the very much alive McCartney) were rumors that, when played backward, the band's songs revealed "hints" such as John Lennon saying "Paul is a dead man. Miss him." Though the Beatles, along with many other artists, had indeed at times included hidden back-recorded messages in some of their songs, something known as *backmasking*, this was definitely not one of them.

Now, you might be wondering what the heck the Beatles and backward recordings have to do with accents. Well, though less famous than John, Paul, George, or Ringo, language researchers have also made a few backward recordings of speakers, in this case with and without foreign accents, to see what listeners made of them. Remarkably, even with garbling of sounds and words in speech played backward, listeners were better than chance at picking out the speakers with native versus foreign accents. Even more remarkable was the fact that they could often recognize foreign-accented speech on the basis of just a single word played backward. Azwow.*

A slightly more traditional approach looked at how much non-backward speech it took to identify English spoken with a French accent. In this study, researcher James Flege found that American listeners only needed to hear the single consonant "t" or the single vowel "u"—roughly about 30 milliseconds of speech—to detect a French accent. This tells us that listeners are extremely sensitive to very subtle cross-language differences since both French and English have "t" and "u" sounds, just produced in slightly different ways from a phonetic perspective. We're good at noticing foreign accents—even more so than our chops at identifying race, which, by comparison, takes a leisurely 400 milliseconds. Of course, this is something most of us probably already know simply from personal experience meeting or being non-native speakers.

Still, these mad skills we have for recognizing accents leave us linguists with more than just a few questions to ponder. Like, what are the greatest difficulties for non-native speakers to overcome and what makes some accents so much more noticeable—and difficult to understand—than others? What might help or hinder? And, most intriguingly, how much of an accent is in the mouth of a speaker versus the ear of a listener?

* In case you didn't follow, that's "wowza" spelled backward.

RURAL SQUIRRELS?

First of all, just to make sure we are on the same page, let's talk about what exactly we mean when we talk about a "foreign accent." All of the accents we've so far chatted about mainly reflected socially salient pronunciation differences between speakers of the *same* language. In contrast, foreign accents involve pronunciations that a native speaker hears as unusual sounding and, for that reason, suggests that the speaker likely grew up speaking a different language.

One's childhood language is what we are referring to when we talk about someone's first, or native, language. When talking about a second language, we generally mean any language a person learned after that native language, and though it might include another language learned in childhood, it is more often a language acquired in late adolescence or adulthood. Of course, children often grow up acquiring more than one language at the same time; in this case, we would talk of them having more than one native or first language. We are also mainly talking here about second-language acquisition in places where that new language is the dominant one, rather than, say, a classroom-based foreign language experience like you might find in an American high school.

While we all would like to think we are capable of surmounting any obstacles that get in our way, our native language makes for some cognitive and linguistic hurdles when learning a second one that are not easy to leap, no matter how many Rosetta Stone or Duolingo levels we master.

There is much debate about why it's so hard to learn a second language once you're past your childhood, with explanations ranging from age-related neurobiological changes to attentional and motivational factors to interference from the native language programming we acquired alongside our marvelous ability to say "rural" and "squirrel" without blinking. In the 1970s, a very prominent theory was that young children had a more elastic brain, allowing for more implicit language learning. The downside? Our neurobiological flexibility dried up around the onset of puberty, leaving us with an accent in any later languages learned. There is certainly a large body of research that shows that kids are typically better at playing second-language limbo than adults, but it is harder to tease out how much of this is because of changing brains versus simply that once we know more and are more practiced (with our first language), it's harder for our brains and mouths to shift course. As with most long-standing linguistic debates, the answer lies somewhere in the middle. Research suggests that both neurological differences—such as enlarged language processing areas and more dense gray matter in kids—and knowledge from our first language contribute to the linguistic rigidity we experience once we are old enough to realize tequila shots were never our friend.

It might seem hard to believe that just being wiser and more experienced could have such a massive impact, but, because our first language-learning experience comes so early and without much conscious effort, we tend not to realize just how many different factors are at play.

We touched briefly on some of these in our baby talk chapter, but let's take a deeper tour of the types of complexities we encounter as adults—or sassy post-pubescent teens—trying on a new language for size. First, language learners often have to try to master completely new sounds, since, as mentioned earlier, each language selects only a small number (twenty to forty) of sounds found in languages worldwide. That means if you come from a home language like English, you will be hard-pressed to sound like a native when learning to speak a Khoisan language, which makes use of click consonants that don't exist in English. It's not even so much that the click sound itself is impossible for us to make—in fact, anytime an English speaker makes a "tsk-tsk" sound to scold a child or call over a horse, they are making one type of click. It's just that, in such cases, we aren't combining it with other speech sounds, as click languages do, to make different words, and therein lies our problem: our old tongues have particular problems with combinatory new tricks. In most languages using clicks, there is not just one singular click consonant but many, all with different articulations. Also, clicks can combine with other aspects, like being nasalized or voiced, to multiply yet again the number of unique sounds made. In short, trying to learn a click language ain't no joke.

Because of the way English has become a powerful global language, a more likely scenario than an English speaker learning a click language would be a speaker of a click language finding it necessary to learn English. In the same way, though, the rarity of the English "th" sound would pose similar learner pronunciation problems. This lack of a cross-linguistically shared "th" is, of course, why we often notice it as a common aspect in foreign-accented

English, with non-native pronunciations ranging from "ze" instead of "the" from a French, German, or Egyptian Arabic speaker's lips to a "de" falling from those of a French Canadian, Russian, or Hindi speaker. These substitutions may seem somewhat random, but if that were truly the case, we would expect variation between "ze" and "de" in the same non-native individual's speech—which doesn't typically happen.

Instead, the choice of substitute seems to do with how certain types of sounds are unconsciously organized as more primary or typical in a speaker's first language—and that mental programming influences which sound a specific language's speakers would perceive as a closer fit to "th."* This type of first-language interference makes it hard to take a one-size-fits-all approach to language instruction, as the sounds speakers encounter in a new language are filtered by the way they've come to understand the sounds of their first language.

GETTING THE MELODY DOWN

As if figuring out different sounds and how they pattern isn't enough of a complication to sounding like a native, toss in the fact that it is not just new or subtly different sounds we are dealing with when learning a new language: we also must become familiar with

* This is a vast simplification of a much more complex topic that involves things like phonological underspecification and markedness. Suffice it to say that the difference in which sounds speakers use to substitute for "th" depends on the ways in which some aspects of the sound system are structured in their first language.

the new stress and rhythm patterns that ride shotgun. When learning to speak a new language, there is much more to it than simply getting our mouths around some new grammatical forms and unfamiliar sounds. We also have to be able to use all of these new skills in connected sentences with the goal of competently communicating with another human.

This brings us to things like the intonational patterns that speakers use to convey additional information such as that a statement is actually a (sometimes accusatory) question, as in "You like Nickelback?" or like which syllable takes the stress within a word (compare "puh-LICE" to "PO-lice")—all things we have to figure out over and above knowing how to pronounce "r," conjugate our verbs, and be aware that the answer to "What's up?" doesn't involve a glance toward the sky. The real question is how would we *not* have an accent?

To see how such issues create additional—and often unacknowledged—difficulties for second-language learners, let's just consider a few examples of how prosodic patterns, meaning things like stress, tone, and intonation, can make one come across as native sounding versus noticeably non-native.

Say it was your birthday and someone asked a seemingly simple little question like "How old are you?" Now, since I personally have turned twenty-five every birthday since I was actually twenty-five, I would just answer, "I'm twenty-five years old." Reading that sentence, anyone proficient in English should have no problems regardless of their first language. But *saying* that sentence with the right American style of intonation is less simple.

Americans typically increase the duration and loudness of whatever word they may want to highlight in a sentence, and they also signal they are done with their speaking turn by shifting to a lower pitch on the final word of a sentence, if not a question or if not using an uptalk pattern to signal an intent to continue talking. Since I have no interest in chatting extensively about my aging process, I'd pronounce it with an intonational pattern like "I'm **TWENTY**-five years old," with *twenty* taking more of the sentence stress to make sure no one mistakes me for thirty-five and hitting a coming-to-the-end-of-my-turn lower pitch as I get to the *old*. However, these patterns are culturally determined, so second-language speakers will not automatically know such stress and intonational patterns.

In case you're not hip to the difference between stress and intonation, stress is a prominence associated with particular syllables or words, while intonation is the overall rising or falling pitch pattern associated with sentences. Since language classes focus a lot on learning grammar, vocabulary, and basic sounds, intonation and stress are often not given a lot of play, and the type of prosodic difficulties a speaker may have will depend a lot on the language background they are coming from.

For example, Mandarin is what is called a *syllable-timed language*, where every syllable is said with roughly the same duration and intensity. As a result, Chinese speakers speaking English often stress each syllable to the same degree, making it harder for English listeners to figure out the intended sentence focus or topic. As well, Chinese is what we call a *tone language*, a language in which words are composed not only of consonants and vowels but also of various patterns of tones. This means that a word like *mā*, with a level high tone, is actually a different word than *mǎ*, with a low to high tone, each with its own meaning—namely, *mā* for mother and *mǎ* for horse. These tones on words can interact with sentence intonations, so it's not always clear to native English speakers whether non-native intonation patterns signal statements or questions.

None of these cross-linguistic difficulties are a matter of a speaker's ability with the language system itself but rather with the unconscious rhythms and intonation patterns that American English speakers follow compared to those that Mandarin speakers follow. The bottom line is that learning English is difficult for Mandarin speakers, and vice versa, and the tone differences add one extra layer to an already challenging task. As someone who struggled to learn Mandarin in college, I can absolutely attest that learning Mandarin is no walk in the park. I admit that I have insulted probably more than a few fellow students by accident when using the wrong tone. Imagine calling someone's mother a horse!

Perhaps you don't have much experience with Mandarin, so let's shift to a language that, if you live in the United States, you are bound to either speak yourself or know someone else who does, namely Spanish. Spanish is also considered a syllable-timed language, and, just as for Chinese speakers, this can create particular problems for Spanish native speakers when switching to a language like English. English is instead what is known as a *stress-timed language.** What this means is that certain syllables in a sentence receive more prominence—e.g., are louder and longer—and intervening syllables that don't have heavy stress, including words like articles and auxiliary verbs, have to be said faster to make up for their attention-hogging syllable mates.

This is one of the reasons why we have such a fondness for contracting and deleting in English, as unstressed syllables are shortened or dropped to keep things humming along. So, if I say "ToDAY is my BIRTHday" (stressed syllables in caps) because I am so excited to share the gift of my birth twenty-five years ago, I basically smush the unstressed syllables into "t'DAYzmaBIRTHday." Crucially, this pattern also creates a substantive change to the vowel in unstressed words, something we call *vowel reduction.* Vowel reduction is what causes *today* to come out as "tuhday," instead of with more of a "to" sound. Spanish, with its syllable timing, doesn't have vowel reduction. This fact makes this seemingly weird thing English speakers do with their vowels, on top of this dropping of parts of words, particularly head-scratching.

If you are a native English speaker, you probably never even noticed that you regularly reduce very different vowel sounds to an "uh" sound because it has become so automatic, like when saying

---

* In reality, the stress versus syllable timing is more of a continuum than a dualism, but for our purposes here the way a language leans on this dimension can make it harder for those coming from languages on the other side of the continuum.

"thuh" for *the*. But hear a non-native speaker say "exorcise" for *exercise*, using a full vowel instead of a reduced syllable, and, boy, if some people's heads don't spin around just like Linda Blair's. Vowel reduction rules are quite complex to learn as they are tied up with the stress patterns that English speakers have unconsciously learned in childhood and are very much a part of what makes speakers sound "accented" even when they have conquered the words and grammar.

Not only does Spanish not have vowel reduction, it also only has about one-third the number of vowels that English does. That means that Spanish speakers learning English also have to learn how to say vowel distinctions that don't exist in their native language—which is why we hear frequent substitutions like "eat doesn't feet" for *it doesn't fit*. To top it off, a Spanish native speaker then has to go on to figure out exactly when they are supposed to reduce all these vowels to correctly follow the English stress patterns. As Gen Alpha might say, big yikes.

Of course, differences in the tune of speech like the ones we've just been talking about might not seem like that big a deal, but they have been found to have quite a strong effect on how well listeners understand what a non-native speaker says.

In fact, several studies suggest prosodic issues may impact intelligibility and comprehension on par with mismatches in vowel and consonant sounds. One study looked at lectures given by an international teaching assistant (TA) who used either typical or non-typical stress patterns when lecturing. Researcher Laura Hahn found that students listening to TAs using more natively placed stress were better able to understand and recall the main points and content of the lecture. On top of increased difficulty in understanding speakers, differences in stress and intonation patterns can also affect how native speakers feel toward non-native speakers. In the study just mentioned, students rated the speaker much more positively when stress was used in a more native-like fashion.

Here's one last example, this time showing us how English speakers can be on the receiving end of cross-linguistic intonational judgment. German varies less in up and down pitch across a sentence compared to English and typically uses a lower pitch. As a result, English speakers, especially women, are often heard as "überspannt" and "zu stark aufgedreht," or, putting it in English, a bit overexcited and over the top. In contrast, Germans can come across as stiff or overly assertive with their lower, more monotone pitch. Interestingly, while being seen as overexcited may not be awesome, research suggests that speakers who use more intonational variation are often viewed more positively and as having greater charisma, so the news is not all bad for Americans who plan to travel abroad to get their fill of schnitzel.

What this brings home is that, even though we know that it is not the case that all English speakers are overenthusiastic or all Germans austere and gruff, the way we sound affects how others come to see us. And that, in a nutshell, is where we really start wading into troubled accent waters—particularly for speakers with lower-prestige non-native accents compared to American ones.

ACCENT-UATION

Remember a couple chapters back where I said that an extremely robust research finding is that speakers with nonstandard accents are heard as less intelligent, less credible, and lower in status than standard-accented speakers? Well, take that finding and double it when we are talking about non-native accents. In part, our preference for an accent that sounds more like our own is due to our inherent spidey sense for noticing "outsiders," but it turns out that this is just the tip of the perceptual iceberg: sometimes even just the effort our brains have to make to process non-native speech and certain expectations we bring to the listening event impact how we hear those around us. But before I explain why our brains have issues, let's go back to the beginning.

We've already talked a bit about how youngsters tend to prefer those with accents more similar to their own. For instance, little babies prefer taking toys from adults sharing the same linguistic background, and foreign accents seem more noticeable to young kids than regional ones. But, while we may be born predisposed to notice accents as a way to assess who's in our tribe and who's not, it doesn't explain why we view some foreign accents quite positively while others are maligned. After all, how many of James Bond's archenemies does one need to hear to get the hint that a Russian accent oozes evil villainy?

More surprising perhaps is the number of villains who speak the King's English. Consider regal-sounding English-accented antagonists like Scar in *The Lion King* or Shere Khan in *The Jungle Book*, or, if cartoons are not your thing, how about Ash, the undercover android from the horror movie *Alien*, whose highbrow English accent hid his treacherous alien-protecting-at-all-cost intentions. On the flip side, would Netflix's popular show *Emily in Paris* channel high-fashion romance as easily without the sexy allure of the French accent? So why is a Russian or fancy English accent the mark of a baddie while the French accent is the mark of a hottie?

The crux is that we hear accents not simply as marking someone as like us or not like us, we also hear them in ways shaped by our in-group norms as well as beliefs we've come to have about speakers of those accents. In short, these social-categorizing skills we've had since birth come to trigger negative or positive stereotypes. These may come in the shape of classist and protectionist attitudes spurred by immigrants speaking Spanish working in low-status jobs, nationalist attitudes shaped by a long history of Russian-American hostility, or slightly covetous attitudes stoked by Paris's elegant allure and its reputation as the City of Love. And why would British accents trigger thoughts of villainy? Because Americans tend to associate powerful, but also pretentious, cold, and uptight traits with Standard Southern British accents, and there is also a sense of postcolonial linguistic inferiority thrown into the mix. Noticing accents may be an evolutionary gift, but judging them is very much a product of our environment.

Of course, accents clue us into far more than simply someone's different nationality—what really shapes how we react to them is our view of the relative social standing of the speakers to whom they belong. Consider, for example, the social traits and status Americans might unconsciously associate with a Haitian immigrant compared to a Swiss immigrant, i.e., who would typically be cast in a movie as the housekeeper versus the banker? Because more Haitian immigrants come to the United States from an impoverished background relative to Swiss immigrants, as well as the fact that the ethnic background of most White Americans is European, reactions to a Haitian Creole versus a Swiss accent are filtered through this experiential lens.

Of course, a multitude of studies indicate that simply being heard as a linguistic outsider makes a person come across as less competent, loyal, and trustworthy, but toss in being poor and from a less desirable place on top of just being an outsider and you get extra bonus points in the negative ratings game.

What this means is that, though foreign accents of any type might be recognizable signals of being a nonlocal, how people evaluate the speakers who own them will depend on where they fall on what researchers have called the *evaluative hierarchy*, meaning whether they're associated with high prestige or low prestige. When issues of national identity are relevant, i.e., during international sporting events or worldwide pandemics, all non-native accents can spur negative feelings merely because they heighten our sense of in-group allegiance and solidarity.

This is why we sometimes find ourselves oddly attracted to other American English speakers when we are traveling abroad, despite the fact that the whole point was to experience a different language and culture. After all, being able to commiserate with someone over the difficulty of finding bathrooms—or, more importantly, the shortage of toilet paper—is reassuring, even if we would never actually have anything in common were we both back home. But, particularly when in our own country, negative biases are triggered when hearing accents of speakers viewed as coming from areas considered to be low prestige because of our ingrained notions about class, ethnicity, and cultural fit.

As an example of how this plays out, one recent study explored how attitudes toward different types of foreign accents factored into listeners' ratings of status and solidarity—meaning essentially how successful and pleasant they judged speakers to be. The researchers asked American listeners to listen to nine different non-English accents and to rate them on a variety of evaluative scales. While an accent-categorization question was phrased in such a way that listeners were simply asked to describe the speakers' accent (i.e., they could have just answered "foreign"), most tried to identify the accent more specifically in terms of place. When listeners identified accents as belonging to more prestigious, that is, Western European, groups, ratings on both status and solidarity scales went up compared to less prestigious ones like Asian.

The funny part was that listeners were often mistaken in their identification of accents: for instance, the German accent was misidentified over 60 percent of the time. But the pattern of receiving higher evaluations when it was heard as an accent belonging to a non-stigmatized group compared to a more stigmatized one was constant. Clearly, not all accents are equal in the ears of listeners, and a mistaken attribution of an accent to a less favored group changes how it is rated. This finding highlights a theme coming up again and again in research: accents are not only about how we speak, they are also profoundly about how we listen.

THE LISTENER'S POINT OF VIEW

To see just how crucial a role the listener plays, consider this: In a well-known experiment from the 1990s, a researcher had groups of undergraduates listen to an audio recording of an American-accented speaker from Central Ohio giving an academic lecture. Though they were all listening to the same voice, some students were shown a picture of a White woman as the purported lecturer, while another group was shown a picture of an Asian woman as the lecturer.

After listening to the recording, all students participated in a follow-up test measuring how well they recalled the lecture as well as rating the speaker on different dimensions, including how accented she was. Strikingly, those shown the photo of an Asian woman performed worse on the recollection test and rated her speech as more strongly accented—despite the fact that all students actually heard the same native English speaker.

This is a bit similar to the studies we talked about last chapter where people gave a different rating to how standard a voice sounded when they were shown a photo of a Black person versus one of a White person. Here, though, listeners imagined a foreign accent based on seeing a face that they *assumed* to be foreign—and this affected not just their accent ratings but also how much they took away from the lecture material itself. Such a finding of so-called *accent hallucination* has been replicated a number of times since. Other studies testing how speakers heard Indian English, American English, and Canadian English when seeing photos of White versus Asian faces showed somewhat similar "more accent, less intelligibility" effects, even though the same voice was always heard.

This is not something we find only in research settings—it's a common experience in everyday life for many Americans who were born here but look like they might be from elsewhere. In fact, a friend of Japanese descent told me that, when doing his medical residency, sometimes patients asked his supervisor for a different doctor because they couldn't understand his accent, even though he was a native English speaker born and raised in the Northeast. Ironically, he had never even traveled outside of the United States, nor did he speak any language other than English.

This certainly seems to indicate that our biases are so strong that they cause us to imagine accents even when there aren't any, and our stereotypes and beliefs absolutely do play a role in the way we hear and interact with others. For example, studies have shown that those with negative attitudes toward non-native speakers rate interactions less positively and comprehension more poorly as well as adopt more avoidance strategies than those with positive attitudes. Likewise, people who scored high on ethnocentrism scales, i.e., viewing their own culture as the cat's pajamas, rated a non-native speaker more physically and socially unattractive and less credible than those who scored lower on ethnocentrism. Finally, the very fact that not all foreign accents are judged equally harshly drives home the point that our sociocultural biases influence our evaluative behavior.

But we also need to be careful to not assume that attitudes are all there is to the story. After all, most people don't walk around wanting to be accent assholes, just waiting for an opportunity to keep non-native speakers down. The reality is we can still experience difficulty understanding speech that doesn't sound like what we are used to even if we are pretty fair people. Why? Because of how our brains react when hearing something unexpected.

It turns out that our expectations based on experience with past speakers as well as cultural stereotypes prime our brain in ways that make receiving information that matches expectations easier to process, while information that doesn't match is harder. As a result, incongruent information—like a native-speaker accent paired with a photo of what's perceived as a non-native-looking person—throws off our cognitive processing. This processing disruption, in turn, screws with our perception, making us hear more of an accent or understand less than when such information matches.*

In other words, at an unconscious level, our social expectations can actually alter what we hear in others' speech. This doesn't let us entirely off the hook, though, because this effect stems primarily from the fact that we have developed a limited perspective of what American identity looks like, and this narrow experience can negatively affect others, as happened with my friend the doctor.

---

* And, in fact, recent research with Canadian listeners finds that showing Asian and White faces while playing Chinese-accented English showed a similar incongruent intelligibility hit when the White face was shown.

But what about when a listener hears speech that *is* actually from a second-language speaker, a.k.a. non-native speech? Well, first of all, a listener generally hears not just an accent, but also gets a sense of a heavy or light accent based on how far it deviates from their own speech. On top of that, there is also the question of how well the listener can understand what is said, something linguists refer to as *intelligibility*.

In research contexts, intelligibility is something often measured via the listener's ability to accurately write down or repeat a speaker's words. Though people might think of them as one and the same, intelligibility is not really the same thing as comprehensibility. Intelligibility is about how much someone actually understands when hearing another's speech and comprehensibility is about how well someone *feels* like they understand (i.e., their perception).

While it might seem like heavy accents and low intelligibility would go hand in hand, we can often still understand what someone says even if we might hear their speech as heavily accented. Indeed, studies that look at how these dimensions correlate find that their relationship is not straightforward, i.e., a heavy accent will probably make it *feel* hard to understand someone but it may not actually impact intelligibility. Listeners are often able to accurately transcribe heavily accented speech, though at the same time they rate it as not very comprehensible. The finding that a heavy accent doesn't necessarily hinder intelligibility has to do with the fact that not every accent feature, even if prevalent, equally impairs a listener's understanding.

Still, as with the perceived face/accent mismatch, it takes more mental-processing power to decode a foreign accent, using more areas of our brain and for a longer period. In short, our brain works a bit harder, especially for un- or less-familiar accents. What's interesting is that our subjective experience of such increased effort is as something uncomfortable, sort of like how it feels as if your head might explode when reading about the physics of wormholes or just trying to keep up with the plot of a Christopher Nolan movie. This sense of ease or difficulty when performing a mental task is something those of us who read academic texts way too often refer to as *processing fluency*. And here is where things get crazy: the way we experience this increased brain effort—giving us the impression of something hard—has a substantial impact on how positively or negatively we perceive a speaker *and* how well we understand their speech.

What's fascinating is that the finding that we more negatively judge something when it feels harder to process is not limited to accents. Any information that feels more taxing can influence evaluations of things such as intelligence and likability and even future economic performance. For instance, psychologists Adam Alter and Daniel Oppenheimer discovered that how hard it seemed to pronounce a company's name influenced investors' judgment of its value. In their study, stocks with names that are easier to pronounce for people used to American English, like "Adderley" versus "Aegeadux," consistently performed better on both the New York Stock Exchange and the American Stock Exchange in the first few weeks after their initial offerings. This relationship held no matter the size, industry type, or national origin of the company. As mentioned in the study, "People tend to prefer easily processed information," and it turns out this holds true whether we're talking company names or accents.

Of course, while company creators have a choice in what names they select, non-native speakers don't have as much choice about their accents, and, as we discussed earlier, even looking the part—without any non-native accent—can create mental-processing disruptions. As a result, it sucks to be the speaker in this equation because listeners attribute the discomfiting sense of increased mental effort to a speaker issue, rather than a cognitive-processing issue. Not surprisingly, when we experience things as more difficult, we don't find it as pleasant as when things feel easy. And these negative feels don't just make us hear someone as less intelligent or friendly; research suggests we also find them less trustworthy—a fact that doesn't bode well for anyone with a foreign accent needing a job, a place to rent, or a not-guilty verdict.

ACCENTED BLISS?

Herein lies our quandary—no matter what, speakers gonna speak and listeners gonna listen. The question is how, when a non-native accent is involved, do we make this a non-frustrating, non-discriminatory, and productive experience for everyone?

From just our short foray into the mechanics of accent, it should be clear that the idea that adults who speak a second language must aim to sound like native speakers is not very realistic—or fair. For many, a more reasonable and achievable goal is to aim for intelligibility; outside of the rare neighbor's sister's roommate's friend who manages to sound like a local, the rest of us will always have an accent when learning another tongue after acne and braces.

Interestingly, research shows that certain traits appear common across the cases we hear of adults who are able to sound like a native. For example, those with better mimicry abilities or musical aptitude are found to do better at second-language pronunciation. As well, a brain imaging study found that those with more native-like speech showed distinctive brain activity, suggestive of differences in how they processed speech. But, if we are not one of these few naturally gifted people, we probably need a little more help when we are looking to improve our pronunciation, especially for language learners who have a personal goal of sounding less accented. There are some ways people can reduce their accent if they feel it would make them more self-assured and their speech easier to understand.

Getting explicit instruction in pronunciation does help, despite the fact that pronunciation is often secondary in language classes compared to grammar and vocabulary learning.* In particular, attention to things like native patterns of vowel reduction as well as intonation, speaking rate, and sentence stress can be very helpful in gaining skills and confidence with a new language. Studies have

* These days language apps can also often provide help with oral proficiency, though they are not able typically to provide specific corrective feedback as an instructor can. Overall, apps seem to help most with the acquisition of vocabulary and grammar, as they can't replace the back-and-forth of real-life oral communication (though generative AI may be changing that).

suggested that speaking rate plays a role, though probably not as you would expect: faster speaking rates are usually judged as more intelligible than slower speaking rates.

Word to the wise, though: while pronunciation instruction can definitely improve oral proficiency, many so-called accent-reduction courses are run for profit by people without any training making unrealistic promises ("Lose your accent in twelve weeks or less!"). Some approaches they use may even make speakers less intelligible. Better are university or community-based courses or speech therapists familiar with the research about best practices in teaching pronunciation.

Even in reputable programs, trying to be native-like will not be the goalpost for everyone, nor should it be. While some second-language learners might want to sound native-like and to integrate into the new culture as much as possible, others may have very different reasons for acquiring a new language and might be fine keeping an accent that represents their own sociocultural and linguistic identity. Instead, being intelligible, which we learned earlier can absolutely happen with an accent, is really what will be most beneficial for people who, whatever their motivation, want to be able to communicate successfully in their new language. To that end, blanket approaches to pronunciation (e.g., drilling sounds over and over) are not that useful for most non-native speakers who are having trouble being understood by others. That is because not all sounds are equally likely to contribute to comprehension difficulties, even if not pronounced correctly.

For example, as mentioned before, a lot of learners have difficulty with "th" sounds, and there are certainly a lot of "th" words in English like *the* or *think*. Yet there is not a lot of confusion caused by saying them incorrectly, since resulting words like "de" and "tink" don't exist as different words in English. When a specific sound doesn't do that much in terms of distinguishing different words like this,* a listener can generally glean what an accented speaker meant.

In contrast, substituting "s" for "sh," sounds, as, for instance, Korean- or Japanese-accented speakers learning English sometimes do, can create overlap with other existing words. Similarly, Spanish-accented speakers often substitute "ch" for "sh" sounds. In both cases, all these sounds do create a bunch of word distinctions, so saying "I'm taking a sip" (or "chip") instead of "ship" can definitely cause more confusion. The takeaway here is that targeted pronunciation instruction with the specific sounds causing difficulty for a speaker is often more beneficial than a one-size-fits-all approach.

An example of how even just focusing on recurrent words or sounds that are problematic for understanding can help make linguistic interactions more successful comes from a situation my neighbor's son, Alex, found himself in. Alex had just started college and had placed into a reasonably advanced math class. The problem he encountered, though, was that he really struggled to understand his new instructor, a TA with a foreign accent. This is a classic complaint we hear on college campuses, and it causes angst on both the part of the student and the teacher.

* This is referred to as having a *low functional load.*

However, it turned out that some of the difficulty Alex was experiencing came from a single word that the instructor used extremely often and, since the instructor's pronunciation of this frequent word was different from that of a native speaker's, it caused Alex and his peers to feel like they were not understanding the lecture. Finally, one student asked the instructor if he could write the word on the board, and lo and behold, it was *zero*, a word that not surprisingly comes up quite a lot in the context of a math class. Clarifying that one word managed to help Alex adjust to the speaker's accent and he felt he was much better able to understand the content of the lectures going forward.

Along the same lines, in a well-known book on pronunciation research, there is the story of a speaker who was having difficulties because of how he said the word *targets*, which sounded more like "stockitts." Since the word came up frequently at work, he was being consistently misunderstood and getting frustrated. Working with him specifically on that word improved his intelligibility and, importantly, his confidence. This type of pronunciation clarification can be accomplished without formal classroom instruction—if a speaker knows there is a specific word that they could use some assistance with, and feels supported in asking for help, most native speakers could provide some guidance on this type of limited scale.

The investment of a little effort on the part of a native speaker provides something else found to be very important: authentic interaction in that new language. When looking at which speakers tend to have the most success at second-language pronunciation, research suggests exposure to that new language is a big help. By exposure, I am not talking just about the passive exposure one might get doing daily life tasks like shopping or having *The Real Housewives* on in the background, although truly active listening probably provides some benefit. What I really mean by exposure is conversation with native or proficient non-native speakers.

How long someone has been in a new place is often less important to their pronunciation success than how much they interact with others using that language. This means that when you find yourself in a new place with a new language, seeking out opportunities to use your emerging skills is crucial. Of course, this is difficult for speakers who are already viewed as outsiders, especially those who come from what are considered less prestigious national backgrounds. Native speakers can sometimes respond with frustration or annoyance rather than openness to helping such speakers practice new linguistic skills, as anyone trying out fledgling French skills in Paris has doubtless already encountered.

Opportunities for interaction are also not helped along by some institutional training that suggests that things like asking a colleague with a non-native accent where they are from is a blanket no-no. While there might be times when such questions are targeted or inappropriate, genuinely engaging with newcomers by having conversations that allow us to get to know one another as individuals helps us get past the stereotypes that interactional avoidance encourages people to adopt. Respectful discussion of our linguistic differences and the comprehension difficulties we encounter can make attitudes toward accents more accepting, not less. For instance, channeling positive feelings toward non-native accents (e.g., "I really like your accent, where are you from?") and setting some procedural norms around how to bring up comprehension issues that arise in workplace contexts can help alleviate perceptions of cultural distance and communicative difficulty.

This brings us back around to the fact that comprehension comes not just from the mouth of the speaker but also the ear of the listener. Simply the experience of accented speech being harder to process impacts a listener's understanding and may lead to more negative evaluations of the speaker.

For instance, one study showed that even when a speaker is known to be simply reciting information from someone else (like the researcher), listeners heard information passed along by an accented speaker as less trustworthy than that same information passed along by a native speaker. But, when listeners were told beforehand that processing accented speech makes people more likely to find information less credible, the effect was reduced, except when the accent was very heavy. Similarly, prepping listener expectations to reduce the potential for incongruent information, like when expecting a native accent but instead hearing a foreign one, can also help increase intelligibility. In other words, if a listener simply knows what accent to expect so there is no mismatch, research suggests processing effort may decrease and understanding increase. Another suggestion is to make sure that interactions occur outside of noisy environments, which research shows reduce listener intelligibility even more for unfamiliar voices and accents than for familiar ones. So keep in mind that playing background music or being in large multispeaker situations will make understanding one another a bit more challenging.

Time and time again, research on accent adaptation has shown that listeners are quite good at acclimating to new accents after they have received some exposure. Exposure in this experimental sense meant that listeners showed improvement in how well they transcribed unfamiliar accented speech after hearing a first few sentences by a non-native speaker. But a more casual kind of accent exposure happens in daily life all the time, without us even being aware of it: for instance, my neighbor's son Alex got better at understanding his TA once he had spent more time hearing his accent, especially after he was able to match up the sound variances different from his own (i.e., *zero*).

But here is where accent bias can definitely get in the way: when we have negative feelings toward a sociocultural group and transfer those feelings to their accent, it can make it more likely that we won't understand them. Again, though, studies in social psychology have found that knowing someone as a person (rather than simply as a member of a social group) attenuates our tendency to use stereotypic shortcuts in categorizing them. As well, those who report more experience with non-native speakers in their social circles often do better in adapting to novel accents, likely because this greater exposure decreases the processing effort associated with unexpected and/or unfamiliar accents. While it's natural to categorize people and to identify who's in our group, as we grow older, it's also really helpful to expand our horizons by getting to know "outsiders" on a one-to-one basis. We can learn a lot from their different experiences, and we may just find that we have more in common with them than we ever would have thought.

The most important takeaway here is that speakers and listeners are *partners* in conversation—despite the burden of intelligibility often being placed on non-native shoulders alone. As mentioned before, a big aid to pronunciation proficiency is greater use of a new language, especially with native speakers. And, in turn, one of the biggest influences on increasing listeners' comprehension of accented speech is their amount of exposure to and interaction with non-native-accented speakers. I'd say it doesn't really take a rocket scientist—or a linguist—to connect the dots on that one.

SOUND BITE

What Makes a Language Beautiful?

Before I met my husband, I had an Australian boyfriend. I'll admit that, though he was a nice guy, he wasn't much of a keeper. In fact, after meeting him, my father summed him up this way: "Some people don't talk much because they think carefully before they speak. Others simply have nothing to say." Not exactly a ringing endorsement.

Needless to say, it wasn't long before we broke up, but the hardest thing to leave behind was the way he sounded: there was just something about his Aussie accent that made me swoon. Turns out, I was not alone in feeling an attraction to an accent. Surveys of the "sexiest" accents routinely return ranked lists of desirable accents, as witnessed by this CNN headline: "Sexiest accents poll: Where do people have the voice of seduction?" Or *Esquire*'s "The 10 Sexiest Accents."

Now, linguists might not have a lot of personal experience with linguistic sexiness, but we do have some chops in figuring out what it is exactly that makes us find some accents appealing and others not so much. For our final little sound bite foray, I thought it might be fun to share a few of our insights into what makes for a linguistic aphrodisiac.

LOVE LANGUAGES?

Most of us have some sense about which languages we find aesthetically pleasing and which we don't. In fact, we often liberally share our opinions on the matter, at least to go by the amount of internet chatter. French and Italian make frequent appearances on lists ranking languages we love, which seems a bit of a cheat since they also happen to be known as Romance languages, but rarely do we find German, Chinese, or Arabic at the top of those same charts. Why exactly do some languages sound hot while others do not?

While such a question might, on the surface, be a tad silly, underneath its tongue-in-cheekness lies a more important theoretical question: Is there something intrinsic in certain sounds that draws us toward languages that have a preponderance of them? On the flip side, can we pinpoint the features that make a language sound harsh, grating, or unpleasant? Or are we just conditioned by the languages we know best to have an affinity for those that sound more familiar?

Studies aimed at figuring out the answers to these questions started to ramp up in the 1970s, with much of the work at first led by social psychologist Howard Giles. Giles and his research team suggested there were two possible reasons why we get good or bad vibes hearing certain languages. One possibility was that there is something inherent in the language itself that we are reacting to, such as the sounds or the tones that are most prevalent. This idea became known as the *inherent value hypothesis*. The other possibility was that it is mainly social and cultural things like status, power, or even our amount of exposure that influences the feels we get from one language versus another. This idea became known as the *imposed norm hypothesis*. Another idea floated around is that we have a preference for hearing more intelligible and/or more familiar speech—something related to the idea we explored earlier about cognitive fluency and how easy a language is for us to process.

Giles and his colleagues might have started the ball rolling, but more recent research has continued to explore whether humans have ingrained bias toward certain sounds as well as test out these different theories about what makes our love language sensors tick. The answer turns out to be a bit, in the words of singer Avril Lavigne, complicated.

THE DEVIL YOU KNOW

In the earliest experiments on the question of what drives our linguistic preferences, Giles's research team decided to have people rate different dialects of languages they didn't know.* They wanted to do this to tease out whether people had particular feelings for some accents over others even in the absence of the social associations we develop with languages we do know, such as links to class,

* In this study, Welsh speakers were asked to rate various French varieties, ranging from Standard Parisian French to working-class French to Canadian French.

rurality, or region. If people who were cultural outsiders still made the same aesthetic distinctions among dialects of foreign languages, even with no previous experience with or ability to understand them, that would lend support to the idea that there is something inherent in the sound characteristics that people responded to.

Instead, the results of these experiments suggested that our loves and hates, linguistically speaking, are more about what we have come to know through exposure to societal beliefs and attitudes, rather than any intrinsic qualities. When rating various dialects in an unknown language, listeners showed no predictable patterns of aesthetic preferences. This result stands in contrast to when subjects were asked to rank dialects in a language they were familiar with—like the strong preference English raters showed for the high-status Received Pronunciation dialect or the more cultivated ratings given to Parisian French by French Canadians.

Much more recently, a group of researchers published the results of a more rigorous and larger-scale study looking at the same question of whether our preferences are driven by some inherent linguistic quality or by social associations and exposure. Using recordings of multiple speakers from each of 228 different languages, native English-, Chinese-, and Semitic-speaking listeners were asked which recorded language excerpts sounded most attractive as well as whether they recognized the language spoken and could place it geographically. As with the early studies, no clear patterns of aesthetic preferences emerged—except when speakers believed they recognized a language. More familiar languages tended to get a boost in pleasantness ratings. This boost occurred even when listeners misidentified languages (something that happened over half the time!).

What this means is that just thinking a language sounded familiar made it sound more pleasing. While English speakers simply found any familiar-sounding language to be more pleasant, Chinese speakers preferred languages they believed were spoken in North Asia or North America and downrated those they believed were spoken in Africa. Semitic-language speakers felt languages they thought came from the Americas (North and South) sounded nicer. It appears that social and cultural beliefs as well as how familiar a language sounds were the biggest factors in governing linguistic likes and dislikes. Among languages they didn't recognize, listeners did not show any kumbaya-like agreement on which sounded more pleasant than others, suggesting no clear underlying universal preferences that make some languages inherently more beautiful than others.

Still, the researchers did find evidence that some linguistic traits might play into pleasantness scales, something they determined by looking at what sound characteristics were shared across the languages that speakers tended to like more than others. What they found was that, no matter the language, low-pitched speakers tended to be rated more attractive than higher-pitched voices (for both men and women), and that non-tonal languages tended to be slightly preferred over tonal ones. But the particular type or complexity of sounds a language had—or even the more overlap in sounds languages had with one's native variety—did not seem to play a significant role in making a language more or less beautiful.

SOUND AND SENSIBILITY

Outside the specific question of what it is that makes some languages come across as more appealing than others, there has also been work on whether or not sounds themselves have intrinsic aesthetic appeal, an area of (relatively little) study that linguist David Crystal tagged *phonaesthetics*. The topic of phonaesthetics usually comes up when we talk about which words sound prettier or more melodious than others. For instance, there has been a weirdly large amount written about the pleasantness associated with hearing the combo *cellar door*, while, as we discussed previously, overuse of the word *moist* can ruin otherwise solid friendships. While a lot of this work on intrinsic properties of sounds falls under the larger rubric of sound symbolism, which examines how sounds themselves contain meaning of some sort, phonaesthetics looks specifically at how specific sounds or sound qualities can provoke affective reactions, absent of ties to the actual meaning of the words in which they appear.

One recent study, for example, looked at the phonetic qualities shared by words heard as beautiful or ugly in German, finding that the more sonorant sounds a word had, the more likely it was heard as beautiful. As mentioned before, vowels are what define syllables, but what makes vowels a boon to syllabification is a phonetic property known as *sonority*. Sonority has to do with how much acoustic energy—something related to its loudness and airflow—a sound contains. Vowels have more acoustic energy than consonants, but consonants like "l," "r," "m," and "n" also have more acoustic energy than other consonants. This could explain why *cellar*, a word that doesn't mean anything particularly enticing unless a tornado is approaching, is heard as pretty. All but one of the sounds it contains are what linguists would call sonorant sounds. Other research finds that a lot of popping and hissing consonants like "p," "t," "s," and "sh" can be somewhat aversive to listeners, making *piss* and *shit* winners in the rough- and rude-sounding department.*

In a similar vein, some work has tried to home in on the phonetic qualities that might explain what attracts us more to some languages than others. Researchers have suggested that languages with more open syllables (like Italian or Spanish) are more attractive than languages with high numbers of consonants and consonant clusters (like English, which allows consonant orgies like in "strengths" or "widths"). This again has to do with the acoustic energy vowels contain and the more open articulation they involve, something that makes a language with lots of syllables ending in vowels seem to have greater musicality and singability.† Sonorant consonants are also high on the list of possible promoters of preferred languages, for much the same reason.

The melodious flowing nature of languages with high numbers of open syllables and sonorant consonants may also be what makes people link them with softness and sensuality, essentially giving

---

* As well, these words contain a short vowel ("ih"), something also found to be less preferred than the sound of long vowels, as found in the perhaps less rude-sounding *pee*.

† Open syllables, like "fa" or "la," are easier to sing and hold, and languages with limited consonants and consonant clusters tend to have more open syllables.

off what has been referred to as a "phonetic chill factor." On the other hand, languages like German or Russian that have throaty guttural consonants and consonant clusters are often perceived as hard and less melodious sounding. The perceptual contrast between languages with greater sonority and open syllables versus those with less sonority and consonant clusters might also have to do with speech rate, since languages with the former tend to be faster, something perceived more positively in general.

Other rhythmic properties beyond speech rate have also been hypothesized as making a language sound beautiful. For instance, it has been suggested that stress-timed languages like English, German, or Russian (where stressed syllables pop out more) are less appealing to listeners than the more steady rhythm of syllable-timed languages like French, Italian, Spanish, or Icelandic. This preference might explain why, in the sixteenth-century, Holy Roman Emperor Charles V reportedly said he spoke "Spanish to God, Italian to women, French to men, and German to my horse." Along the same rhythmic lines, a preference for less up and down pitchiness might make for the slight preference found for non-tonal languages, since tonal languages have more pitch variation in general.

There has not been a lot of empirical research testing out such hypotheses, but the studies that have been done have not turned up strongly compelling evidence that phonetic traits like these are the main factors driving how beautiful we perceive a language to be. While sonority, faster speech rate, and *isochrony* (the fancy name for stress- versus syllable-timing properties) have been found to contribute in some part to linguistic attraction, social factors like familiarity, relative status, and exposure account for the lion's share of our linguistic likes and dislikes.

In other words, our learned preferences and language experience tend to dampen any influence of intrinsic properties that, in a social vacuum, might otherwise incline us toward preferring the way one language sounds over another. After all, Hawaiian has only open syllables and a high relative proportion of sonorant consonants but rarely hits the top of the sexiest language lists. English, on the other hand, lacks many such preferred traits, yet is often ranked highly.* The fact that the top languages in most such polls tend to lean Western European heavy, but also vary depending on where the majority of respondents hail from, points to cultural hierarchies and values at work.

Still, when social attitudes and linguistic preferences line up, a language's phonetic properties probably help tip it into the beautiful language zone. Consider, for instance, the enduring aesthetic appreciation of and interest in learning Italian, a language that is neither globally powerful nor super professionally useful, but that has both a culturally sexy ethos and a syllable-timed, sonority-heavy profile that, together, seem to make for a powerful linguistic aphrodisiac.

What this really points to is something that has come up a lot over these pages: beauty, as with what sounds "good" or "bad," is

* English has lower sonority, much more consonant clustering, a slower speech rate, and is stress timed, all of which have not been found among the most appealing linguistic traits.

just as much in the ear and mind of the beholder as in the mouth of the speaker. While intrinsic properties and tendencies of languages might plant the seed for the direction languages grow, it's the environment in which they find themselves that really has the most impact on whether we envision a weed or a flower.

CONCLUSION

Accent-uating the Positive

When I first started researching different accents of American English as a fresh-faced graduate student, it was because I was tired of hearing about what Southerners sounded like from people who clearly hadn't been there recently. The Southern I knew, the accent I had, was nothing like the slow Southern caricature that was so prevalent in the American psyche. Instead, while maybe we still had "y'all" and "bah bah," our *pins* no longer overlapped our *pens* and our drawl was in much shorter supply. That's why I was stunned when, years later, as a young professor at the University of Nevada, Reno, a brilliant graduate student I had recruited from Tennessee complained that one of her professors had called out her accent during class. Though her Southern lilt was certainly noticeable, the snarky fun they had at her expense relied on stereotypes about the bumpkin Southerner and made her feel like the ultimate unwanted outsider.

Up to that point, my work had focused mainly on how American speech had evolved in terms of the way it was spoken, but this experience brought home to me that just as important was understanding how it was perceived and why it was perceived that way. In that spirit, it is my sincere hope that you have found within these pages some fun and fascinating facts about the accents that surround you, but my greatest hope about what you take away is that the idea that there exists only one "right" way to sound is both historically and linguistically misguided.

OUR VERY ORIGINAL TONGUES

It is undeniable that, over the course of human history, accents have proved advantageous as a quick and dirty way to recognize who is in our tribe. Still, today, accents that don't sound like our own draw our notice—with many speakers believing that their own reference group speaks "normally," while everyone else speaks with an accent. Of course, modern speakers are far from the first to have been led astray by thinking their own group's way of speaking is the most "pure" form of language from which others deviate.

For instance, writing in the fifth century BCE, the Greek historian Herodotus relayed a story told to him by Egyptian priests in Memphis of early attempts to definitively answer the question of the most ancient race by discovering whose language was the first or primordial language. The story they shared involved the world's earliest social experiment, one devised by the Egyptian pharaoh Psammetichus, who ruled from 664 to 610 BCE.

Psammetichus had come up with what seemed a most ingenious way to illustrate that the Egyptian language was *the* original, and thus would prove the Egyptians to be the most hallowed and ancient people. His idea? Snatch up a couple of babies (after all, he was the king), send them off to live in isolation with nothing but a few goats for company, and see what happened. Psammetichus presumed that, after the babies stopped babbling baby nonsense, some pure form of language would naturally develop, just as the first language must have sprung forth in the earliest articulate humans (presumably Egyptian). To avoid having the experiment end too prematurely, Psammetichus did allow for a goatherder to keep them fed and relatively cared for, but he was instructed to do so in strict silence.*

So, did Psammetichus end up with more than murderously mad moms and babies who could bleat? According to the legend, yes. Unfortunately for the pharaoh, it didn't add up to be a commanding victory for the primacy of the Egyptians.

As the tale goes, after about two years, the goatherder who was their de facto and silent custodian walked into their rustic cottage, only to be greeted by the enthusiastic toddlers repeatedly saying the word *bekos*. If this sounds suspiciously a bit like the sound a goat might make, you are not alone in that thought. Many later discussions of Psammetichus's experiment have suggested the babies were

---

* Other versions of the story suggest their caretakers were nursemaids with their tongues cut out, so let's root for the goatherder being the way it went down.

merely imitating the goats amongst whom they flocked, a claim that would support our old friend Darwin's view of how language began (e.g., via the imitation of sounds heard in nature).

But this similarity was allegedly lost on the pharaoh, who instead dejectedly determined that this "first" word was not Egyptian, but instead the word for wheat bread in Phrygian, the language of the Phrygian people who lived contemporaneously in Asia Minor. Considering the babies had been on a strict goat milk diet since birth, it doesn't surprise me in the least that their first word would be a request for something with a bit more chew, and perhaps they simply thought the Phrygians were a safer bet for something more epicurean. Yet, in the face of such undeniable evidence, Psammetichus had no choice but to concede that the honor of greater antiquity rested with the Phrygians, whose language appeared to be the original language.

There are a couple of morals to this story. For one, babies left to their own devices are not the most reliable experimental subjects. This is a moral not heeded by other royal types ranging from Holy Roman Emperor Frederick II in the twelfth century to Emperor Akbar the Great of India in the sixteenth, both of whom undertook their own emergent language projects involving infant neglect. In those cases, the babies fared far worse, with death or muteness the reported and none-too-surprising result.

The rumored exception to these early experimental failures was King James IV of Scotland, who was well-known for his interest in medical and scientific experimentation. King James apparently had great success raising isolated and linguistically deprived infants who turned out speaking Hebrew, but considering he sent them to live on an island used to quarantine those with syphilis, I am guessing their story did not ultimately end well. Assuming this first moral is now squarely a lesson learned, the second and more relevant moral to our endeavor here is that being too deeply invested in believing in the primacy of your own speech has always been bound to get you into trouble.

The Greeks, from whom we learned of Psammetichus's tale, called those who spoke a different tongue *barbaroi*, or barbarians. At the time of Herodotus, this meant those who spoke a foreign tongue, but the pejorative connotation of the word *barbarian* comes from the way those with a different language came to be viewed as uncivilized and ignorant. The word *barbaros* itself appears to be an onomatopoeic form, imitating the incomprehensible muttering of strange sounds, as in it's all "bar . . . bar . . ." to the Greeks.* Of course, the Greeks included the Romans under this label, but the joke was on them after the Roman conquest of Greece and their subsequent embrace of the word to describe all non-Romans. Though suspicion and disdain for those who speak differently certainly has a long history, the advantage we have now is a couple of centuries of linguistic science to help us tackle the question of the original tongue and how we came to sound so different today.

If there is one lesson I hope you've learned by now, it is that

---

* Which is amusing considering the modern-day English expression "Sounds like Greek to me" for something hard to understand.

when people become separated by land, by tribe, by economics, or by ideology, natural linguistic processes affect their speech in different ways, leading to divergence—and our recognizable accents—over time. In other words, languages, like people, never stand still, and our accents are a signal of who we are and where we've been.

But when we look to the bigger picture, what's as important is that our accents don't always set us apart; they also bring us together. When we both put our groceries in "begs" instead of "bags," share "ahnts" instead of "ants," or eat "brefas" in the morning, it means we share something much deeper than a pronunciation habit—we also share experiences and a history that brought us to speak the way we do. And it is this community-forging facet of accent—and the scientific research that tells us why and how sounds morph and change over time—that is so often missing from our national conversations about the funny ways we think people talk.

Together, over these pages, we've unlocked the secrets of what linguistic science, psychology, and history can tell us about the evolution of human speech, why accents develop, and how it impacts the social lives of speakers and listeners when they do. Looking deeper into the ways that small differences in speech sounds unite and divide us—by nation, by region, by class, and by race—we have come to see that accents are grounded not in ignorance, indifference, or inability, but in the remarkable way we are wired for speech, allowing us to be simultaneously communicative *and* remarkably efficient. To me as a linguist, this is the greatest power of accents: They teach us how much we have in common—especially once we are able to see how what sounds different on the surface derives from the same underlying social desires and linguistic predispositions we all share as human language speakers.

ACKNOWLEDGMENTS

I certainly could never hope to elucidate the evolution of accents without an amazing linguistic village behind me. My broad appreciation goes to all the linguists who have guided me during my career and all the scholars whose research provided the basis for these pages. Particularly, though, I want to pay tribute to the late Dr. William Labov. As is evident from his many mentions in this book, his influence on the way we have come to understand language variation and change has been profound and far-reaching. Bill was to me, as he was to so many others, a man whose tireless devotion to the field provided a model I could only hope to follow. I am grateful that I had the opportunity to know him and benefit from his work, his wisdom, and his support. I also want to recognize Dr. Robert "Bob" Bayley, another linguist no longer with us but whose mentorship and friendship left an indelible mark on the careers and in the hearts of not just me but so many who had the great honor of working with him.

In addition, I want to extend my deepest thanks to the many

friends and colleagues who helped me craft this book, whether it came in the form of brainstorming cover ideas or reading chapters or just making sure my "t"s were crossed and my "i"s were dotted. Natalie Schilling, Mignon Fogarty, Karen Azoulay, Lieselotte Anderwald, Tyler Kendall, Chris Sapp, Julie Palmer, Julie Roberts, Rachel Curran, and Mahmoud Abdi Tabari—I will forever be grateful for your help! To my students, thank you for lighting a fire by asking questions that pushed me to find better answers than our texts could provide. To my colleagues at the University of Nevada, Reno—I could not ask for more than to have spent my career at a place where my work is valued. I also want to acknowledge the important role played by the National Endowment for the Humanities in this project. As a Public Scholars Fellow, I was given the gift of time to write, an invaluable aid in the completion of this work.

To my team at Viking/Penguin, my agent, Becky, and especially my editor, Terezia, I know that I have hit the literary equivalent of a jackpot, which is no small feat considering I live in Nevada, where jackpots are often promised but rarely delivered. You have proven time and time again to be great allies in developing my work and getting it out into the world. Thank you for putting up with my many drafts, multiple emails, and endless requests for memos.

As for those a bit closer to home: my kids, Cole and Taylor, might not have inspired this book topic as they did the last, but, as Gen Z Westerners, they will eternally be both my favorite linguistic subjects and my favorite people. To my husband, Craig, whose confidence in my ability to get this book written never wavered even when my own did, your support and love has meant the world. Thank you for going down this road with me and helping me always keep my eye on the destination, even when things seemed a bit fuzzy at the outset. Finally, I owe many treats and long overdue pets to my sweet dog friends, Shadow, Aspen, and Juneau, who worked hard to keep my feet warm and my keyboard in constant need of de-furring.

NOTES

INTRODUCTION

5 **spelling/sound mismatches:** This is unsurprisingly known as the *meet/meat merger*, which was complete in English by about 1700. Simplifying somewhat, before this merger, the vowel spelled "ea" was pronounced like the modern vowel in *mate*, while "ee" was pronounced as it is today in *meet*. Between 1600 and 1700, the "ea" vowel became pronounced with a more raised tongue like "ee," resulting in the merger, which is why pairs like *meet/meat*, *see/sea*, and *beet/beat* all sound the same. While many words with "ea" were affected, some vowels in words like *great* never raised to "ee," and this is why we have different-sounding vowels in word pairs like *greet* and *great*.

6 **variant of another sound:** This is because both "r" sounds and "l" sounds are produced in a phonetically similar manner (both are known as *liquids* in linguistic lingo), which makes them very likely candidates across languages to be simply variants of the same sound.

10 ***LA Times* put it:** Robert Schwartz, "Expert on Dialects Deciphers Dilemma of Accused Airline Employee: His Acquittal Is a Matter of Sound Judgment," *LA Times*, July 8, 1985, https://www.latimes.com/archives/la-xpm-1985-07-08-mn-9706-story.html.

11 **linguists have found:** For instance, see Joshua L. Martin and Kelly

Elizabeth Wright, "Bias in Automatic Speech Recognition: The Case of African American Language," *Applied Linguistics* 400, no. 4 (2023): 613–30, https://doi.org/10.1093/applin/amac066. For Southern speech recognition issues, see Li-Fang Lai, Janet G. van Hell, and John Lipski, "Dialect Bias in Automatic Speech Recognition: Analysis of Appalachian English," *American Speech* 100, no. 2 (2025): 190–207.

12 **"shtreets" and "shtrings":** There has been a lot of interest in "s" retraction as of late in sociolinguistics. A couple of good (but technical) studies are Eric Wilbanks, "Social and Structural Constraints on a Phonetically-Motivated Change in Progress: (str) Retraction in Raleigh, NC," *University of Pennsylvania Working Papers in Linguistics* 23 (2016): 301–10, https://doi.org/10.5070/P7121040720; and David Durian, "Getting [S]tronger Every Day?: More on Urbanization and the Sociogeographic Diffusion of (str) in Columbus, OH," *University of Pennsylvania Working Papers in Linguistics* 13 (2007): 13–16, https://repository.upenn.edu/handle/20.500.14332/44654.

13 **attractive social meaning:** For instance, a sense of youth and coolness was hypothesized for its growing presence in Cockney English; for more, see Ulrike Altendorf, *Estuary English: Levelling at the Interface of RP and South-Eastern British English* (Narr, 2003).

14 **have them at "Hello":** Thomas Purnell, William Idsardi, and John Baugh, "Perceptual and Phonetic Experiments on American English Dialect Identification," *Journal of Language and Social Psychology* 18, no. 1 (1999): 10–30, https://doi.org/10.1177/0261927X99018001002.

15 **possible speech sounds:** English, at thirty-nine-ish (depending on dialect), has more than average because we really like our vowels. To find out more about sound inventories and preferences across languages, Ian Maddieson's *Patterns of Sounds* (Cambridge University Press, 1984) is a great text.

19 **perceived traits and habits:** The way in which this type of linguistic "enregisterment" happens has been discussed most thoroughly in Asif Agha, "The Social Life of Cultural Value," *Language and Communication* 23, no. 3–4 (2003): 231–73, https://doi.org/10.1016/S0271-5309(03)00012-0, as well as in Michael Silverstein, "Indexical Order and the Dialectics of Sociolinguistic Life," *Language and Communication* 23, no. 3–4 (2003): 193–229, doi:10.1016/S0271-5309(03)00013-2.

CHAPTER 1: BABY STEPS

21 **Tiny infants might babble:** Janet F. Werker and Richard C. Tees, "Cross-Language Speech Perception: Evidence for Perceptual Reorganization During the First Year of Life," *Infant Behavior and Development* 7, no. 1 (1984): 49–63, https://doi.org/10.1016/S0163-6383(84)80022-3.

25 **especially the vowel sounds:** These are the vowels /i/, /a/, and /u/ in the International Phonetic Alphabet.

25 **unique acoustic signature:** For a fascinating glimpse of the impressive and largely hidden nature of speech production, see Peter MacNeilage, *The Origin of Speech* (Oxford University Press, 2010).

25 **Other sounds, like "sh" or "r":** For example, an "r" sound involves the tongue tip gesturing at the hard ridge right behind your teeth. A "sh," on the other hand, lifts a more flattened tongue toward the hard palate, just a bit farther back than for "s." Other differences involve how the tongue is positioned, as in whether it touches the upper mouth or is instead just close to it and how the tongue is shaped, like curled back, rolled, or spread out. All of this happens simultaneously to imbue the air with the resonances we hear as particular speech sounds.

25 **motor cortex system:** Hugo Théoret and Alvaro Pascual-Leone, "Language Acquisition: Do as You Hear," *Current Biology* (2002): 736–37, https://doi.org/10.1016/s0960-9822(02)01251-4.

26 **babies practice early on:** A range of speech sounds are really only possible once a baby's larynx has lowered. Earlier in life (around six to eight weeks), babies do make cooing noises that are speech-like.

26 **the same set of consonants:** This list of consonant sounds was established by John Locke, *Phonological Acquisition and Change* (Academic Press, 1983).

26 **always the earliest ones:** These sounds as well as others of the same type (called *stops*) were the earliest acquired by children across languages. In English specifically, sounds like "b," "p," "m," "n," "d," and "t" were found to be the earliest sounds after vowels and vowel-like consonants such as "y" and "w" sounds.

27 **narrows down which specific sounds:** A seminal work on perceptual development in infants is Janet F. Werker and Richard C. Tees, "Cross-Language Speech Perception: Evidence for Perceptual

Reorganization During the First Year of Life," *Infant Behavior and Development* 7, no. 1 (1984): 49–63.

28 **first language a hindrance:** Many of these different factors affecting L2 (second language) accents are discussed in more detail in Tracy M. Derwing and Murray J. Munro, *Pronunciation Fundamentals: Evidence-Based Perspectives for L2 Teaching and Research* (John Benjamins Publishing Company, 2015).

29 **Spanish in those contexts:** This ease or difficulty is related to the way that a speaker's native language perceives a sound as a member of a single sound in their language (i.e., dark "l" and light "l" in English), known as *single category assimilation*, or two separate sounds ("l" and "r" in English), known as *dual category assimilation*, an idea more fully developed in C. T. Best and M. D. Tyler, "Nonnative and Second-Language Speech Perception: Commonalities and Complementarities," in *Language Experience in Second Language Speech Learning: In Honor of James Emil Flege*, ed. Ocke-Schwen Bohn and Murray J. Munro (John Benjamins Publishing Company, 2007), 13–34. The idea that a non-native speaker can more accurately produce a sound that doesn't exist in one's native language compared to similar (but not identical) sounds draws from Flege's speech learning model (1995).

30 **found in Swahili:** In Swahili, many of these "n" or "m" sounds that come before another consonant at the beginning of a word are pronounced as their own syllable the same way English speakers sometimes pronounce "m" or "n" at the end of a word like *bottom* ("bott'm") or *button* ("butt'n"). In English, this type of pronunciation only occurs at the ends of words, which is why we stick in an extra vowel sound at the beginning of a word like *mzazi*.

31 **pops up for Spanish speakers:** As found, for instance, for Spanish speakers in Matthew T. Carlson, Matthew Goldrick, Michael Blasingame, and Angela Fink, "Navigating Conflicting Phonotactic Constraints in Bilingual Speech Perception," *Bilingualism: Language and Cognition* 19, no. 5 (2016): 939–54, https://doi.org/10.1017/S1366728915000334, or for Japanese speakers in Emmanuel Dupoux, Kazuhiko Kakehi, Yuki Hirose, et al., "Epenthetic Vowels in Japanese: A Perceptual Illusion?" *Journal of Experimental Psychology: Human Perception and Performance* 25, no. 6 (1999): 1568–78, https://doi.org/10.1037/0096-1523.25.6.1568.

31 **English speakers who learned German:** Alene Moyer, "Ultimate Attainment in L2 Phonology: The Critical Factors of Age, Motivation, and Instruction," *Studies in Second Language Acquisition* 21, no. 1 (1999): 81–108, https://doi.org/10.1017/S0272263199001035.

33 **value of baby talk:** See, for instance, Anne Fernald, "The Perceptual, Affective, and Linguistic Salience of Mothers' Speech to Infants," *Infant Behavior and Development* (1984): 113, or Debora S. Herold, Lynne C. Nygaard, and Laura L. Namy, "Say It Like You Mean It: Mothers' Use of Prosody to Convey Word Meaning," *Language and Speech* (2011): 423–36, https://doi.org/10.1177/0023830911422212.

34 **mothers tend to be hyperarticulate:** Patricia K. Kuhl, Jean E. Andruski, Inna A. Chistovich, et al., "Cross-Language Analysis of Phonetic Units in Language Addressed to Infants," *Science* (1997): 684–86, https://doi.org/10.1126/science.277.5326.684.

34 **when talking to adults:** Each of these consonant pairs differs only in terms of the vibrating or not vibrating of the vocal cords, a contrast that is often important to creating meaning differences between words (e.g., *kin* versus *gin*) and known as a *voicing contrast* in linguistics.

35 **echoed in other studies:** J. Roberts, "Shifting Vowels in Tiny Mouths: Toddlers' Acquisition of Southern American English," paper presented at New Ways of Analyzing Variation (NWAV) Conference, Toronto, October 1999.

35 **when speaking to other adults:** Paul Foulkes, Gerard J. Docherty, and Dominic Watt, "Phonological Variation in Child-Directed Speech," *Language* 81, no. 5 (2005): 177–206, https://doi.org/10.1353/lan.2005.0018.

35 **as babies get older:** As found, for instance, in the previously mentioned study by Foulkes, Docherty, and Watt (2005), as well as Huei-Mei Liu, Feng-Ming Tsao, and Patricia K. Kuhl, "Age-Related Changes in Acoustic Modifications of Mandarin Maternal Speech to Preverbal Infants and Five-Year-Old Children: A Longitudinal Study," *Journal of Child Language* 36, no. 4 (2009): 909–22, https://doi.org/10.1017/s030500090800929x.

35 **moms started using more:** For more on moms' changing use of Geordie features as their kids age, see Foulkes, Docherty, and Watt (2005).

36 **a boy thing:** In Foulkes, Docherty, and Watt's examination (2005) of Geordie features in Tyneside, England, a few dads wandered in during

the recording sessions, providing a small amount of comparative data on dad talk.

37 **compared to their older siblings:** Sali A. Tagliamonte and Sonja Molfenter, "How'd You Get That Accent?: Acquiring a Second Dialect of the Same Language," *Language in Society* 36, no. 5 (2007): 649–75, https://doi.org/10.1017/S0047404507070911.

37 **similar to Philly natives:** Arvilla Payne, "Factors Controlling the Acquisition of the Philadelphia Dialect by Out-of-State Children," in *Locating Language in Time and Space*, ed. W. Labov (Academic Press, 1980), 143–78.

38 **mother's speech in utero:** Birgit Mampe, Angela D. Friederici, Anne Christophe, and Kathleen Wermke, "Newborns' Cry Melody Is Shaped by Their Native Language," *Current Biology* 19, no. 23 (2009): 1994–97, https://doi.org/10.1016/j.cub.2009.09.064.

39 **recognizing and associating accents:** Two great summaries of what we know about kids' production and social perception are Katherine D. Kinzler, "Language as a Social Cue," *Annual Review of Psychology* 72 (2021): 241–64, https://doi.org/10.1146/annurev-psych-010418-103034; and Elizabeth K. Johnson and Katherine S. White, "Developmental Sociolinguistics: Children's Acquisition of Language Variation," Wiley Interdisciplinary Reviews, *Cognitive Science* (2020), https://doi.org/10.1002/wcs.1515.

40 **just nonlocal accents:** Melissa Paquette-Smith, Helen Buckler, and Elizabeth K. Johnson, "How Sociolinguistic Factors Shape Children's Subjective Impressions of Teacher Quality," *Quarterly Journal of Experimental Psychology* 76, no. 3 (2023): 485–96, https://doi.org/10.1177/17470218221094312.

40 **more accent experience:** Melissa Paquette-Smith, Helen Buckler, Katherine S. White, et al., "The Effect of Accent Exposure on Children's Sociolinguistic Evaluation of Peers," *Developmental Psychology* 55, no. 4 (2019): 809–22, https://doi.org/10.1037/dev0000659.

41 **upper-elementary ages:** As found in Katherine D. Kinzler and Jasmine M. DeJesus, "Northern = Smart and Southern = Nice: The Development of Accent Attitudes in the United States," *Quarterly Journal of Experimental Psychology* 66, no. 6 (2013): 1146–58, https://doi.org/10.1080/17470218.2012.731695.

43 **hypothesized ancient root /ra:** This root for *tea* is hypothesized to

have existed in a language that preceded modern Chinese dialects (where our word for tea comes from) by thousands of years and was likely derived from an early Mon-Khmer language. See Dan Jurafsky, "Tea," in *Encyclopedia of Chinese Language and Linguistics*, ed. R. P. E. Sybesma, Wolfgang Behr, Yueguo Gu, et al. (Brill, 2017), https://doi.org/10.1163/2210-7363_ecll_COM_00000431.

44 **words resistant to the changes:** There are a number of discussions of how these terms ended up so similar across languages. A few seminal ones include John L. Locke, "'Mama' and 'Papa' in Child Language. Parent Reference or Phonetic Preference?," in *Symposium Balticum*, ed. B. Metuzale-Kangere and H. D. Ringholm (Buske, 1990): 267–73; Roman Jakobson, "Why Mama and Papa?," in *Perspectives in Psychological Theory: Essays in Honor of Heinz Werner*, ed. B. Kaplan and S. Wapner (International Universities Press, 1960): 124–34; Peter MacNeilage, *The Origin of Speech* (Oxford University Press, 2008); and Pierre J. Bancel and Alain Matthey de l'Etang, "Kin Tongue. A Study of Kin Nursery Terms in Relation to Language Acquisition, with a Historical and Evolutionary Perspective," *Mother Tongue* 9 (2005): 171–90.

44 **descendants of the primordial language:** An interesting empirically based discussion can be found in Doug Jones and Bojka Milicic, *Kinship, Language, and Prehistory: Per Hage and the Renaissance in Kinship Studies* (University of Utah Press, 2015), particularly chapters 3 and 4, https://dx.doi.org/10.1353/book41603.

CHAPTER 2: OUR ORIGIN STORY

47 **advent of language:** A good overview on this topic is provided in Mark Pagel, "Q&A: What Is Human Language, When Did It Evolve and Why Should We Care?" *BMC Biology* 64 (2017), https://bmcbiol.biomedcentral.com/articles/10.1186/s12915-017-0405-3.

48 **symbolic thinking necessary for language:** For a deeper dive into the evolution of modern human cultural and linguistic behavior, see Kim Sterelny, "From Hominins to Humans: How *Sapiens* Became Behaviourally Modern," *Philosophical Transactions of the Royal Society B* 366, no. 1566 (2011): 809–22, or Richard G. Klein, "Language and

Human Evolution," *Journal of Neurolinguistics* 43 (2017): 204–21, https://doi.org/10.1016/j.jneuroling.2016.11.004.

48 **The origin of language:** For an overview of some of these early theories on the origin of language, see chapter 1 of George Yule, *The Study of Language* (Cambridge University Press, 2022).

50 **known as *sound symbolism*:** For more details on these types of associations, see Aleksandra Ćwiek, Susanne Fuchs, Christoph Draxler, et al., "The *Bouba/Kiki* Effect Is Robust across Cultures and Writing Systems," *Philosophical Transactions of the Royal Society B: Biological Sciences* (2021): 377, https://doi.org/10.1098/rstb.2020.0390.

50 **evidence of such patterning:** Damián E. Blasi, Søren Wichmann, Harald Hammarström, et al., "Sound-Meaning Association Biases Evidenced across Thousands of Languages," *Proceedings of the National Academy of Sciences of the United States of America* 113, no. 39 (2016): 10818–23, https://doi.org/10.1073/pnas.1605782113.

52 **Indo-European people spread:** There has been much debate about and research into where these Indo-Europeans started and how they spread. Two competing theories have posited the Indo-European origin in Anatolia or with the Kurgan culture of the Black Sea region. Recent scholarship takes a hybrid approach and suggests that an original Indo-European society existed south of the Caucasus Mountains (modern Armenia, Azerbaijan, Georgia, and Turkey), which began spreading out into Europe and Asia about eight thousand years ago. Then, around five thousand years ago, another major migration, this time coming from an area of what is now Southern Russia and Ukraine, created further separation among speakers, and as a result, more new languages that could be ultimately traced back to this same Indo-European source. See Paul Heggarty, Cormac Anderson, Matthew Scarborough, et al., "Language Trees with Sampled Ancestors Support a Hybrid Model for the Origin of Indo-European Languages," *Science* 381, no. 6656 (2023), https://doi.org/10.1126/science.abg0818.

53 **common Germanic language:** The complete list of Germanic-descended languages is too exhaustive to include here but can be found in M. Durrel, "Germanic Languages," in *Encyclopedia of Language and Linguistics*, ed. Keith Brown (Elsevier, 2005), 53–55.

58 **the groundbreaking work of linguist Bill Labov:** William (Bill)

Labov is known to most of us working in the field as the father of modern sociolinguistics. Some of his most influential early works include: Uriel Weinreich, William Labov, and Marvin I. Herzog, "Empirical Foundations for a Theory of Language Change," in *Directions for Historical Linguistics: A Symposium*, ed. W. P. Lehmann and Yakov Malkiel (University of Texas Press, 1968), 95–188; William Labov, "The Social Motivation of a Sound Change," *Word* 19, no. 3 (1963): 273–309; William Labov, *The Social Stratification of English in New York City* (Center for Applied Linguistics, 1966).

60 **some socially symbolic way:** Spatial effects alone (i.e., geographic dispersal) do not sufficiently explain the changes that have occurred in the historical record. For more on this, see James Burridge and Tamsin Blaxter, "Inferring the Drivers of Language Change Using Spatial Models," *Journal of Physics: Complexity* 2, no. 3 (2021), https://doi.org/10.48550/arXiv.2107.02056.

60 **Educated Greeks, in the first:** Simon Swain, *Hellenism and Empire: Language, Classicism, and Power in the Greek World, AD 50–250* (Clarendon Press, 1996).

61 **"outlandish" regional pronunciations:** As cited in Jack Chambers, "Studying Language Variation: An Informal Epistemology," in *The Handbook of Language Variation and Change*, ed. J. K. Chambers and N. Schilling (John Wiley & Sons, 2013): 2–15.

61 **elite Roman society:** For a highly readable discussion of ancient Roman attitudes toward accents, I suggest the wonderful article by Wolfgang de Melo, "Latin with an Accent," *Antigone*, https://antigonejournal.com/2022/05/latin-accent/.

61 **Book of Judges:** Judges 12:1–15.

61 **weed out German spies:** For more on the German difficulty with pronunciation of this word, see Natalie Wolchover, "Why Can't Germans Say 'Squirrel'?" NBC, March 8, 2012, https://www.nbcnews.com/id/wbna46669535#.

62 **the Parsley Massacre:** The Dominican "r" sound here is what linguists call a *flapped "r,"* a bit reminiscent of the "d"-like sound Americans make when they say the "t" in *water*. Examples of the pronunciation difference can be heard at https://languagelog.ldc.upenn.edu/nll/?p=19987. For a detailed account of the massacre, and the history of conflict between Haiti and the Dominican Republic, a great source is

Michelle Wucker, *Why the Cocks Fight: Dominicans, Haitians, and the Struggle for Hispaniola* (Hill and Wang, 1999).

63 **Jewish/Yiddish background:** The substitution of "s" for "z" as a Jewish ethnic marker was discussed in Rebecca Knack, "Ethnic Boundaries in Linguistic Variation," in *New Ways of Analyzing Sound Change*, ed. Penelope Eckert (Academic, 1991): 251–72.

64 **This social categorizing:** Recent research in evolutionary psychology suggests that accent variation might have developed to serve a "recurrent and informative feature of ancestral environments," p. 48 in David Pietraszewski and Alex Schwartz, "Evidence That Accent Is a Dimension of Social Categorization, Not a Byproduct of Perceptual Salience, Familiarity, or Ease-of-Processing," *Evolution and Human Behavior* 35, no. 1 (2014): 43–50, https://doi.org/10.1016/j.evolhumbehav.2013.09.006.

64 **linguist Jack Chambers:** As mentioned in his chapter "Studying Language Variation: An Informal Epistemology," in *The Handbook of Language Variation and Change*, ed. J. K. Chambers, Peter Trudgill, and Natalie Schilling-Estes (Blackwell, 2002), 3–14.

SOUND BITE: HATE *MOIST*? JOIN THE CLUB.

68 **substantial reader backlash:** Emily Johnson, "Stop Getting Mad at Me for Using the Word 'Moist,'" *Epicurious*, June 21, 2017, https://www.epicurious.com/expert-advice/stop-getting-mad-at-me-for-using-the-word-moist-article.

68 ***moist* was borrowed:** "Moist, Adj. and N.," *OED Online*, Oxford University Press, September 2022, https://doi.org/10.1093/OED/2346822180.

70 **disdain for *moist*:** Paul H. Thibodeau, "A Moist Crevice for Word Aversion: In Semantics Not Sounds," *PLOS One* 11, no. 4 (2016), https://doi.org/10.1371/journal.pone.0153686.

72 **isolated speech sounds:** David M. Sidhu and Penny M. Pexman, "Five Mechanisms of Sound Symbolic Association," *Psychonomic Bulletin and Review* 25 (2018): 1619–43, https://doi.org/10.3758/s13423-017-1361-1.

73 **sound-meaning correspondence:** Damián E. Blasi, Søren Wich-

mann, Harald Hammarström, et al., "Sound-Meaning Association Biases Evidenced across Thousands of Languages," *Proceedings of the National Academy of Sciences of the United States of America* 113, no. 39 (2016): 10818–23, https://doi.org/10.1073/pnas.1605782113.

75 **"sexy men saying 'moist'":** "These Sexy Men Make the Worst Word Sound Hot," *People*, 2013, https://www.youtube.com/watch?v=HrLE4RJuUgg.

CHAPTER 3: LINGUISTIC (R)-EVOLUTIONARY

78 **some type of "r" sound:** As estimated in James Scobbie, "(R) as a Variable," in *Encyclopedia of Language & Linguistics*, 2nd ed., ed. Keith Brown (Elsevier, 2006): 337–44, https://doi.org/10.1016/B0-08-044854-2/04711-8.

81 **most modern English varieties:** Phoneticians Peter Ladefoged and Ian Maddieson suggest trilled "r" as the prototypical "r" sound in their 1995 book *The Sounds of the World's Languages* (Wiley-Blackwell, 1995).

82 **Indo-European-derived languages:** Though this is not without substantial debate in historical linguistic circles. See the following works if you are interested in a (fairly technical) discussion of the various kinds of evidence for different "r" types in Indo-European languages: J. C. Catford, "On Rs, Rhotacism and Paleophony," *Journal of the International Phonetic Association* 31, no. 2 (2001): 171–85, https://www.jstor.org/stable/44645159, or Jeffrey Wollock, "Views on the Decline of Apical R in Europe: Historical Study," *Folia Linguistica Historica* 16, no. 2 (1982): 185–238, https://doi.org/10.1515/flih.1982.3.2.185.

82 **tap of the tongue:** The loss of the classic trill has been noted by a number of linguists studying "r" sounds in Scottish English, starting with sociolinguist Suzanne Romaine in 1978. See Suzanne Romaine, "Postvocalic /r/ in Scottish English: Sound Change in Progress?," in *Sociolinguistic Patterns in British English*, ed. P. Trudgill (Edward Arnold, 1979), 145–57.

85 **"r" sounds got dropped:** As discussed by linguist April McMahon in her work exploring the history of "r" in English and Scots: April McMahon, "On the Use of the Past to Explain the Present: The History of /r/ in English and Scots," in *English Historical Linguistics 1994*,

ed. Derek Britton (John Benjamins Publishing Company, 1996), 73–89.

86 **"R . . . is sounded firme"**: Ben Jonson, *The English Grammar, Made by Ben Jonson for the Benefit of All Strangers Out of His Observation of the English Language Now Spoken and in Use* (Richard Bishop, 1640).

86 **R "is often too feebly sounded"**: John Walker, *A Critical Pronouncing Dictionary* (G. G. J. & J. Robinson, 1791).

87 **famed as a pirates' nest**: If you are interested in a deeper dive into the world of pirates than you get once a year on Talk Like a Pirate Day, a fascinating read is Mark Hanna's *Pirate Nests and the Rise of the British Empire, 1570–1740* (University of North Carolina Press, 2015).

90 **"vergin, virgin and vurgin"**: This charming example comes to you by way of Roger Lass as cited in his chapter "Phonology and Morphology" in *A History of the English Language*, ed. Richard Hogg and David Denison (Cambridge University Press, 2006), 43–108.

92 **vowel becoming *rhotacized***: Exactly why "r" affects the preceding vowel in this way has been widely explored, but it is quite technical in terms of phonetic and phonological background; for example, see Raymond Hickey's *Vowels Before /r/ in the History of English* in *Contact, Variation, and Change in the History of English*, ed. Simone E. Pfenninger et al. (John Benjamins Publishing Company, 2014), 95–110.

97 **among the Scots Irish**: The Scots had moved from Scotland to Ulster in the North of Ireland in the 1600s, where they had little economic or political power. The New World offered much greater opportunity.

CHAPTER 4: THE DIVIDED TONGUE OF A DIVIDED NATION

99 **"England and America are two"**: Though whether Shaw actually said this is up for debate: https://quoteinvestigator.com/2016/04/03/common/.

100 **"The language of the immediate descendants"**: Written in 1770 by William Eddis: As cited in J. Dillard, "On Leveling and Diversity in the Early Period," in *Toward a Social History of American English*, 51–72 (De Gruyter Mouton, 1985).

102 **we might call "spares"**: More about the origins of Southern American English can be read in *English in the Southern United States*, ed.

Stephen J. Nagle and Sara L. Sande, Studies in English Language (Cambridge University Press, 2003), 6–16.

103 **But aristocratic settlers:** Richard W. Bailey, "American English: Its Origins and History," in *Language in the USA: Themes for the Twenty-First Century*, ed. Edward Finegan and John R. Rickford (Cambridge University Press, 2004), 3–17.

103 **give rise to an American tongue:** A great discussion of the early settler mix in New England, and how it contributed to the dialect that developed there, can be found in Merja Kytö, "The Emergence of American English: Evidence from Seventeenth-Century Records in New England," in *Legacies of Colonial English: Studies in Transported Dialects*, ed. R. Hickey, Studies in English Language (Cambridge University Press, 2005), 121–57.

103 **evidence of such pronunciations:** There are a good number of early writings and transcripts from the New England colonies, where literacy and education were prized. Unfortunately, we have far fewer early documents from the Middle or Southern colonies. A great source to see some of these early spelling variations, which provide a hint of what these colonists sounded like, is Kytö, "The Emergence of American English." Also, see Ann Louise Frisinger Sen, "Dialect Variation in Early American English," *Journal of English Linguistics* 8, no. 1 (1974): 41–46, https://doi.org/10.1177/007542427400800105.

107 **distinct cultural hearths:** Gleb V. Aleksandrov, "A Civil Body Politick: Governance, Community, and Accountability in Early New England," *Frontiers in Political Science* 4 (2022): 804673, https://doi.org/10.3389/fpos.2022.804673.

109 **"hit" instead of "it":** "Hit" is the older form, dating back to Old English, until "h" dropping in English became prevalent. Scots preserved this original "h" initial form much longer than Southern British varieties.

109 **The Scots gave us:** For more on Scots Irish influence, particularly on Pennsylvania and Pittsburgh speech, a great source is Barbara Johnstone, Daniel Baumgardt, Maeve Eberhardt, and Scott Kiesling, *Pittsburgh Speech and Pittsburghese* (De Gruyter, 2015).

110 **this mix is responsible:** These examples, along with a great discussion of the influence of German on English, can be found in Michael Putnam and Joseph Salmons, "Multilingualism in the Midwest: How

German Has Shaped (and Still Shapes) the Midwest," *Middle West Review* 1, no. 2 (2015): 29–52, https://doi.org/10.1353/mwr.2015.0008.

111 **The Germans too came:** As the 1790 census did not specifically ask for information on nationality, estimates of background of the foreign-born population have been made mainly using surname data, making it a very inexact science. For more on these difficulties and some updated estimates of the ethnic makeup of those in the United States at the time of the 1790 census, see Forrest McDonald and Ellen Shapiro McDonald, "The Ethnic Origins of the American People, 1790," *The William and Mary Quarterly* 37, no. 2 (1980): 181–99, https://doi.org/10.2307/1919495.

111 **the *three-generation pattern*:** For research on how this has played out with Spanish in the past several decades, see Jens Manuel Krogstad, "Rise in English Proficiency among U.S. Hispanics Is Driven by the Young," Pew Research Center, April 20, 2016, https://www.pewresearch.org/short-reads/2016/04/20/rise-in-english-proficiency-among-u-s-hispanics-is-driven-by-the-young/.

112 **the colonists "generally talk good English":** For more detailed discussion, see Paul Longmore's wonderful chapter "'Good English without Idiom or Tone'—The Colonial Origins of American Speech," appearing in *The Journal of Interdisciplinary History* 37, no. 4 (2007): 513–42. As well, the quotes from Jones cited in this chapter are drawn from Longmore's work.

113 **this type of linguistic reworking:** As discussed in Longmore, "'Good English without Idiom or Tone.'"

114 **Southern colonies had their own thing:** For more on the different cultures and rivalries among the colonies, David Hockett Fischers's *Albion's Seed* is a great source. David Hackett Fischer, *Albion's Seed: Four British Folkways in America* (Oxford University Press, 1989).

115 **The plantation culture:** Edgar Schneider, "The Cycle in Hindsight: The Emergence of American English," in *Postcolonial English*, 251–308 (Cambridge University Press, 2007), https://doi.org/10.1017/CBO9780511618901.008.

115 **This pre-Revolutionary South:** Much of this movement was inspired by the increasing number of enslaved people brought in to do the backbreaking work required to grow sugarcane compared to tobacco, pushing out many White laborers.

115 co-opt African American speech patterns: For more discussion of this tendency and parodies of American regional speech from that era, see Gavin Jones, "American English Dialects," in *A Companion to the History of the English Language*, ed. H. Momma and M. Matto (Wiley, 2008), https://doi.org/10.1002/9781444302851.ch27.

116 the development of "r" dropping: As discussed by linguist Crawford Feagin in "The African Contribution to Southern States English," in *Language Variety in the South Revisited*, ed. Cynthia Bernstein, Thomas Nunnally, and Robin Sabino (University of Alabama Press, 1997), 123–39.

117 linguistic atlas data: Based on the *Linguistic Atlas of the Gulf States*, ed. Lee Pederson, Susan L. McDaniel, and Carol M. Adams (University of Georgia Press, 1986–1993).

118 preserving nineteenth-century Southern English: Michael Montgomery and Cecil Ataide Melo, "The Phonology of the Lost Cause: The English of the Confederados in Brazil," *English World-Wide* 11, no. 2 (1990): 195–216, https://doi.org/10.1075/eww.11.2.03mon.

119 codify American speech forms: Jones, "American English Dialects."

119 exists "proper" English: For more background on Webster and his sociopolitical linguistic agenda, see J. C. Kendall, *The Forgotten Founding Father: Noah Webster's Obsession and the Creation of an American Culture* (Berkley Publishing Group, 2012).

122 "moun-TEN" pronunciation: Another earlier study also investigated this feature; see David Eddington and Matthew Savage, "Where Are the Moun[ʔə]ns in Utah?" *American Speech* 87, no. 3 (2012): 336–49, https://doi.org/10.1215/00031283-1958345.

123 blame it on vowel shifts: For more on our melky habits, see Jack Chambers and Erin Hall, "The Melky Way: Lexicalized /I/-Lowering in Toronto," *Toronto Working Papers in Linguistics* 40, no. 1 (2018).

125 baby boomers and Generation X: "An Introduction to Language Change at the Intersection of Movement, Economy, and Orientation," ed. Joseph A. Stanley, Margaret E. L. Renwick, and Monica Nesbitt, *Publications of the American Dialect Society* 109 (2024).

126 experienced explosive corporate growth: Robin Dodsworth and Mary Kohn, "Urban Rejection of the Vernacular: The SVS Undone," *Language Variation and Change* 24, no. 2 (2012): 221–45, doi:10.1017/S0954394512000105.

127 **shifted away from accents:** Monica Nesbitt, "The Rise and Fall of the Northern Cities Shift: Social and Linguistic Reorganization of *TRAP* in Twentieth-Century Lansing, Michigan," *American Speech* 96, no. 3 (2021): 332–70, https://doi.org/10.1215/00031283-8791754.

127 **altered their sense of rootedness:** The idea of rootedness as being impactful on speech choices has been the topic of much of linguist Paul Reed's work on Appalachian English (see, for example, Paul E. Reed, "Sounding Appalachian: /ai/ Monophthongization, Rising Pitch Accents, and Rootedness," PhD diss., University of South Carolina, 2016).

129 **Upper Midwestern tendency:** If you are not familiar with this pronunciation, you can find a great discussion as well as sound clips at https://wep.csumc.wisc.edu/a-bag-of-bagels/.

130 **preliminary research suggests:** The study of vowels and politics has a fairly short history, with much of it engendered by none other than the very wise and prescient Dr. William Labov in his 2012 book, *Dialect Diversity in America: The Politics of Language Change* (University of Virginia Press). If you are interested in an overview of work done on language and politics from a sociolinguistics perspective, see Lauren Hall-Lew and Sarah van Eyndhoven, "Linguistic Variation and Political Identity," in *Dimensions of Linguistic Variation*, ed. Christopher Cieri, Lauren Hall-Lew, Katie Drager, and Malcah Yaeger-Dror (Oxford University Press, 2025). For more specific studies, see Natalie Schrimpf, "Politics and Dialect Variation: A Sociophonetic Analysis of the Southern Vowel Shift in Middle TN," *Linguistic Society of America Annual Meeting Extended Abstracts* 4 (2013).

SOUND BITE: A LOST COLONY AND A LOST LANGUAGE

132 **the ship's captain refused:** It is not entirely clear what really transpired between White and the captain of the ship and whether White had agreed with or been involved in the change of plan to any degree.

134 **the pivotal connection:** Much of what I've written here about the ancestry and heritage of the Lumbee comes from the work of Lumbee member and Emory University professor and historian Melinda Maylor Lowery. For more on the Lumbee and their history, see her book

The Lumbee Indians: An American Struggle (University of North Carolina Press, 2018).

134 **historical account of the Lost Colony:** Hamilton McMillan, *Sir Walter Raleigh's Lost Colony: An Historical Sketch of the Attempts of Sir Walter Raleigh to Establish a Colony in Virginia, with the Traditions of an Indian Tribe in North Carolina. Indicating the Fate of the Colony of Englishmen Left on Roanoke Island in 1587* (Advance Presses, 1888).

135 **Tree-ring data:** David W. Stahle, Malcolm K. Cleaveland, Dennis B. Blanton, and Matthew D. Therrel, "The Lost Colony and Jamestown Droughts," *Science* 280, no. 5363 (1998): 564–67, https://doi.org/10.1126/science.280.5363.564.

135 **In his journal:** John Lawson, *A New Voyage to Carolina: Containing the Exact Description and Natural History of That Country; Together with the Present State Thereof; and a Journal of a Thousand Miles, Travel'd Thro' Several Nations of Indians; Giving a Particular Account of Their Customs, Manners, Etc.* (1709).

136 **rapid adaptation to their new reality:** This section draws from the great discussion of the linguistic history of the Lumbee tribe in Clare Danneberg, "The Roots of Lumbee Language," *Publication of the American Dialect Society* 87, no. 1 (2002): 9–35.

137 **lack of a specific heritage language:** As of this writing, the fight for official federal acknowledgment is not yet over. In early 2025, President Trump ordered the secretary of the interior to develop a plan to grant the Lumbee full recognition, but, despite a ninety-day deadline, that requested plan had yet to be delivered. Many other tribes contest Lumbee recognition, feeling that such a plan would skirt the established process and criteria set forth by the Office of Federal Acknowledgment to which they were subject. For more on the struggle to be recognized and the construction of Lumbee ethnic identity, see Natalie Schilling-Estes, "Constructing Ethnicity in Interaction," *Journal of Sociolinguistics* 8 (2004): 163–95, https://doi.org/10.1111/j.1467-9841.2004.00257.x. For more on the current complexities behind this recognition, including the concerns voiced by other tribal nations, see Laken Kincaid, "Trump's Push for Lumbee Recognition Causes Concern among Other Native Tribes," NBC News, May 26, 2025, https://www.nbcnews.com/politics/trump-administration/trumps-push-lumbee-recognition-causes-concern-native-tribes-rcna208174.

137 **the Lumbee absolutely sound:** Walt Wolfram and Clare Dannenberg, "Dialect Identity in a Tri-Ethnic Context: The Case of Lumbee American Indian English," *English World-Wide* 20, no. 2 (1999): 179–216.

137 **"exactly who we are":** As cited in Walt Wolfram, "From the Brickhouse to the Swamp," *American Language Review* (2001): 34–38.

138 **this dialect combines relic forms:** A very accessible discussion of Lumbee English features and their origins can be found in Walt Wolfram, Clare Dannenberg, Stanley Knick, and Linda Oxendine, *Fine in the World: Lumbee Language in Time and Place* (University of North Carolina Press, 2002). There's also a short section on Lumbee English in Walt Wolfram and Natalie Schilling's book *American English: Dialects and Variation* (Wiley-Blackwell, 2016) that is quite accessible.

138 **twists on traditional Southern pronunciations:** See, for example Natalie Schilling-Estes, "Investigating Intra-Ethnic Differentiation: /ay/ in Lumbee Native American English," *Language Variation and Change* 12, no. 2 (2001): 141–74, https://doi.org/10.1017/S0954394500122021.

138 **dropping of final consonants:** As discussed in Benjamin Torbert, "Tracing Native American Language History through Consonant Cluster Reduction: The Case of Lumbee English," *American Speech* 76, no. 4 (2001): 361–87.

139 **two-consonant pattern:** For more discussion of such transfer effects, see Walt Wolfram, "Dynamic Dimensions of Language Influence: The Case of American Indian English," in *Language: Social Psychological Perspectives: Selected Papers from the First International Conference on Social Psychology and Language*, ed. Howard Giles, Peter W. Robinson, and Philip M. Smith (Pergamon Press, 1980), 377–88; and Walt Wolfram, Rebecca Childs, and Benjamin Torbert, "Tracing English Dialect History Through Consonant Cluster Reduction: Comparative Evidence from Isolated Dialects," *Journal of Southern Linguistics* 24 (2000): 17–40, https://doi.org/10.1215/00031283-76-4-361.

CHAPTER 5: CLASSING IT UP

142 **in the day of Cicero:** Edgar Sturtevant, *The Pronunciation of Greek and Latin* (University of Chicago Press, 1920).

142 aitches in all the wrong places: Elizabeth Vandiver, "Sound Patterns in Catullus 84," *The Classical Journal* 85, no. 4 (1990): 337–40, https://www.jstor.org/stable/3297680.

145 "Torono" or "Sacramenno": For example, hear from actress Nina Dobrev on "Toronto" as the outsider pronunciation of the city name: https://www.tiktok.com/@podcrushed/video/7259449915535871274?lang=en.

146 a natural linguistic process: For more about this reduction process and its regional distribution, phonetician John Wells has a great blog about it: http://phonetic-blog.blogspot.com/2011/11/winter-and-winner.html.

146 dominant one we hear: This is something referred to as the *obligatory contour principle* (OCP)—when two consonants are adjacent to each other, the more similar they are in how they are articulated, the more likely one will be deleted. If you are dying for more linguistic detail, see Gregory Guy and Charles Boberg, "Inherent Variability and the Obligatory Contour Principle," *Language Variation and Change* 9 (1997): 149–64. Or see William Raymond, Robin Dautricourt, and Elizabeth Hume, "Word-Internal /t,d/ Deletion in Spontaneous Speech: Modeling the Effects of Extra-Linguistic, Lexical, and Phonological Factors," *Language Variation and Change* 18, no. 1 (2006): 55–97.

148 follow a regular pattern: Mark A. Pitt, Laura Dilley, and Michael Tat, "Exploring the Role of Exposure Frequency in Recognizing Pronunciation Variants," *Journal of Phonetics* 39, no. 3 (2011): 304–11, https://doi.org/10.1016/j.wocn.2010.07.004.

148 to decrease deletion rates: Raymond, Dautricourt, and Hume, "Word-Internal /t,d/ Deletion in Spontaneous Speech."

150 The impetus for what: For more on the growth and influence of London more generally during this period, see Peter Borsay, "London, 1660–1800: A Distinctive Culture?," *Proceedings of the British Academy* 107 (2001): 167–84.

151 need for a professional class: A great chapter that surveys these changes from a rank-based to class-based system is Paul Kerswill, "Language and Social Class," in *English Language*, ed. Jonathan Culpeper, Francis Katamba, Paul Kerswill, et al. (Palgrave Macmillan, 2009), 358–72.

151 nineteenth-century shipping magnate: The book *Talking Proper: The Rise of Accent as Social Symbol* by Lynda Mugglestone (Oxford

University Press, 2003) is an invaluable resource to the chapter in elucidating the way sounds became markers of class during the eighteenth and nineteenth centuries. This particular anecdote is discussed in chapter 2, "Accent as Social Symbol."

153 **desire for acceptance and respect**: Thomas Paul Bonfiglio, *Race and the Rise of Standard American* (De Gruyter Mouton, 2002).

153 **in New Zealand English**: The result discussed here is a somewhat simplified takeaway of the complex interactions reported between class and degree of merger found in the speaker's vowels as well as in listeners' own speech, but the gist is that listeners seem to have expectations based on their daily experience with linguistic variation due to social characteristics (like a speaker's class and age) that affect how they hear the speech of those around them. The study itself is Jennifer Hay, Paul Warren, and Katie Drager, "Factors Influencing Speech Perception in the Context of a Merger-in-Progress," *Journal of Phonetics* 34 (2006): 458–84, https://doi.org/10.1016/j.wocn.2005.10.001.

155 **more Canadian vowels**: Nancy Niedzielski, "The Effect of Social Information on the Perception of Sociolinguistic Variables," *Journal of Language and Social Psychology* 18, no. 1 (1999): 62–85, https://doi.org/10.1177/0261927X99018001005.

155 **class affects linguistic perception**: Katie Drager, "The Influence of Social Characteristics on Speech Perception," MA thesis, University of Canterbury, 2005.

157 **listeners assessed deviations**: Michael Kraus, Brittany Torrez, Jun Won Park, and Fariba Ghayebi, "Evidence for the Reproduction of Social Class in Brief Speech," *Proceedings of the National Academy of Sciences of the United States of America* 116, no. 46 (2019): 22998–3003, https://doi.org/10.1073/pnas.1900500116.

158 **nonstandard-accented speakers**: Jairo Fuertes, William Gottdiener, Helena Martin, et al., "A Meta-Analysis of the Effects of Speakers' Accents on Interpersonal Evaluations," *European Journal of Social Psychology* 42 (2012): 120–33, http://dx.doi.org/10.1002/ejsp.862.

158 **A recent project**: The work discussed here is part of the Accent Bias in Britain project, which takes a multipronged approach to looking at language attitudes and accent bias in Britain. Visit their website (https://accentbiasbritain.org) to learn more about the project and the results of their extensive work.

159 **judgments about professional suitability:** Erez Levon, Devyani Sharma, Dominic Watt, et al., "Accent Bias and Perceptions of Professional Competence in England," *Journal of English Linguistics* 49, no. 4 (2021): 355–88, http://dx.doi.org/10.1177/00754242211046316.

161 **positive or negative social associations:** The ideas discussed here are developed more fully, though with quite a bit more complexity, in the important work of Asif Agha, "The Social Life of Cultural Value," *Language and Communication* 23, no. 3–4 (2003): 231–73, https://doi.org/10.1016/S0271-5309(03)00012-0; and Michael Silverstein, "Indexical Order and the Dialectics of Sociolinguistic Life," *Language and Communication* 23, no. 3–4 (2003): 193–229, doi:10.1016/S0271-5309(03)00013-2.

163 **dialect of an "alien" language:** Betsy Sneller and Gareth Roberts, "Why Some Behaviors Spread While Others Don't: A Laboratory Simulation of Dialect Contact," *Cognition* 170 (2018): 298–311, https://doi.org/10.1016/J.COGNITION.2017.10.014.

164 **"educated" speech forms:** Read more about these newer varieties and what makes them tick in Stefan Marzo and Stefan Grodelaers, "Why Does the Shtyle Spread? Street Prestige Boosts the Diffusion of Urban Vernacular Features," *Language in Society* 52, no. 2 (2023): 295–320, https://doi.org/10.1017/S0047404521001202.

165 **lower- instead of middle-class:** Mark Stewart, Ellen Bouchard Ryan, and Howard Giles, "Accent and Social Class Effects on Status and Solidarity Evaluations," *Personality and Social Psychology Bulletin* 11, no. 1 (1985): 98–105, https://doi.org/10.1177/0146167285111009.

165 **more material possessions:** Kristin Shutts, Elizabeth L. Brey, Leah A. Dornbusch, et al., "Children Use Wealth Cues to Evaluate Others," *PLOS One* 11, no. 3 (2016): e0149360, https://doi.org/10.1371/journal.pone.0149360.

166 **even one nonstandard pronunciation:** For more discussion of this issue of the trade-off and problems with class-based accentism, see this great piece for the Conversation by Professor Amanda Cole: https://theconversation.com/posh-spice-sounds-posher-but-changing-your-working-class-accent-isnt-a-ticket-out-of-discrimination-189401.

168 **play for leadership:** Sean R. Martin, Benjamin D. Innis, and Ray G. Ward, "Social Class, Leaders and Leadership: A Critical Review and

Suggestions for Development," *Current Opinion in Psychology* 18 (2017): 49–54, https://doi.org/10.1016/j.copsyc.2017.08.001.

169 **mitigating accent bias:** A great summary of several studies on accent bias as well as intervention strategies can be found at https://accentbiasbritain.org/wp-content/uploads/2020/03/Accent-Bias-Britain-Report-2020.pdf.

CHAPTER 6: WHAT COLOR IS YOUR ACCENT?

174 **hundreds of thousands of:** During the colonial period, estimates of the Black population range from 300,000 to almost 500,000. By the 1790 census, the number of African Americans living in the United States was around 750,000. For more discussion, see Mary B. Zeigler, "Migration and Motivation in the Development of African American Vernacular English," in *A Companion to the History of the English Language*, ed. Haruko Momma and Michael Matto (John Wiley & Sons, 2008), 509–20. For a breakdown of population by various decades see Guy Bailey, "The Relationship Between African American and White Vernaculars in the American South: A Sociocultural History and Some Phonological Evidence," in *Sociocultural and Historical Contexts of African American English*, ed. Sonja Lanehart (John Benjamins Publishing Company, 53–92).

174 **a deficient form of English:** This view that AAE is the result of deficient learning is also known as the *pre-linguistic deficit perspective*, as discussed in Mary Zeigler, "Migration and Motivation in the Development of African American Vernacular English," 509–20.

177 **were considered uncouth:** For instance, see complaints about those vulgar contractions in John Witherspoon and John Rodgers, *The Works of the Rev. John Witherspoon . . . : to Which Is Prefixed an Account of the Author's Life, in a Sermon Occasioned by His Death* (Printed and published by William W. Woodward, 1800/1801).

177 **Some linguists put their money:** For more on the history of *ain't*, see Martin Stevens, "The Derivation of 'Ain't,' *American Speech* 29, no. 3 (1954): 196–201, https://doi.org/10.2307/454240.

178 **"and yet give no thousand crowns":** William Shakespeare, *As You*

Like It, ed. Barbara A. Mowat and Paul Werstine (Simon & Schuster, 2009): 1.1.85–86.

178 **Chaucer's impressive negation rate:** Iyeiri Yoko, "Multiple Negation in Early Modern English," *Bulletin des anglicistes médiévistes* 47 (1995): 69–86.

180 **"Yow loueris axe":** As cited in "ask (*v.*)," *The Oxford English Dictionary*, online edition, June 2025, https://doi.org/10.1093/OED/1077422768.

181 **marker of class and region:** See further discussion of metathesis and *ask* as well as *wasp* in Southern and African American speech in Erik R. Thomas, "Phonological and Phonetic Characteristics of African American Vernacular English," *Language and Linguistics Compass* 1 (2007): 450–75, http://dx.doi.org/10.1111/j.1749-818X.2007.00029.x.

182 **Many of the features:** For an accessible and somewhat deeper overview of the various theories about the origins of AAE discussed in this chapter, see chapter 2 of Sonja Lanehart's *Language in African American Communities* (Routledge, 2023), 18–40.

186 **a striking similarity:** As discussed in Ian Hancock, "A Provisional Comparison of the English-Based Atlantic Creoles," *African Language Review* 8 (1970): 7–72.

186 **early pidgins formed:** Whether shared creole features were inherited from a single source or developed in each creole separately based on similar shared input and contact situations is a debated topic; for example, see various views in Michael Montgomery, ed., *The Crucible of Carolina: Essays in the Development of Gullah Language and Culture* (University of Georgia Press, 1994).

187 **new creole developing:** For a deeper discussion of the development of AAE via contact with colonial varieties, see Salikoko S. Mufwene, "The Emergence of African American English: Monogenetic or Polygenetic? With or Without 'Decreolization'? Under How Much Substrate Influence?," in *The Oxford Handbook of African American Language*, ed. Jennifer Bloomquist, Lisa J. Green, and Sonja L. Lanehart (Oxford University Press, 2015), 57–84.

187 **pattern of consonant deletion:** The exact constraints on these patterns of deletion are much more complex than I am able to go into here, as they require some basic knowledge of linguistic principles and distributions. The deletion pattern found for speakers with potential

substrate influence like Lumbee and African American English involves particular unique conditions (like being monomorphemic and bimorphemic and prevocalic and prepausal environments), which set them apart from the dominant Anglo pattern and provide more support for an early language-transfer explanation.

188 **influx of African influence:** See, for example, Walt Wolfram, "Reexamining the Development of African American English: Evidence from Isolated Communities," *Language* 79, no. 2 (2003): 282–316; and Becky Childs and Christine Mallinson, "African American English in Appalachia: Dialect Accommodation and Substrate Influence," *English World-Wide* 25 (2004): 27–50.

188 **boot on their backs:** For a fascinating and in-depth discussion of the importance of this era to the development of English vernaculars in the South, see Guy Bailey, "The Relationship between African American and White Vernaculars in the American South: A Sociocultural History and Some Phonological Evidence," in *Sociocultural and Historical Contexts of African American English*, ed. Sonja Lanehart (John Benjamins Publishing Company, 53–92).

189 **this bidirectional influence:** As discussed in G. Jones, "American English Dialects," in *A Companion to the History of the English Language*, ed. Haruko Momma and Michael Matto (Wiley-Blackwell, 2008), 274-80; and in Edgar Schneider, *American Earlier Black English: Morphological and Syntactic Variables* (University of Alabama Press, 1989).

190 **over 80 percent:** A much fuller and accessible discussion of both origins and contemporary factors in the development of AAE can be found in Guy Bailey, "The History of African-American Vernacular English," *Oxford Research Encyclopedia of Linguistics* (Oxford University Press, 2022).

191 **having "ahnts" (for *aunts*):** The transport of Southern features to the North with the Great Migration, as well as the "ahnt" for *aunt* path, is discussed in Thomas, "Phonological and Phonetic Characteristics of African American Vernacular English."

192 **the Northern Cities Shift:** For an interesting analysis of the interaction between the Great Migration and White flight, see https://lboustan.scholar.princeton.edu/sites/g/files/toruqf4146/files/lboustan/files/research02_whiteflight.pdf.

193 older African Americans: Walt Wolfram and Erik Thomas, *Development of African American English* (John Wiley & Sons, 2008).

193 "intensifying the ethnolinguistic divide": Walt Wolfram and Erik Thomas, "Beyond Hyde County: The Past and Present Development of AAVE," in *Development of African American English* (John Wiley & Sons, 2008).

193 African American Standard English (AASE): Arthur K. Spears, "African American Standard English," in *The Oxford Handbook of African American Language*, ed. Jennifer Bloomquist, Lisa J. Green, and Sonja L. Lanehart (Oxford University Press, 2015), 786–99.

194 exemplified in the speech: A fascinating study that compares Martin Luther King Jr.'s use of AAE features over a series of different contexts and audiences is Walt Wolfram, Caroline Myrick, Jon Forrest, and Michael J. Fox, "The Significance of Linguistic Variation in the Speeches of Rev. Dr. Martin Luther King Jr.," *American Speech* 91, no. 3 (2016): 269–300.

194 cadences, pausing, vowels, and rhythm: For more on Obama's stylistic code-switching, see Geneva Smitherman and H. Samy Alim's chapter 1 of *Articulate While Black: Barack Obama, Language, and Race in the U.S.* (Oxford University Press, 2012), 1–30.

194 the Southern "ay" vowel: Jen Hay, Stefanie Jannedy, and Norma C. Mendoza-Denton, "Oprah and /ay/: Lexical Frequency, Referee Design, and Style," in *The Routledge Sociolinguistic Reader*, ed. Miriam Meyerhoff and Erik Schleef (Routledge, 2010), 53–58.

194 "our view of the African American community": Quote from Spears, "African American Standard English," 788.

195 People have been shown: Wow, we are speedy when it comes to identifying a voice as male or female. If you are interested in learning just how fast, here are a couple of studies you might find interesting: S. P. Whiteside, "Identification of a Speaker's Sex: A Study of Vowels," *Perceptual and Motor Skills* 86, no. 2 (April 1998): 579–84, https://doi.org/10.2466/pms.1998.86.2.579; and Michael J. Owren, Michael Berkowitz, and Jo-Anne Bachorowski, "Listeners Judge Talker Sex More Efficiently from Male than from Female Vowels," *Perception & Psychophysics* 69, no. 6 (2007): 930–41, https://link.springer.com/content/pdf/10.3758/bf03193930.pdf.

195 Racial identification starts: As was the finding of Thomas Purnell,

William Idsardi, and John Baugh, "Perceptual and Phonetic Experiments on American English Dialect Identification," *Journal of Language and Social Psychology* 18, no. 1 (1999): 10–30, https://doi.org/10.1177/0261927X99018001002.

196 **rate AAVE speakers more positively:** For more discussion of these complex feelings about "sounding Black," see Tracey L. Weldon, "Sounding Black," in *Middle-Class African American English* (Cambridge University Press, 2021).

197 **Studies looking at the consequences:** For specific studies that explored the various ways in which sounding Black affects finances, guilt attribution, and perceived criminality, here are some sources. Jason A. Cantone, Leslie N. Martinez, Cynthia Willis-Esqueda, and Taija Miller, "Sounding Guilty: How Accent Bias Affects Juror Judgments of Culpability," *Journal of Ethnicity in Criminal Justice* 17, no. 3 (2019): 228–53; Jeffrey Grogger, "Speech Patterns and Racial Wage Inequality," *Journal of Human Resources* 46, no. 1 (2011): 1–25; Courtney A. Kurinec and Charles A. Weaver III, "Dialect on Trial: Use of African American Vernacular English Influences Juror Appraisals," *Psychology, Crime & Law* 25, no. 8 (2019): 803–28; Rebecca K. Rosen, *What's in a Voice? Effects of Dialect Perception on Activation of Crime Stereotypes* (University of Chicago, 2017).

197 **a heavy AAVE accent:** John R. Rickford and Sharese King, "Language and Linguistics on Trial: Hearing Rachel Jeantel (and Other Vernacular Speakers) in the Courtroom and Beyond," *Language* 92 (2016): 948–88.

197 **make inferences about:** Purnell, Idsardi, and Baugh, "Perceptual and Phonetic Experiments on American English Dialect Identification," 10–30.

198 **when speaking Standard English:** Sharese King, Charlotte Vaughn, and Adam Dunbar, "Dialect on Trial: Raciolinguistic Ideologies in Perceptions of AAVE and MAE Codeswitching." *University of Pennsylvania Working Papers in Linguistics* 28, no. 2 (2022).

198 **participants tend to report:** For instance, Frederick Williams, Jack L. Whitehead, and Leslie Miller, "Relations between Language Attitudes and Teacher Expectancy," *American Educational Research Journal* 9, no. 2 (1972): 263–77, https://doi.org/10.3102/00028312009002263.

198 **Such ideas are what also:** A great discussion of this tendency is found in "A.W.B. Articulate While Black" in H. S. Alim and G.

Smitherman, *Articulate While Black: Barack Obama, Language, and Race in the U.S.* (Oxford University Press 2012).

199 **When teachers come armed:** See, for example, William Labov and Clarence Robins, "A Note on the Relation of Reading Failure to Peer-Group Status in Urban Ghettos," *Teachers College Record* 70 (1969): 395–405.

200 **program designed by linguist Bill Labov:** For more on this program in practice, check out https://www.ling.upenn.edu/~wlabov/PRI/ or https://web.sas.upenn.edu/penn-reading/. See also William Labov and Bettina Baker, "African American Vernacular English and Reading," in *The Oxford Handbook of African American Language*, ed. Jennifer Bloomquist, Lisa J. Green, and Sonja L. Lanehart (Oxford University Press, 2015), 617–36.

CHAPTER 7: STRANGERS WITHIN THE LINGUISTIC GATES

203 **Fueling this myth:** For more on this urban legend, see https://www.bbc.com/culture/article/20141003-the-hidden-messages-in-songs.

204 **recognize foreign-accented speech:** Murray J. Munro, Tracey M. Derwing, and Clifford S. Burgess, "The Detection of Foreign Accent in Backwards Speech," in *Proceedings of the 15th International Congress of Phonetic Sciences*, ed. M. J. Solé, D. Recasens, and J. Romero (Futurgraphic, 2003).

204 **30 milliseconds of speech:** James Emil Flege, "The Detection of French Accent by American Listeners," *Journal of the Acoustical Society of America* 76, no. 3 (1984): 692–707.

204 **We're good at noticing:** In the study mentioned in the previous chapter on the perception of ethnicity from simply hearing the word "hello," the average length of the "hello" stimuli participants heard was 414 milliseconds. For full details on the study, see the discussion of experiment three in: Thomas Purnell, William Idsardi, and John Baugh, "Perceptual and Phonetic Experiments on American English Dialect Identification," *Journal of Language and Social Psychology* 18, no. 1 (1999): 10–30, https://doi.org/10.1177/0261927X99018001002.

206 **a more elastic brain:** This was related to the critical period hypothesis (CPH) first proposed by Wilder Penfield and Lamar Roberts in

Speech and Brain Mechanisms (Princeton University Press, 1959), but refined and propelled to star-theory status by Eric Lenneberg in *Biological Foundations of Language* (John Wiley and Sons, 1967).

206 **somewhere in the middle:** For a discussion of these different viewpoints, see Wendy Baker, Pavel Trofimovich, James E. Flege, et al., "Child-Adult Differences in Second-Language Phonological Learning: The Role of Cross-Language Similarity," *Language and Speech* 51, no. 4 (2008): 317–42, https://doi.org/10.1177/0023830908099068.

206 **both neurological differences:** Andrea Mechelli et al., "Structural Plasticity in the Bilingual Brain," *Nature* 431, no. 757 (October 13, 2004), https://doi.org/10.1038/431757a.

207 **the click sound itself:** For more on clicks (though somewhat technical), see Peter Ladefoged and Anthony Traill, "Clicks and Their Accompaniments," *Journal of Phonetics* 22, no. 1 (1994): 33–64, https://doi.org/10.1016/S0095-4470(19)30266-9.

207 **rarity of the English "th":** Ian Maddieson, "Presence of Uncommon Consonants," in *WALS Online* v2020.4, ed. Matthew Dryer and Martin Haspelmath (2013), https://doi.org/10.5281/zenodo.13950591.

212 **fondness for contracting and deleting:** Though a bit technical, this happens because in stress-timed languages, stressed syllables are said at equal intervals within a sentence, which means that, however many unstressed syllables there are between these stressed ones, they all get crammed into that interval.

213 **prosodic issues may impact intelligibility:** For an early such study, see Janet Anderson-Hsieh, Ruth Johnson, and Kenneth Koehler, "The Relationship between Native Speaker Judgments of Non-Native Pronunciation and Deviance in Segmentals, Prosody, and Syllable Structure," *Language Learning* 42 (1992): 529–55. A more recent study that specifically looked at stress misallocation, finding that it impacted intelligibility, is John Field, "Intelligibility and the Listener: The Role of Lexical Stress," *TESOL Quarterly* 39 (2005): 399–423, http://dx.doi.org/10.2307/3588487. Other studies, though, still point to segmental (i.e., sound) properties as being the biggest hurdle in sounding accented and difficult to understand.

214 **more natively placed stress:** Laura D. Hahn, "Primary Stress and Intelligibility: Research to Motivate the Teaching of Suprasegmentals," *TESOL Quarterly* 38, no. 2 (2004): 201–23.

214 **overexcited and over the top:** From Hartwig Eckert and John Laver, *Menschen und ihre Stimmen: Aspekte der vokalen Kommunikation* (Psychologie Verlags Union, 1994), 145, as cited in Ineke Mennen, "Phonological and Phonetic Influences in Non-Native Intonation," in *Non-Native Prosody: Phonetic Description and Teaching Practice*, ed. Jürgen Trouvain and Ulrike Gut (De Gruyter Mouton, 2007). For more on German versus English pitch, see Matthias Jilka's "Different Manifestations and Perceptions of Foreign Accent in Intonation" in the same text.

214 **use more intonational variation:** For example, see Renee Bezooijen, "The Relative Importance of Pronunciation, Prosody, and Voice Quality for the Attribution of Social Status and Personality Characteristics," *Language Attitudes in the Dutch Language Area*, ed. Roeland van Hout and Uus Knops (De Gruyter, Inc., 1988), 85–103.

215 **heard as less intelligent:** An overview of all the bad juju loaded on those with non-native accents can be found in Agata Gluszek and John F. Dovidio, "The Way They Speak: A Social Psychological Perspective on the Stigma of Nonnative Accents in Communication," *Personality and Social Psychology Review* 14, no. 2 (2010): 214–37, http://dx.doi.org/10.1177/1088868309359288.

215 **foreign accents seem more noticeable:** For more specifics, see Katherine D. Kinzler, Emmanuel Dupoux, and Elizabeth S. Seplke, "The Native Language of Social Cognition," *Proceedings of the National Academy of Sciences of the United States of America* 104 (2007): 12577–80, https://doi.org/10.1073/pnas.0705345104; and Frédérique Girard, Caroline Floccia, and Jeremy Goslin, "Perception and Awareness of Accents in Young Children," *British Journal of Developmental Psychology* 26 (2008): 409–33, https://doi.org/10.1348/026151007X251712.

216 **an evolutionary gift:** A great overview of much of the research on language attitudes discussed in this chapter is provided in Marko Dragojevic, Fabio Fasoli, Jennifer Cramer, and Tamra Rakić, "Toward a Century of Language Attitudes Research: Looking Back and Moving Forward," *Journal of Language and Social Psychology* 40, no. 1 (2021): 60–79.

218 **ratings of status and solidarity:** Marko Dragojevic and Sean Goatley-Soan, "Americans' Attitudes Toward Foreign Accents: Evaluative Hierarchies and Underlying Processes," *Journal of Multilingual and Multicultural Development* 43, no. 2 (2022): 167–81.

219 a well-known experiment from the 1990s: Donald Rubin, "Non-Language Factors Affecting Undergraduates' Judgments of Nonnative English-Speaking Teaching Assistants," *Research in Higher Education* 33 (1992): 511–31.

220 seeing photos of White versus Asian faces: For more discussion of this topic (and different views of why accent hallucination happens), two great papers are Molly Babel and Jamie Russell, "Expectations and Speech Intelligibility," *Journal of the Acoustical Society of America* 137, no. 5 (2015): 2823–33; and Ethan Kutlu, "Now You See Me, Now You Mishear Me: Raciolinguistic Accounts of Speech Perception in Different English Varieties," *Journal of Multilingual and Multicultural Development* 44, no. 6 (2020): 511–25, http://dx.doi.org/10.1080/01434632.2020.1835929.

220 high on ethnocentrism scales: James W. Neuliep and Kendall M. Speten-Hansen, "The Influence of Ethnocentrism on Social Perceptions of Nonnative Accents," *Language & Communication* 33, no. 3 (2013): 167–76, http://dx.doi.org/10.1016/j.langcom.2013.05.001.

220 not all foreign accents: For example, see Stephanie Lindemann, "Listening with an Attitude: A Model of Native-Speaker Comprehension of Non-Native Speakers in the United States," *Language in Society* 31, no. 3 (2002): 419–41, http://dx.doi.org/10.1017/S0047404502020286. Extensive discussion of the role of stereotypes and attitudes in evaluating accents can be found in Rosina Lippi-Green's very well-known book *English with an Accent: Language, Ideology and Discrimination* (Routledge, 2012).

221 As a result, incongruent information: For instance, see work by Kevin B. McGowan, "Social Expectation Improves Speech Perception in Noise," *Language and Speech* 58, no. 4 (2015): 502–21, https://doi.org/10.1177/0023830914565191.

221 our social expectations: Though much more complex than described here, linguists ascribe this to social information stored in memory alongside phonetic information in something referred to as *exemplar theory.*

222 how well the listener can understand: For more on this relative relationship, a seminal source is Murray J. Munro and Tracey M. Derwing, "Foreign Accent, Intelligibility and Comprehensibility in the Speech of Second Language Learners," *Language Learning* 45, no. 1 (1995): 73–97, https://doi.org/10.1111/0023-8333.49.S1.8.

223 names that are easier to pronounce: Adam L. Alter and Daniel M. Oppenheimer, "Predicting Short-Term Stock Fluctuations by Using Processing Fluency," *Proceedings of the National Academy of Sciences of the United States of America* 103, no. 24 (2006): 9369–72.

225 distinctive brain activity: This fascinating research is discussed in chapter 3 of Tracey M. Derwing and Murray J. Munro's *Pronunciation Fundamentals: Evidence-Based Perspectives for L2 Teaching and Research* (John Benjamins Publishing Company, 2015).

226 faster speaking rates: As discussed in Derwing and Munro, *Pronunciation Fundamentals*.

227 distinguishing different words: See more on the topic of functional load and how it interacts with pronunciation and intelligibility in Murray J. Munro and Tracey M. Derwing, "The Functional Load Principle in ESL Pronunciation Instruction: An Exploratory Study," *System* (Linköping) 34, no. 4 (2006): 520–31, http://dx.doi.org/10.1016/j.system.2006.09.004.

229 conversation with native: See, for example, Tracey M. Derwing, Ron I. Thomson, and Murray J. Munro, "English Pronunciation and Fluency Development in Mandarin and Slavic Speakers," *System* (Linköping) 34, no. 2 (2006): 183–93, http://dx.doi.org/10.1016/j.system.2006.01.005.

230 attitudes toward accents: For more actionable recommendations within a corporate context, see Regina Kim, Loriann Roberson, Marcello Russo, and Paola Briganti, "Language Diversity, Nonnative Accents, and Their Consequences at the Workplace: Recommendations for Individuals, Teams, and Organizations," *Journal of Applied Behavioral Science* 55, no. 1 (2019): 73–95, https://doi.org/10.1177/0021886318800997.

230 reciting information from someone else: Shiri Lev-Ari and Boaz Keysar, "Why Don't We Believe Non-Native Speakers? The Influence of Accent on Credibility," *Journal of Experimental Social Psychology* 46, no. 6 (2010): 1093–96, https://doi.org/10.1016/j.jesp.2010.05.025.

230 what accent to expect: Charlotte R. Vaughn, "Expectations about the Source of a Speaker's Accent Affect Accent Adaptation," *Journal of the Acoustical Society of America* 145, no. 5 (2019): 3218–32.

231 listeners showed improvement: Ann R. Bradlow and Tessa Bent,

"Perceptual Adaptation to Non-Native Speech," *Cognition* 106, no. 2 (2008): 707–29, https://doi.org/10.1016/j.cognition.2007.04.005.

SOUND BITE: WHAT MAKES A LANGUAGE BEAUTIFUL?

233 **"the voice of seduction":** For instance, check out https://www.cnn.com/travel/article/sexy-accents/index.html and https://www.esquire.com/entertainment/g1625/sexiest-accents/.

235 ***imposed norm hypothesis*:** As used here, "imposed norm" is a cover for two slightly different sides of the same coin, the imposed norm and social connotations hypotheses. See Howard Giles, Richard Bourhis, and Ann Davies, "Prestige Speech Styles: The Imposed Norm and Inherent Value Hypotheses," *Language and Society: Anthropological Issues*, ed. William C. McCormack and Stephen A. Wurm (De Gruyter Mouton, 1979), 589–96; and Peter Trudgill and Howard Giles, "Sociolinguistics and Linguistic Value Judgements: Correctness, Adequacy, and Aesthetics," *Functional Studies in Language and Literature Studies*, ed. F. Coppieters and D. L. Goyvaerts (Story-Scientia 1978), 167–80.

236 **some inherent linguistic quality:** Andrey Anikin, Nikolay Aseyev, and Niklas Erben Johansson, "Do Some Languages Sound More Beautiful Than Others?" *Proceedings of the National Academy of Sciences of the United States of America* 120, no. 17 (2025): e2218367120, https://doi.org/10.1073/pnas.2218367120.

238 **the combo *cellar door*:** If you think I am overstating our long-standing attraction to *cellar door*, check out more on the topic in Grant Barrett's fun article, "Cellar Door," *The New York Times*, February 11, 2010, https://www.nytimes.com/2010/02/14/magazine/14FOB-onlanguage-t.html.

238 **the more sonorant sounds:** Arthur M. Jacobs, "Quantifying the Beauty of Words: A Neurocognitive Poetics Perspective," *Frontiers in Human Neuroscience* 11 (2017): 622, https://doi.org/10.3389/fnhum.2017.00622.

239 **popping and hissing consonants:** Arash Aryani, Markus Conrad, David Schmidtke, and Arthur Jacobs, "Why 'Piss' Is Ruder Than 'Pee'? The Role of Sound in Affective Meaning Making," *PLOS One* 13, no. 6 (2018): e0198430, https://doi.org/10.1371/journal.pone.0198430.

240 "phonetic chill factor": As discussed in Vita V. Kogan and Susanne M. Reiterer, "Eros, Beauty, and Phon-Aesthetic Judgements of Language Sound. We Like It Flat and Fast, but Not Melodious. Comparing Phonetic and Acoustic Features of 16 European Languages," *Frontiers in Human Neuroscience* (2021), https://doi.org/10.3389/fnhum.2021.578594.

240 something perceived more positively: Also discussed in Kogan and Reiterer, "Eros, Beauty, and Phon-Aesthetic Judgements of Language Sound."

240 This preference might explain: Bernd Brunner, "The Sound of Difference. Why We Find Some Languages More Beautiful Than Others," *The Smart Set*, 2014, https://www.thesmartset.com/article03041401/.

240 the main factors driving: Susanne M. Reiterer, Vita Kogan, Annemarie Seither-Preisler, and Gasper Pesek, "Foreign Language Learning Motivation: Phonetic Chill or Latin Lover Effect? Does Sound Structure or Social Stereotyping Drive FLL?," in *The Psychology of Learning and Motivation: Adult and Second Language Learning*, ed. Kara D. Federmeier and Hsu-Wen Huang (Elsevier Academic Press, 2020), 165–205.

241 lacks many such preferred traits: For more discussion of English's best of both worlds positioning, see Reiterer, Kogan, Seither-Preisler, and Pesek, "Foreign Language Learning Motivation," 165–205.

CONCLUSION: ACCENT-UATING THE POSITIVE

244 the first or primordial language: The myth as reported by Herodotus is well-known but my retelling here was greatly assisted by Antoni Sułek, "The Experiment of Psammetichus: Fact, Fiction, and Model to Follow," *Journal of the History of Ideas* 50, no. 4 (1989): 645–51; and Deborah Gera, "Psammetichus' Children," in *Ancient Greek Ideas on Speech, Language, and Civilization* (Oxford University Press, 2003).

245 Many later discussions: Darwin's theory that language came about via our vocal mimicry of natural sounds appears in his 1871 work *The Descent of Man*.

247 linguistically deprived infants: To read more about this and his other scientific activities, see Douglas Guthrie, "The Medical and Scientific Exploits of King James IV of Scotland," *The British Medical Journal* 1, no. 4821 (1953): 1191–93.

INDEX